# Agates
## of Lake Superior
### Stunning Varieties and How They Are Formed

**Dan R. Lynch and Bob Lynch**

Adventure Publications, Inc.
Cambridge, MN

## Dedication

To Nancy Lynch, wife of Bob and mother of Dan, for her continued support of our book projects.

And to Julie Kirsch, Dan's fiancée, for her love and incredible patience throughout the process of writing this book.

## Acknowledgements

A special thank you to the following for providing specimens and/or information: George Robinson, PhD, Jim Cordes, Christopher Cordes, Dave Woerheide, David Gredzens, Terry and Bobbi House, Dean Montour, Bradley A. Hansen, Phil Burgess, John Perona, Wally Crabtree, Zack Jacobson, Terry Roses, Eric Powers and Mike Wendt (www.agate-beach.com)

All photos by Dan R. Lynch, except page 24-Courtesy of Visible Earth, Jacques Descloitres, MODIS Rapid Response Team, NASA/GSFC (http://visibleearth.nasa.gov/)

Book and cover design by Jonathan Norberg

Edited by Brett Ortler

10 9 8 7 6 5 4 3 2 1

# Table of Contents

# Introduction

*Agates are some of the most beautiful—and mysterious—of all natural formations*

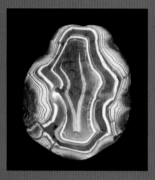

**ADHESIONAL BANDED AGATE**

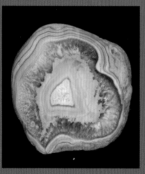

**FLOATER AGATE**

**VEIN AGATE**

**COPPER REPLACEMENT AGATE**

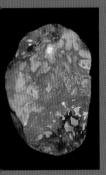

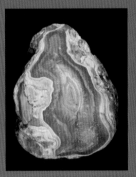
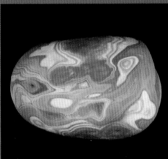

**MOSS AGATE**  **STALACTITIC AGATE**  **COLORED MACROCRYSTALLINE QUARTZ**  **PAINT AGATE**  **WATER-WASHED AGATE**

Agates are mineral formations famous for their concentric, ring–like banding and beautiful coloration. Found around the world and revered for thousands of years, agates are undoubtedly one of the most spectacular results of geology, yet for all their popularity we know comparatively little about them. For centuries, researchers have tried to explain their wild patterns and puzzling origins, but details surrounding the enigmatic stones' formation remain mostly a mystery. Throughout this book we will discuss what we know about agates (and what we think we know) as we explore these ancient gemstones of Lake Superior.

## THE AGATE ENIGMA

Despite centuries of research, many mysteries remain in the sciences of geology, petrology and mineralogy. However, few scientific enigmas are as intriguing and beautiful as the agate, the colorfully banded variety of quartz. Although agates have been collected and appreciated since antiquity, we still have only theories, conjecture and educated guesses to account not only for the many varied formations and structures found within them, but for how they form at all.

Several key problems are at the center of the conundrum; the primary issue is that we don't yet understand the mechanisms that give agates their characteristic concentric banding. Another major problem is that none of the existing historical or contemporary theories account for all of the unique structures found in the many different varieties of agates, although some do come close. A satisfactory explanation of agate formation must take into consideration the often overlooked external geological conditions under which agate formation takes place as well as the source of the material from which agates are made. While the earth sciences will no doubt play the largest role in answering our many questions about agates, we must acknowledge that the physical sciences, such as chemistry and physics, will also be essential to determining the origin of agates and their mysterious bands.

Agates can be found in thousands of locations and on every continent, and though every agate may differ in structure and age, they all share the same uncertain past. The agates found in and around Lake Superior, the world's largest freshwater lake by surface area, are no exception. Formed approximately 1.1 billion years ago, their considerable age has shrouded the history of these agates more so than many of those found in other parts of the world. As a result, it seems as though researchers have historically ignored Lake Superior agates in favor of studying more accessible agates. Such agates are less than half as old as Lake Superior agates and originate from other countries, such as Germany, England, Brazil, Mexico and Australia. Only in recent years have Lake Superior agates been consistently included in scientific studies. With the increase in attention afforded them by researchers and hobbyists alike, more and more unusual structures unique to Lake Superior agates are being discovered, providing more insight into the origin of agates.

It is clear that the puzzle of agate formation requires a very complex answer, an answer that Lake Superior's agates may help discover. But just when we think that an answer presents itself, further observations or new discoveries bring us back to where we started. In this book we will explore the most prominent agate formation theories and how they relate to the Lake Superior region and the distinctive varieties of agates found there. So where do we begin? To attempt an educated discussion of agates, their possible genesis, their many varieties, and their significance, we must first know exactly what an agate is and the terminology necessary to analyze it.

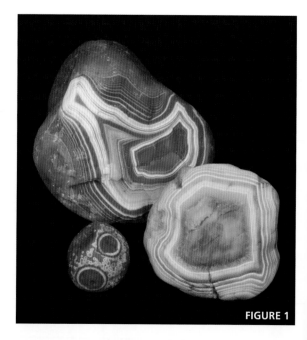

**FIGURE 1**
An assortment of natural Lake Superior agates. Largest agate 1.5" x 1.5" (3.8 cm x 3.8 cm)

FIGURE 1

## ETYMOLOGY OF "AGATE"

While there was once some dispute where the word "agate" (pronounced "AG-it") originated, the colorful stones are now generally thought to have been named in ancient Greece. The earliest known written record of agates, produced by Greek philosophers, dates to approximately the year 300 BC. They called them "achates," after the Achates River in southern Sicily where agates were commonly found. Throughout the course of history, French and Italian rulers have controlled Sicily, resulting in an evolution of the word. Today, the French word for agate is *acate* while the Italian word is *agata*. Our current spelling and pronunciation of "agate" is most likely from the French, but could also be attributed to a combination of both the French and Italian words. The Achates River is now known as the Dirillo, though some modern maps still refer to it by its French name, the Acate River. The 34-mile-long river carries agates down from mountainsides toward the Mediterranean Sea and today, over two thousand years later, agates can still be collected along its banks.

## AGATES THROUGHOUT HISTORY

Though the first known written record of agates was produced in Greece around the year 300 BC, evidence of people using agates for various purposes predates historical records by thousands of years. Renowned throughout history for their great hardness and durability, their ability to take a high polish, their potential to produce a razor-sharp edge when carefully broken, and, of course, their colorful appearances, agates have been used for decorative and utilitarian purposes for at least 12,000 years. Some of the most ancient examples of agate use have been found in the United States. Knives, arrowheads and spear points carefully shaped from agates and other varieties of quartz have been discovered in several states, and these

artifacts date back to the last ice age, 10,000 years ago. In Bulgaria, agate beads were found alongside gold artifacts in ancient burial tombs constructed by the people of the Varna culture, providing evidence of spiritual reverence given to agates as early as 6,500 years ago. The ancient Egyptians used agate for beadwork and carving earlier than the year 3000 BC, and both the Greeks and Phoenicians were sculpting with agates prior to the fifth century BC. Roman and Byzantine artisans used agates to create bowls, vases, beads, seals and other carvings around the first century AD, which led to centuries of decorative use in Europe through the Middle Ages. Agate cameos, or small carved portraits, were fashionable jewelry in Italy during the Renaissance. In Germany, the city of Idar-Oberstein's economy depended on agate mining (and agate sculpting) for centuries, and the city became one of the world's most important sources of decorative agate material until the 1900s. More recently, agates have been employed in a great number of uses; agates have been used in everything from aviation equipment to clock crystals and scientific instruments. Clearly, agates have played a significant cultural role throughout human history. While there are far fewer utilitarian uses for agate today, as collectible gems agates are enjoyed by more people than ever before. While many view them as merely a curiosity, who knows what importance they may hold once we've unlocked their secrets?

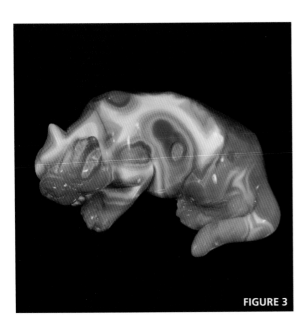

FIGURE 2
This agate displays some of the great variations in color displayed by Lake Superior agates. Approx. 3" x 2" (7.6 cm x 5 cm)

FIGURE 3
Agate carvings, such as this Lake Superior agate cougar, have been produced for centuries. Approx. 3" x 1.5" (7.6 cm x 3.8 cm)

# Quartz and Chalcedony

## WHAT IS AN AGATE?

Any agate expert will tell you that the question he or she is most often asked is, "What is an agate?" A concise reply is that agates are a banded variety of chalcedony, a microcrystalline form of the mineral quartz that is often colored by impurities. But this answer doesn't help a novice. To understand what an agate is, one must first have a working knowledge of quartz, its properties and its many varieties. Only then can we discuss agates in further detail.

## QUARTZ

Quartz is the most abundant mineral on earth; it is the crystallized form of silica, a chemical compound also known as silicon dioxide. When ample amounts of silicon and oxygen come into contact with each other, a chemical reaction takes place that bonds the two elements together. When two or more atoms of any element (or elements) bond, they take on a specific orientation determined by the properties of each element and form a structural unit called a molecule. In this case, four oxygen atoms attach themselves to one silicon atom to form a specific structural arrangement called a silica tetrahedron. A silica tetrahedron is a molecule that has the specific shape of a triangular pyramid. If more silicon and oxygen are added, additional tetrahedra begin forming from all four tips of each pre-existing tetrahedron, sharing the oxygen atoms in the process. When enough microscopic silica molecules have developed and grown upon each other, they form an intricate

three-dimensional framework called a crystal lattice. When the crystal lattice has grown to a size that we can see, we simply refer to it as a crystal. This process is similar for all minerals. But it doesn't take a geologist to see the difference between a quartz crystal and an agate. So if agates are made almost entirely of quartz, why did they form so much differently?

Quartz can form in a number of different environments, but it typically grows when silica molecules that have been dissolved in warm water begin to bond with each other and accumulate on a solid surface. When quartz forms in this way, it can be greatly affected by the conditions surrounding it. The developing silica crystal lattice can be altered by heat, pressure or impurities, which can result in a different form of quartz or another mineral entirely. Under ideal conditions, a pure, unaltered quartz crystal will grow into an elongated, six-sided prism that terminates, or ends, with a pointed tip. But agates form under different conditions; when a solution high in silica solidifies in an environment with low temperature and low

FIGURE 6

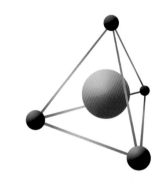

FIGURE 4

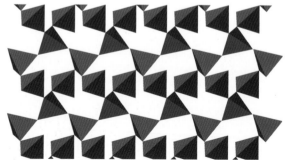

FIGURE 5

FIGURE 7

pressure, the resulting quartz formation consists of minute stacks of flat, plate-like quartz crystals referred to as chalcedony (pronounced "kal-SED-oh-nee"). If the temperature had been higher or the silica content had been lower, a quartz crystal or another form of solidified silica, such as opal, may have been the result instead.

Quartz not only takes different forms depending on the circumstances present when it crystallized, but it is also extremely common. It is found in every geological environment on earth; in fact, approximately 12% of the earth's crust consists of quartz, more than any other single mineral. Given this abundance and variability, it is clear why so many varieties can exist. Arguably the most well-known and popular types of quartz are the large, finely developed, translucent "rock crystals" found across the globe, and their colored variants, such as purple amethyst, yellow citrine, pink rose quartz and black smoky quartz. These are all examples of macrocrystalline quartz, or quartz formations with crystals large enough to be seen with the naked eye. Microcrystalline quartz, which consists of crystals that are so small that significant magnification is required to see them, occurs in many forms and is much more common throughout the world.

No matter what form it takes, quartz is always very hard. The hardness of a mineral is determined by how resistant it is to abrasion. The standard of measurement is the Mohs hardness scale, which ranges from 1 to 10. An example of a mineral with a hardness of 1 is talc, an extremely soft mineral that you can easily scratch with your fingernail; diamond, the hardest known natural substance on earth, is at the opposite end of the scale, with a hardness of 10. Most minerals fall in the range of 2 to 7. On this scale, quartz is a 7, and of the over 4,000 known minerals, only a few dozen are harder. As agates consist of countless tiny quartz crystals, they also measure 7 in hardness. This makes them extremely durable and is the primary reason that Lake Superior's agates have survived over one billion years of weathering.

## CHALCEDONY

Agates are formed almost entirely of chalcedony and are undoubtedly its most striking and beautiful form. However, while agates can be easily defined as a banded variety of chalcedony, the definition of chalcedony itself is more complicated.

Chalcedony forms as irregularly shaped masses composed of microscopic, flat, plate-like quartz

crystals arranged into parallel stacks. When viewed under a microscope, these very small crystals appear as delicate fibers. While few sharp details can be seen at lower than 1,000x magnification, indications of the fibrous structure are noticeable at magnifications as low as 30x. This is especially true within the white bands of an agate. Each fiber is actually a tiny crystal seen in cross-section, comparable to holding a book so that you can only see its spine rather than the cover. For this reason, chalcedony is often referred to as fibrous quartz. Despite decades of study, it is not clear why quartz sometimes forms in this way instead of in its more typical macrocrystalline habit.

While we may not fully understand chalcedony, we do know some of the conditions required for its development. As mentioned earlier, quartz can crystallize in several different ways, depending on its surroundings, and there are three prerequisites that seem to be most important for chalcedony's formation. First, laboratory tests have generally shown that chalcedony forms at temperatures typically around 100 degrees Celsius (212 degrees Fahrenheit), which, in a geological context, is very low. Second, it is also known that chalcedony can form at low pressures. Both of these conditions are corroborated by observation; chalcedony, including agates, forms relatively close to the earth's surface rather than deeper in the earth's crust where temperatures and pressures are much greater. Finally, recent findings suggest that an acidic solution of silica dissolved in water, called silicic acid, is required to transport the silica and begin the crystallization of chalcedony. Silicic acid is a particularly mobile solution and can easily permeate the tiny pores and spaces within rock. However, the mechanism by which the dissolved silica develops into chalcedony is one of the aspects of this process that is not yet understood. The problem becomes even more puzzling when agate banding is considered. Therefore, the mystery of chalcedony formation has resulted in many hypotheses, several of which specifically focus on agate formation. We will discuss these theories later in the book.

So, what is chalcedony? Clearly it is a complex and puzzling form of quartz that is not easy to define, given the uncertainty that surrounds its formation. We do know some things for sure: chalcedony is the fibrous, plate-like, microcrystalline variety of quartz that forms as hard, irregular masses in cavities within rock. It's important to keep in mind that while agates are made almost entirely

**FIGURE 8**
Chert, very common on Lake Superior's shores, can appear banded or uniform in color. Largest stone 2" x 2" (5 cm x 5 cm)

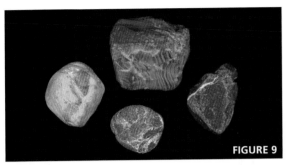

**FIGURE 9**
Four samples of multicolored jasper, found on the shores of Lake Superior. Largest stone 1.5" x 1.5" (3.8 cm x 3.8 cm)

**FIGURE 10**
Not all chalcedony is banded. Shown here are three masses of translucent colored chalcedony found on Lake Superior's shores. Largest stone 1.5" x 1" (3.8 cm x 2.5 cm)

allowing no light to pass through its surface, unless the chert is cut very thinly. In comparison, chalcedony's fibrous, organized structure allows light to easily penetrate into a specimen. Jasper is the colorful, impurity-rich form of chert and flint is the glassy, black variety known for its ability to create a spark (despite the fact that any form of quartz will produce a spark when struck with steel). Chert and jasper are often layered and can exhibit agate-like banding, but due to their opacity and abundance, only novices are likely to confuse them with agate.

When macrocrystalline quartz is allowed the proper conditions and space to fully form, its shape will mimic that of other quartz crystals. A distinct, predefined, repeatable crystal structure is a trait of all minerals, and it is one of the key ways to distinguish one mineral from another. But microcrystalline forms of quartz do not work the same way. Chert, chalcedony and agates typically form in shapes and sizes determined by their surroundings. Chert often develops in large beds on sea floors as well as in smaller concentrated pockets encased in rock. And most kinds of chalcedony form in cracks as well as in vesicles (gas bubbles) trapped within volcanic rock. The result is not unlike plaster poured into a mold— once the material hardens, it retains the shape of the mold even after it has been removed.

## CHALCEDONY'S COLORS

Chalcedony (and other forms of microcrystalline quartz, including chert and jasper) can be found in a wide range of colors. Particularly pure chalcedony is colorless or pale gray, but it is more often stained brown, red or orange by minute particles of iron-based minerals, such as hematite. The particles, called impurities, are carried by groundwater and therefore easily make their way into a developing chalcedony formation. Under a powerful microscope, the tiny flecks of iron minerals can be seen among the quartz microcrystals. Other colors, such as black, green or pink, are caused by impurities of other minerals.

of chalcedony, not all specimens of chalcedony are agates. Agates are a very particular variety of chalcedony made of many layers, each enclosing the next, much like the layers of an onion. When cut, broken or viewed in cross-section, we see the characteristic concentric banding common to many agates; this is just one of the many structures and characteristics found in agates that are found in few other minerals, ranking them as one of the most intriguing and beautiful mineral formations found on earth.

## CHERT AND JASPER

It is important to note that chalcedony is not the only form of microcrystalline quartz. Chert is an extremely common variety found virtually everywhere. Some of chert's varieties are well known, such as jasper and flint, and all are more abundant than chalcedony. Chert develops in a wide range of geological environments, appearing as irregular masses of hard, dull, brown or gray rocks. Often the result of sediment-rich waters depositing silica into large, layered formations, chert consists of tiny, nonuniform crystalline grains of quartz that are tightly intergrown together. This compact granular formation makes chert very opaque,

# Agate Basics

## AGATES

Agates are undoubtedly one of the most spectacular and mysterious results of earth's geology. Formed within rock, they develop in a process that has never been observed and has yet to be fully replicated in a lab. And although they are defined as the banded variety of chalcedony, we don't yet know exactly how chalcedony forms or what causes it to develop banding. Therefore, by default, we cannot know exactly how agates form. To make matters more confusing, when we look at Lake Superior agates, or "lakers" as collectors call them, we see a great number of variations, some of which are not found anywhere else in the world, and each is more complex than the last. The many varieties make agates amazing and unpredictable, but even more difficult to understand. We do know what agates are made of, where they form, what causes their shapes and colors, and we have some knowledge about the conditions in which they develop, but while there are many theories and opinionated researchers, the agate enigma persists. For 300 years scientists have been trying to solve the riddle of the agate, and whatever the cause for agate formation may turn out to be, it certainly won't be simple to explain.

## GEOLOGICAL SETTINGS

Like most other forms of chalcedony, agates develop in cavities within rock. Cracks, gas bubbles and virtually any other small, hollow opening can provide chalcedony the space to begin accumulating and forming an agate. An agate is a secondary mineralization, which means that it is a mineral formation that develops later than the rock in which it forms. Therefore, agate formation is not dependent on a single type of rock and agates can be found in several different kinds of material. Consequently, to begin to fully understand agates, we need to have a sufficient knowledge of the types of rock they can form

within. As tempting as it may be to immediately begin examining the causes of the beautiful banding, a discussion of agates without consideration of the rocks they form in is like studying fish without first understanding water.

Rocks are comprised of complex mixtures of minerals and can form in many ways. While there are numerous varieties of rock, agates only form within three distinct types: extrusive igneous rocks, clastic igneous rocks and sedimentary rocks. All three kinds can produce unique agates that differ greatly in terms of patterns, colors and sizes. Igneous rocks develop from the products of volcanic activity, such as molten rock or ash, while sedimentary rocks develop when sediments, such as sand, mud or detritus (organic particles) settle into large masses. However, extrusive igneous rocks are the most common hosts for agates, especially in the Lake Superior region.

Extrusive igneous rocks formed directly from volcanic activity. When lava, or molten rock, is spilled onto the earth's surface, it quickly cools

FIGURE 11

and solidifies to form fine-grained rocks that are fairly uniform in color. These are called lava flows. Not every lava flow contains the same minerals, and this results in different types of rocks being formed. The two most common extrusive igneous rocks in the Lake Superior area,

**FIGURE 11**
Massive sheets of basalt and other extrusive igneous rocks slope downward into Lake Superior and are evidence of the area's volcanic past. Near Two Harbors, Minnesota.

as well as throughout the world, are basalt and rhyolite. Both can be found with little effort anywhere around Lake Superior. Basalt is dark gray, black or bluish in color and is comprised of minerals rich in iron, magnesium and calcium. Rhyolite is much lighter in color, found in shades of gray or red and consists primarily of silica-rich minerals, such as quartz and the feldspars, an extremely abundant family of minerals. Both rocks are common hosts to agates, which form within gas bubbles trapped in the rock.

FIGURE 13

All molten rock, including that which forms basalt and rhyolite, contains large amounts of gases, such as carbon dioxide, sulfur dioxide and water vapor. These volcanic gases are critical for the formation of agates, though not because of the gases themselves, but for the hollow voids they leave behind. Extrusive rocks cooled too quickly for the gases in the lava to rise and escape, so the gases were trapped, frozen in place as bubbles. These gas bubbles are called vesicles and are where the majority of the world's agates form. Like the bubbles in a carbonated drink, most gas bubbles within igneous rocks are at or near the top of the rock formation. Because gases were

FIGURE 15

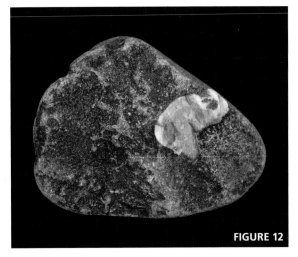
FIGURE 12

rising as the lava cooled, the bottom portion of igneous formations have virtually no vesicles, while the top can contain so many that the rock appears "frothy" or "spongy." When a secondary mineral (sometimes agate) fills in a vesicle, it is referred to as an amygdule. Therefore, agates that form within vesicles in volcanic rocks are called amygdaloidal agates.

Not all igneous rocks form when molten rock solidifies. Clastic igneous rocks develop when violent volcanic eruptions throw tons of dust and

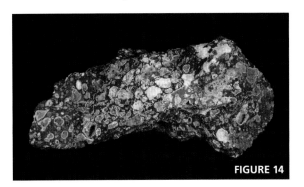
FIGURE 14

ash into the air, which then settles into large beds. The intense heat of the ash causes its tiny particles to partially fuse or weld together, resulting in a solid rock formation. The primary clastic igneous rock in which agates can form is tuff, which is composed of tightly consolidated volcanic ash and tiny shards of volcanic glass. Cavities within a tuff formation are formed when hot gases within the rock are released and rapidly expand, providing the space in which an agate can grow. But tuff is soft, and millions of years of harsh weathering means that virtually no tuff remains in the Lake Superior region.

Sedimentary rocks like sandstone, shale and conglomerate are present throughout the Lake Superior area, but only the area's limestone produces agate. Limestone consists almost entirely

FIGURE 12
A small agate still embedded in the basalt in which it formed. Approx. 2.5" x 2" (6.4 cm x 5 cm)

FIGURE 13
Different samples of basalt collected from multiple sites around Lake Superior. Note the that the bottom-center specimen contains many vesicles, and the bottom-right specimen contains many amygdules of a pink mineral. Largest stone 3" x 3" (7.6 cm x 7.6 cm)

FIGURE 14
This specimen of basalt contains many vesicles that have been filled in with secondary minerals. Here, white calcite, tan laumontite and gray quartz are present as amygdules. Approx. 5" x 2" (12.7 cm x 5 cm)

FIGURE 15
Rhyolite collected from various sites around Lake Superior. Note that the left specimen contains multiple vesicles. Largest stone 3" x 1.5" (7.6 cm x 3.8 cm)

of the fossilized remains of microscopic sea life, making it much softer and more susceptible to weathering. Acidic water can dissolve portions of a limestone formation, leaving behind holes, cracks and even caverns. Agates can form within these cavities, but differ greatly in shape and appearance than those that formed within igneous rocks. Very few areas around Lake Superior contain agate-producing limestone, but one particularly famous deposit is known near Thunder Bay, Canada.

## AGATES OF DIFFERENT ENVIRONMENTS

It is important to note that each geological environment produces different varieties of agates. Amygdaloidal agates, formed within extrusive igneous rocks, are generally round in nature, reflecting the shape of the vesicle they formed within. Their inner patterns generally reflect the "classic" agate appearance and they have a shell, or "husk," of chalcedony. Clastic igneous rocks produce "thunder eggs," a very unique type of agate that forms within irregularly shaped cracks and openings caused by hot gases violently reacting within the rock. Thunder eggs have a shell of rock surrounding a rough, angular formation of agate within. Finally, sedimentary rocks can be home to large agates with no consistent shape. These "sedimentary agates," or "coldwater agates," as they are frequently called, are often impure and contain inclusions of other minerals. The result is a formation of agate with unique colors and structures that cannot be easily confused with amygdaloidal agates or thunder eggs.

Amygdaloidal agates are the most common type worldwide and are generally what the word "agate" refers to. When collectors or researchers wish to discuss a variety other than amygdaloidal agates, they'll most often refer to a specific name, such as "thunder eggs" or "coldwater agates." Similarly, since amygdaloidal agates comprise the vast majority of Lake Superior's agates, usage of the word "agate" in this book refers only to this variety unless otherwise noted. In addition, because basalt is the primary agate-bearing rock worldwide, many researchers concern themselves exclusively with basalt as an agate host; this book will do the same, and host rock will be synonymous with basalt unless otherwise noted.

## THE VESICLE AND THE NODULE

Since basalt and rhyolite are the matrix, or host rock, in which nearly all agates form (including Lake Superior's), some emphasis must be given to the vesicles within the rocks. Vesicles may have been formed by gases simply trying to escape a body of lava, but the cavities left behind posses specific properties that give amygdaloidal agates many of their unique traits.

The shape of the vesicle itself is key. Much like an air bubble rising through water, the gas bubbles that rise through lava have a rounded shape. When lava hardens and gases are trapped in place, the shapes of the resulting vesicles range from near-perfect spheres to elongated teardrops to odd, lumpy formations caused by multiple vesicles that came into contact with each other during formation. Vesicles with an ovoid shape are most common; the bottom end is more pointed than the top. This shape is a result of the fact that lava

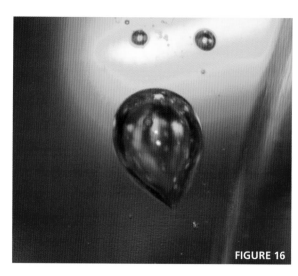

**FIGURE 16**

is an extremely thick and sticky fluid. Though basalt lava is somewhat thinner than rhyolite lava, both are thousands of times thicker than water, so when a bubble tries to rise through such a viscous fluid, the bottommost and weakest portion of the bubble is pinched together by the pressure. The resulting teardrop-shaped vesicle can be observed within many samples of basalt or rhyolite. Vesicles also tend to remain fairly small and rarely measure larger than an adult's fist.

Rocks are porous and contain many tiny channels through which the gases can escape over time. But immediately after the body of basalt or rhyolite solidifies, the hot gases still trapped in the vesicle begin to react with the minerals within the rock, creating new minerals in the process. As the elements within the gas and rock combine and form new molecules, thin coatings of soft minerals begin to line the inside of the vesicle. These vesicle-lining minerals are primarily chlorite, celadonite, various members of the zeolite group of minerals, and clay, all of which are found within many vesicles in the Lake Superior region, especially within basalt. Occasionally, these minerals fill the vesicle entirely, but more commonly they remain as a lining along the inner walls of the vesicle. A shell of chlorite or celadonite can then later be filled in with several different minerals, including agate.

When a vesicle is completely filled with one or more minerals, such as chlorite, celadonite,

FIGURE 18

quartz or agate, it is then called an amygdule. The word "amygdule" is Latin for "almond," and this name is derived from the almond-shaped cross-section of a vesicle that has been filled by a mineral. Of course not all amygdules exhibit the almond-like shape, and instead most are quite irregular. But almond-shaped or not, amygdaloidal minerals are more commonly referred to as nodules. A nodule is any rounded mineral

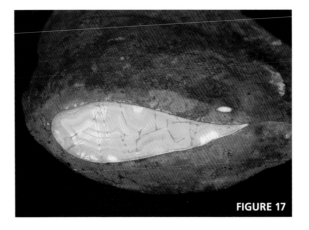

formation found within or separated from its host rock. Not only is the word "nodule" a more accurate description of all the possible shapes an agate can assume, it is also the most commonly used term to address agates, especially whole, unbroken specimens.

Agates often form within a vesicle after a lining of other minerals has formed along the inner walls of the cavity. This coating can affect an agate nodule in several ways. Small dimples or pits are very often observed on the surface of an agate nodule. These concave shapes are created when the minerals lining the vesicle protrude into the agate. As the chalcedony accumulates within the vesicle, it is forced to mold itself around these mineral growths. However, as the agate weathers out of the host rock, the soft vesicle-lining minerals are easily worn away, leaving the pits on the surface of the agate as the only evidence of their existence. Similarly, an agate can exhibit a thin green "skin" on its surface. This coating is actually the vesicle-lining minerals, specifically chlorite and celadonite. But, as mentioned above, these minerals are very soft and normally erode quickly. Given more than one billion years of weathering, Lake Superior

FIGURE 19

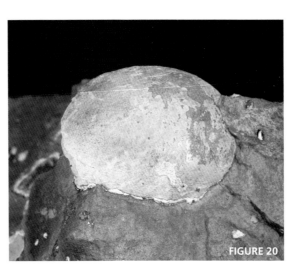
FIGURE 20

**FIGURE 17**
This agate, still embedded in the rhyolite it formed within, exemplifies the "almond" shape of an amygdule. Agate approx. 2" x 1" (5 cm x 2.5 cm)

**FIGURE 18**
A vesicle lined with zeolite minerals is a common sight on Lake Superior's shores. This vesicle is lined with orange and tan laumontite. Imagine the unique agate that would have resulted if one had later formed in this vesicle. Vesicle approx. 0.5" x 0.5" (1.3 cm x 1.3 cm)

**FIGURE 19**
Two large agate nodules still embedded in basalt. Nodules approx. 1.5" x 1" (3.8 cm x 2.5 cm)

**FIGURE 20**
An agate nodule coated with celadonite and still embedded in basalt. Nodule approx. 1.5" x 1.5" (3.8 cm x 3.8 cm) Specimen courtesy of Jim Cordes.

FIGURE 21

FIGURE 21

FIGURE 21
An assortment
of whole, unbroken
agate nodules. Note
that some retain their
original green surface
coatings while others
do not.
Largest nodule
2" x 1.5"
(5 cm x 3.8 cm)

FIGURE 22
This small agate shows
how the agate banding
gradually smooths as it
progresses inward.
Approx. 1.5" x 1"
(3.8 cm x 2.5 cm)

the innermost bands are much smoother in appearance than the outermost bands. These bands are actually layers, or shells, in which smaller layers are contained. Therefore the bands become evident only when an agate is cut or broken open. An onion is a good comparison—from the outside, it appears to be a solid mass, but when cut open, we see the many layers contained within as rings, or bands, because we are seeing them only in cross-section. In agates, there are two types of bands, the most common of which,

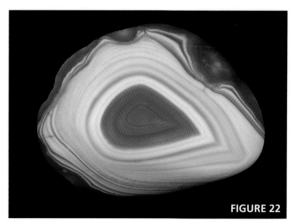

FIGURE 22

agates almost always lack the soft green coating except on nodules that have been freshly broken from their matrix.

## STRUCTURES WITHIN AGATE

It may be the striking banding that most catches our eye, but there are actually dozens of other structures within an agate, many of which are still a mystery. Certain structures are so prominent and unique that we classify those agates as a different variety altogether. From parallel bands and perfectly circular rings to organic, plant-like growths, there is an endless amount of interesting formations and patterns within agates, all of which provide clues toward agate formation. Ignoring these features may make the mystery of agate formation seemingly easier to solve, but doing so would only result in feeble theories that do not account for the many varieties of agate. The more unique and strange agate features, some of which are exclusive to Lake Superior's agates, are discussed in great detail later, but here we will look at the structures common to all banded amygdaloidal agates worldwide.

## BAND COMPOSITION

While no two agates are exactly alike, nearly all amygdaloidal agates share an essential set of structures. Banding is perhaps the most obvious and important. Agates have concentric bands, which means that each band shares the same center. Larger bands enclose smaller bands until a common central point is reached. The bands follow the contours of the vesicle, with each bump and dimple in the surface of the vesicle mirrored in the agate banding. As the banding progresses inward, each inner band loses some of the detail from the previous band, and as a result,

not surprisingly, consists of chalcedony. The chalcedony layers in an agate are primarily the colored bands, including those that are white, gray, red, brown or yellow. Colorless bands, on the other hand, are generally composed of microgranular quartz, or microscopic quartz grains. Many agates will exhibit alternating colored and colorless bands, signifying definite, repeated changes in crystallization and impurity content. However, why these two distinct types of bands form is one of the disputed topics of agate formation.

The exterior of an agate, often called the husk, is unique and differs from the rest of the agate. The outermost layer is generally one of the thickest and most translucent bands, unless heavily weathered. In addition, it is not composed of standard, parallel-oriented chalcedony fibers, but instead is made of chalcedony spherulites. A spherulite is a small spherical arrangement of individual crystals that radiate outward from a central point. It is thought that molecules of silica suspended in a vesicle filled with a silica solution begin to nucleate, or accumulate, around various points on the inner wall of the vesicle. As the many tiny chalcedony spherulites then grow outward from their sources, they eventually contact each other. More and more spherulites develop and become intergrown to form a solid

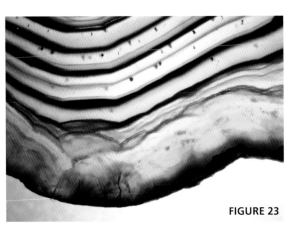

**FIGURE 23**

but more often they can be seen at the very center of an agate. While not all agates contain layers of macrocrystalline quartz, its presence in some specimens is another complication that agate formation theories must explain. Studies have clearly shown that while chalcedony requires a very large amount of silica to form, macrocrystalline quartz growths need much less. It may seem counterintuitive that larger crystals would need less silica, but consider that even a small sample of chalcedony is made of millions of microcrystals, each of which requires its own supply of silica. These many microcrystals

shell, thus forming the first and outermost layer of an agate. As the presence of spherulites have been documented in the husk of many agates, this indicates that one piece of the puzzle of agate formation is at least partially understood.

The presence of macrocrystalline quartz is another topic altogether. Visible as large regions of translucent, colorless material, macrocrystalline quartz often has a fragmented, or "crackled," appearance. Macrocrystalline quartz formations can be observed between layers of agate banding,

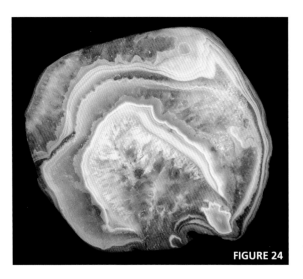

**FIGURE 24**

therefore need more silica than the considerably smaller number of macrocrystalline quartz crystals, which are much larger. The presence of macrocrystalline quartz in an agate is significant because it represents a drop in the amount of silica available during the formation of the agate, which seems understandable when the macrocrystalline quartz is observed at the center of the agate. Since we know that agate bands form inward from the outside, a macrocrystalline center could mean that the bulk of the available silica-rich solution was used in the formation of the chalcedony bands, leaving only a small amount of silica left over at the center of the stone. The remaining silica-poor solution would only be able to create macrocrystalline quartz, which requires much less silica to form. While this theory is very likely, it becomes more difficult to understand when we consider the many agates that have bands of macrocrystalline quartz separated by bands of chalcedony, seemingly indicating alternating rises and drops in the amount of available silica. Agate formation theorists have struggled to identify the mechanisms responsible for creating macrocrystalline

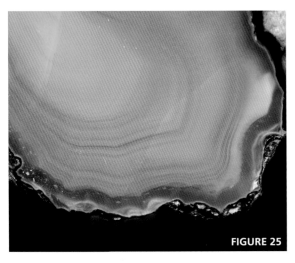

**FIGURE 25**

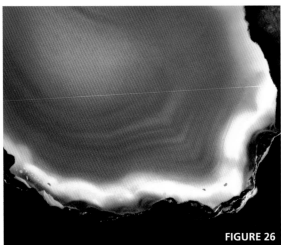

**FIGURE 26**

**FIGURE 23**
The edge of this agate perfectly illustrates the rounded, spherulitic nature of the outermost chalcedony band, clearly formed by a different process than the inner bands.
45x magnification

**FIGURE 24**
Polished agate with ample macrocrystalline quartz.
Approx. 4" x 4"
(10.2 cm x 10.2 cm)

**FIGURE 25**
The outermost layer of chalcedony on this agate slice is clearly thicker and less colorful than the rest of the agate bands. This is characteristic of all agates.
2x magnification

**FIGURE 26**
When the same specimen as in Figure 25 is backlit, the true translucency of the outermost chalcedony layer is shown.
2x magnification

quartz bands in agate. A sufficient theory of agate genesis must account for the growth of chalcedony bands, microgranular quartz bands and macrocrystalline quartz bands, as well as for the fact that some of these structures are completely absent from some agates.

Like the individual spherulites present in an agate's outer layer, there are many other structures within agates that are too small to be seen

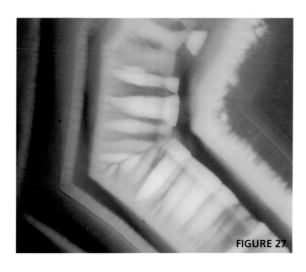

FIGURE 27

without magnification. Odd arrangements of chalcedony fibers are particularly prevalent in many Lake Superior agates. For example, fan- and cone-shaped structures are commonly found within white agate bands when viewed under a microscope. These strange formations, which clearly consist of tiny fibers, are thought to result from the growth of additional, partially formed spherulites within the inner banding of an agate. But since these peculiar chalcedony formations are not evident in all agates, emphasis is rarely placed on them in agate research and not much is known about these odd microscopic structures.

The staggering amount of variations within agates—especially Lake Superior agates—is what makes them so special; this variety is the result of the many unique structures present in agates. But some of the strangest and most perplexing varieties of agate feature inclusions and impurities of other materials. Any number of minerals can form within the vesicle prior to or during the agate formation process. These impurities include minerals such as calcite, barite, zeolites, hematite and goethite, among others. As the agate then fills in around these minerals, their presence impacts the agate's final form, resulting in unique patterns. Many of these minerals are also much softer and more susceptible to weathering than

quartz, so they often dissolve entirely, leaving a void in the agate that may or may not be filled in with more chalcedony later. And in one of the most spectacular examples of inclusions within agates, the developing agate can alter the impurities themselves, as silica replaces the minerals' original crystal structures and turns them into quartz. These odd interactions between agates and other minerals are very common in the Lake Superior region.

These are just a handful of the most common features within agates. There are many others that are less abundant but so unique that we classify them as a different type of agate altogether. One of the most compelling aspects of these variations in structure is that virtually all of them may be absent in an agate. Or, they may all be present, along with other less common structures. If their occurrences were more predictable, we may have understood the genesis of agates long ago. Instead, we have dozens of varieties of agate, each as exciting as the last.

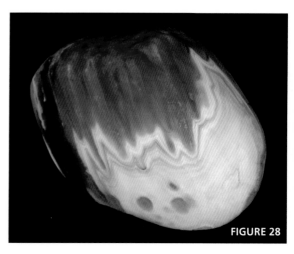

FIGURE 28

## COLORS AND THEIR CAUSES

Chalcedony is colorless to pale gray when pure. But anyone can see that most agates, especially those from Lake Superior, are most often colored in shades of red, brown, yellow, gray and even white. Color within agates is caused by impurities caught in the tiny pores between chalcedony crystals or in the microscopically thin space between agate bands. The primary culprits are particles of iron-bearing minerals and tiny bubbles of water or gas. Trace amounts of aluminum- and manganese-bearing minerals are responsible for some colors as well. Considering that agates form within rocks that contain all of these minerals and elements, it's easy to understand how these impurities can be transported by water and make their way into agates as they're forming. But why neighboring bands can have extreme differences in color (and therefore impurity content) is one of the mysteries of agate formation.

Iron-based minerals are by far the most common colorants within agates, especially in the very iron-rich Lake Superior region. Hematite, a mineral consisting of a combination of iron and oxygen, is responsible for shades of red, orange and brown, and its presence can be assumed in virtually any colored Lake Superior agate. Goethite (pronounced "ger-tite"), a mineral made of iron, oxygen and water, is also very common in agates and produces shades of yellow and golden-brown. Limonite, the name given to unidentified mixtures of several water-bearing iron minerals, also provides yellow coloration, especially in thin layers on the surface of agates that were deposited by groundwater after an agate's formation. Most shades of green, although quite rare in Lake Superior agates, are caused by ferrous iron atoms uncombined with oxygen.

The deep reds and browns of a Lake Superior agate may lead you to believe that there is a large amount of iron present within them. But lab studies have found quite the opposite. Leading agate researcher Terry Moxon shows that even opaque colored bands, which have a high enough concentration of impurities to prevent light from easily penetrating them, consist of as little as 0.5% of iron minerals, and translucent colored bands have an iron mineral content as low as 0.2%. Taking white and gray chalcedony bands and colorless microgranular quartz bands into consideration, the overall iron content of an entire agate is estimated by Götze and his colleagues to be less than 0.3% of the agate's total composition. And after testing agates from all over the world, they found that most agates contain an average iron content of only 0.05%. This very low number may be surprising to some, but looking at an agate under a microscope will provide the answer: the iron-bearing minerals are present as many tiny flecks, or "blobs," that appear as a solid band of color when viewed by the naked eye. This is similar to the way images printed in newspapers actually consist of tiny dots of ink. Even the most opaque and densely colored agates actually contain very little iron.

Aside from the shades of red, brown and yellow caused by iron minerals, there are many other colors that can be found within Lake Superior agates. White bands are formed of compact, densely grown chalcedony fibers that are so tightly packed together that they reflect all light. White bands display the fibrous structure of chalcedony most prominently, and it is sometimes visible even without magnification. The white banding also contains the least amount of pores, therefore making these chalcedony bands the least prone to staining by impurities.

Bluish gray bands, both opaque and translucent, are more complex. Bluish colors in agate are caused by fibrous chalcedony that contains numerous microscopic bubbles of water or gas intergrown among the fibers. Though these bands are actually gray, the bluish coloration is caused when light is scattered and absorbed by the bubbles, and primarily blue tones are reflected back to our eyes. This haphazard light scattering can be frustrating for collectors who may prize a particular agate for its blue coloration, only to find that under more controlled lighting, such as polarized photographic lighting, the blue coloration seems to disappear, leaving gray hues in its place. Even more interesting is the fact that when white, gray or gray-blue bands are lighted from behind, allowing light to transmit through the stone, these bands appear brown. These traits are the result of what is known as the Tyndall effect, which was applied to agate research by Pelto in 1956. The effect can be replicated easily in your kitchen by filling a clear glass with water and then placing a few drops of milk into it. The cloudy water will now appear white or light gray; this represents a chalcedony band that contains microscopic bubbles. Shining a light into the side of the glass and looking down through the top of the water will reveal a bluish coloration, caused by light being bounced around by the milk particles. But if you look through the opposite

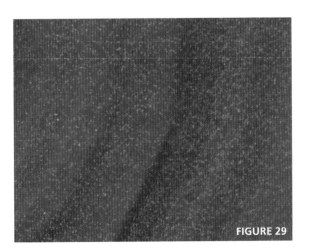

FIGURE 29

FIGURE 29
The purple-red coloration of this agate from Michipicoten Island is caused by tiny grains of hematite. 50x magnification

FIGURE 30
Under natural light, this agate slice appears bluish gray. Approx. 1.5" x 1" (3.8 cm x 2.5 cm)

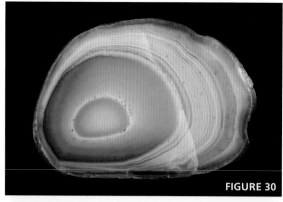

FIGURE 30

FIGURE 31
Under polarized photographic lighting, the same slice appears more brown, losing the bluish tint. Approx. 1.5" x 1" (3.8 cm x 2.5 cm)

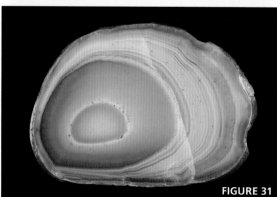

FIGURE 31

FIGURE 32
When backlit, the same agate slice appears brown, due to the Tyndall effect. Approx. 1.5" x 1" (3.8 cm x 2.5 cm)

FIGURE 32

FIGURE 33
Amygdaloidal agates from around the world. (clockwise from left) Scotland, Russia, Morocco, Australia. Largest agate approx. 2" x 2" (5 cm x 5 cm)

agate is caused by a combination of impurities, including bubbles and the presence of aluminum and iron minerals; these scatter nearly all incoming light so that very little color is reflected back to our eyes. Truly colorless bands that are clear and lack a grayish tint are generally microgranular bands, and these tiny, compact grains of quartz contain far fewer pores and spaces where impurities can collect.

Generally speaking, there is no such thing as a "pure" agate, as all agates contain some form of impurity, even if it is just water bubbles. Impurities are simply a side effect of agate formation and result from the surrounding rock, impure groundwater, the pressure and heat present during agate formation and many other possible sources. Because of their prominence, some theorists believe that impurities not only give agates their coloration, but are essential for agate formation. In particular, aluminum is thought to promote chalcedony growth. It was also thought that iron, which is present in the majority of the world's agates, served a similar function in chalcedony creation. However, there are many agates found worldwide that are completely white in color and have extremely low iron content, so this hypothesis has largely been disproved. While the role impurities play in agate formation isn't well understood, the abundance of impurities in agates makes it likely that some are important during agate formation.

## AGATES OF THE WORLD

Lake Superior is far from being the only source of agates. In fact, agates can be found in thousands of locations and on every continent. From world-famous agate sites such as Idar-Oberstein, Germany, and Rio Grande do Sul, Brazil, to lesser-known localities in countries like South

side of the glass, toward the light source, the cloudy water will then appear brown. In agates, the bubbles act in the same manner, scattering light in such a way that the gray or white bands can appear to vary in color depending on the direction and orientation of the light source.

Not all agates with a gray coloration appear bluish because of the Tyndall effect. Translucent gray bands are often very pure chalcedony and contain water or gas bubbles that are larger than those found in agates with bluish bands. These larger bubbles do not scatter light in the same way, and this results in a simple, cloudy, grayish appearance when viewed in normal light. Some theorists also believe that gray banding also contains ample amounts of aluminum impurities and this may contribute to the coloration. Similarly, black or dark gray coloration in an

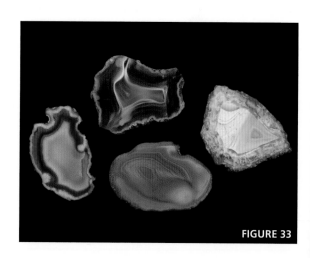

FIGURE 33

Africa, Poland and Mongolia, agates are collected everywhere for both enjoyment and profit. Because the many variables that can affect agate development change from location to location, each agate-producing region throughout the world yields agates distinct in appearance. Many veteran collectors can even use these visual clues to identify exactly where an agate specimen originated based on sight alone.

Not only do the world's agates differ from each other in appearance, but they also vary greatly in age. The work of researcher Keller has shown that some of the youngest agates have been found within rocks in Mexico, and these agates are approximately 38 million years old. On the opposite end of the spectrum are the 1.1 billion-year-old Lake Superior agates, which were long thought to be the world's oldest agates until agates from Warrawoona, Western Australia,

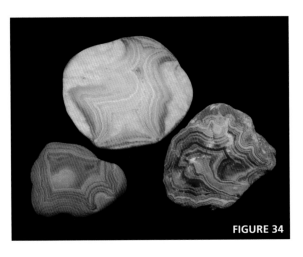

**FIGURE 34**

were discovered. Researcher Moxon described that these ancient Australian agates have been found within rocks that date back a staggering 3.48 billion years, which means these agates formed only approximately one billion years after the formation of the earth itself. Since the age of an agate can differ from the age of its host rock, the age of the agates themselves is unknown, but it is believed to be within a few million years of the rocks in which they were found. But the older an agate is, the more time it has had to undergo observable changes. Young agates, like those from Brazil, have very rough exteriors that show a lack of weathering. The interior patterns of these young agates are also generally intact and complete. In contrast, Lake Superior agates have been tumbled by water, abraded by wind and crushed by glaciers for millions of years, resulting in smooth, worn-down exteriors and interior patterns that are often shattered and cracked. In

addition, chemical alterations produced unique colors and inclusions generally not found in younger agates.

No matter where agates are found, part of their popularity and charm is that they are readily accessible. Many minerals prized by rock hounds are found in mines or other locations where amateurs cannot venture. Agates are not only accessible, they are also fairly common, making them not too difficult to find with practice. Virtually any gravel pit, riverbed or stretch of shoreline in the Lake Superior region can yield agates, and thousands are discovered every year by professionals and novices alike.

## A PICTURE OF AN AGATE

We now have a picture of an agate: An agate is a hard nodule formed within volcanic rock; its outer husk consists of chalcedony spherulites that surround concentric layers of fibrous chalcedony and microgranular quartz. Iron minerals and other inclusions color the chalcedony bands, and macrocrystalline quartz may be present in the agate as well. With this understanding of the structures within agate and the setting in which amygdaloidal agates grow, we can begin to relate these facts to the Lake Superior region and the agates found in Minnesota, Wisconsin, Michigan and Ontario.

**FIGURE 34**
An assortment of agates formed in sedimentary environments. (clockwise from left) Arkansas, England, South Dakota. Largest agate approx. 3" x 3" (7.6 cm x 7.6 cm)

# Lake Superior Agates

*A billion years old, Lake Superior's agates are a reminder of the region's violent geological past*

**LAKE SUPERIOR SHORE**

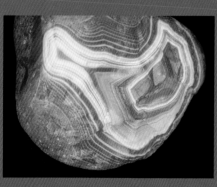

**LAKE SUPERIOR AGATE**

**CARNELIAN**

**JASPER**

Lake Superior, the largest freshwater lake in the world by surface area, played no part in the formation of the agates found on its shores. However, agates and Lake Superior are both evidence of the area's volcanic past and in many ways each can be considered a "side effect" of the same geological event that occurred over one billion years ago— the Midcontinent Rift. And with some help from the glaciers of past ice ages, Lake Superior and the region's agates are now inextricably linked in the minds of collectors and researchers.

## THE BIG LAKE

The French explorers called it *le lac supérieur,* or "the upper lake," when they encountered it in the 1700s, but people of the Ojibwe tribe knew Lake Superior as *Kitchi-gumi,* "big water," for hundreds of years. Later, English explorers named it Lake Superior, honoring the lake's breathtaking size and giving it a fitting title that remains today. Talk to any resident of the Lake Superior area, however, and you'll hear it referred to simply as "The Lake."

Lake Superior is the largest and deepest of the five Great Lakes. With a volume of approximately three quadrillion gallons, it contains more water than the other four Great Lakes combined; in fact, it holds about 10% of the earth's total fresh water. Its surface area measures over 31,000 square miles, it has over 1,000 miles of shoreline, and it is 350 miles long from end to end, making Lake Superior the largest freshwater lake in the world in terms of area. But the lake's watershed is comparatively small, and it takes an incredible 191 years for its water to be completely replaced with new water.

Lake Superior is approximately 10,000 years old—very young, geologically speaking. It formed after the immense glaciers from the previous ice age melted, filling in the trough they'd carved into soft rock. As they scraped through the Lake Superior region, the glaciers also exposed enormous rock formations that were created during one of the continent's most significant geological events—the Midcontinent Rift System. And as these rock formations were exposed, so were Lake Superior's agates. Long entombed within the rocks, the agates were freed by the same glaciers that formed the lake itself.

## MIDCONTINENT RIFT

Around 1.1 billion years ago, North America was situated over the equator and part of a much larger landmass called Rodinia, which began to split in half in an event called the Midcontinent Rift, or the Keweenawan Rift. Tectonic plates, which underlie the earth's crust, were moving apart, tearing the continent in two. As the rift widened, molten rock rose from within the earth to fill the void, creating huge plains of basalt

**FIGURE 35**
Satellite image of Lake Superior. Image courtesy of NASA.

FIGURE 35

and rhyolite, as well as other igneous rocks. The modern-day Red Sea is forming by the same process, and as tectonic plates separate Egypt from Saudi Arabia, basalt fills in the space left between them, widening the Red Sea. But the Red Sea is an important example for another reason, as rift systems (especially continental rifts) usually result in the creation of seas or oceans. Yet the Midcontinent Rift did not develop into a sea, because the rift failed. Rifts form when tectonic plates pull apart, causing a deep void to form. But when plates slam together, rock is forced upwards, creating mountain ranges. It is thought that the same tectonic plate collision that created the Adirondack Mountains in the eastern United States also prevented the Midcontinent Rift from progressing and growing wider, effectively pinching it closed. As its movement ceased, the rift sealed shut with igneous rock, not unlike "scar tissue." Studies probing the depth of Midcontinent Rift rocks have found it to be the world's deepest rift system that failed to become a sea or ocean.

As more lava was forced upwards by the rift and cooled to form basalt and rhyolite, there soon wasn't enough material underneath these igneous rocks to support their weight. In addition, the cooling rocks began to contract, weakening the structure of the formations. As a result, the rocks formed by the Midcontinent Rift began to sag and drop, forming a depression or basin in which water could collect. With water comes sediment, and eventually the rift was filled and covered by limestone, sandstone, shale and other sedimentary rocks. Recent research suggests that agates

form relatively quickly after their host rock; this means that Lake Superior's agates had already formed long before the burial of the Midcontinent Rift rocks.

Over a billion years ago when Lake Superior's agates were forming and the Midcontinent Rift occurred, the earth was a much different place, one we'd hardly recognize. Most of the continents were contained within a single large landmass named Rodinia, which was surrounded by a single, enormous ocean. More incredible, however, is that Lake Superior agates formed in a nearly lifeless world—no life existed on land yet and only microorganisms dwelled in the earth's waters. Land surfaces were barren, dry and covered in loose sand, causing all rain to run off into bodies of water, carrying sediments and nutrients with it. It would take approximately 600 million years for sea life to diversify, for the continents to separate and spread around

**FIGURE 37**
This map depicts a generalized representation of the Midcontinent Rift. Theoretically, a large amount of this rock could contain agates, but only the exposed rocks of Minnesota, Wisconsin, northern Michigan and Ontario have yielded the precious stones.

the globe, and for the first plant life to emerge on land, creating soil and making the earth much more hospitable. In addition to geological changes, throughout the course of earth's history there have been many drastic changes in climate as well. In particular, ice ages (periods of low temperatures accompanied by ice sheets and glaciers that covered much of the planet) were an integral part of Lake Superior's past. The glaciers of the last ice age, which formed approximately 110,000 years ago and lasted until just 10,000 years ago, not only uncovered and exposed the Lake Superior agates, but helped form Lake Superior itself.

## GLACIERS

The Midcontinent Rift System is responsible for much of the landforms and topography of the northern regions of Minnesota, Wisconsin and Michigan, as well as southern Ontario, but none of Lake Superior's magnificent shoreline cliffs, hills and beaches would exist if the glaciers of the last ice agate hadn't uncovered, scoured and shaped the rock. Glaciers are immense sheets of ice, sometimes over a mile thick, that slowly move over land. As they move along, their incredible weight crushes and pulverizes rock (especially soft sedimentary rocks), eventually wearing down the terrain to expose the hard bedrock underneath.

The most recent ice age lasted for approximately 100,000 years, and ice sheets and glaciers covered virtually all of modern-day Canada and much of the northern United States. Over the centuries, there were many advances and retreats of the glaciers, caused by variations in temperature, and each movement removed huge amounts of the sedimentary rocks that buried the Midcontinent Rift. By the time the last glacier receded from the Lake Superior region 10,000 years ago, not only had the large flows of basalt and rhyolite been uncovered, but they had been intensely worn and shaped.

When glaciers crawl across the earth, many of the rocks they crush and break are later picked up by the ice and incorporated within the glacier. Sedimentary rocks are largely pulverized and turned into sediment once again, but harder rocks, such as igneous and metamorphic rocks, can survive. These pieces of stone are rounded and smoothed by the glacier until it begins to melt, dumping its load of rock with it. The gravel

FIGURE 38

and sand deposited by a glacier is called glacial till, and mounds of till, sometimes hundreds of feet deep, can be found throughout the Lake Superior area. The majority of Lake Superior agates are found within glacial till. Because quartz is so hard and weather-resistant, agates that were lifted out of their host rock by glaciers survived, though not always wholly intact.

The hills, beaches and river beds filled with glacial till are of particular interest to agate collectors. Particularly in Minnesota, huge regions of till can yield agates by the thousands, all beautifully glaciated and weathered. Formations of till directly created by glaciers are rounded and generally fairly low-lying, occurring as elongated hills or ridges. Northern Minnesota and Wisconsin have many prominent examples of unique topography formed of glacial till.

Lake Superior agates found within till deposits, particularly in Minnesota, have distinct weathering that makes them instantly identifiable to veteran agate collectors worldwide. The majority of lakers are "glaciated," or have their outer surfaces worn down by the glaciers and always lack the greenish chlorite or celadonite coating often present in unweathered agates. In addition, they are also often missing the outermost layers of chalcedony, including the thick husk. Instead, glaciated agates have smooth, worn-down exteriors and are virtually always cracked and fractured—the result of the crushing weight of the glaciers and repeated freezing-thawing cycles. The smooth, irregular exteriors of glaciated Lake Superior agates are easy to distinguish from agates freshly removed from their matrix, which are rounded and have rough surface textures.

When the glaciers melted and retreated to the far northern reaches of the globe, they didn't just leave till behind, they also left millions of gallons of water. As they plowed and scraped away the sedimentary rocks that once covered the sagging igneous rocks of the Midcontinent Rift, they gouged out a great basin where water would eventually collect. Lake Superior is located in the northern reaches of this basin.

Today, the most prominent evidence of the Midcontinent Rift and the subsequent glacial activity is visible on the northern shores of Minnesota, the southern shores of Ontario and the Keweenaw Peninsula of northern Michigan. Few visitors to the Big Lake know that the cliffs and huge sheets of ledge rock that extend from the shore into Lake Superior are actually part of the Midcontinent Rift, the original home of Lake Superior's agates. Since the Midcontinent Rift is large (over 1,200 miles long) and extends from Nebraska to southern Michigan, one might wonder why other states don't have such dramatic outcrops of Midcontinent Rift rocks (or exposed agates). Again, the glaciers are responsible; as the glaciers only covered portions of the northern states, the sedimentary rocks covering the rift remain in place in more southern areas.

## ROCK FORMATIONS OF LAKE SUPERIOR

There are some amazing rock formations that can be found surrounding Lake Superior, many of which result from the Midcontinent Rift System. Areas like the Silver Creek Cliff and Palisade Head in Minnesota, the Keweenaw Peninsula in Michigan, Sleeping Giant Provincial Park in Ontario and the whole of Isle Royale are some of the most breathtaking examples of igneous rock formed during the rift event. Basalt forms the vast majority of Lake Superior's extrusive igneous rock formations, but rhyolite formations are prominent as well. Both frequently are hosts for

amygdaloidal agates. A third type of igneous rock called diabase is common also, but it does not produce agates.

When glaciers were present, they didn't always scour the land uniformly; sedimentary rock formations are common where the glaciers missed. The Apostle Islands of Wisconsin and Pictured Rocks National Lakeshore of Michigan are spectacular examples of sandstone formations that survived the glaciation. The Nonesuch Shale formation of northern Michigan and Wisconsin provides an amazing view of layered sedimentary formations that were also largely unaffected by the glaciers. But these sedimentary formations don't produce agates. The limestone deposits near Thunder Bay, Ontario, are the only sedimentary rocks in the region that do, but the agates present there do not resemble amygdaloidal agates, instead exhibiting strange, lace-like patterns formed within cracks in rock.

Lake Superior has some of the most magnificent rock formations in the country. But as striking as some of the cliffs and islands may be, agates remind us of what the area has endured. When you're walking along a beach that consists of billion-year-old basalt pebbles and you find a bright red agate glowing in the sunlight, you've just experienced what makes Lake Superior agates special. It is a wonder that agates have survived at all; they formed within rocks during one of the most violent geological events in our continent's history, and then they survived millennia of pummeling after being plucked from their vesicles by glaciers. To many agate collectors, finding and appreciating a beautifully banded Lake Superior agate is more incredible than any of the lake's rock formations.

**FIGURE 39**
A helicopter provides one of the best views of Silver Creek Cliff, an enormous formation of diabase formed atop basalt flows. Sloping basalt ledge rock can be seen on the shoreline in the distance. North of Two Harbors, Minnesota.

27

# Distribution

## WHERE AND WHY

In any agate-producing region in the world, there are two places you'll find agates: where they formed and where weathering transported them. The Lake Superior region is no exception. In fact, Lake Superior's agates are surprisingly widespread, thanks to the glaciers that scoured the area, but these agates actually formed in a more localized area closer to the lake itself.

Although Lake Superior played no part in the formation of the region's agates, agates and the Big Lake are directly related, of course. Lake Superior is centered upon the northernmost reaches of the rocks of the Midcontinent Rift, in which Lake Superior agates formed. Much of the rock formed during the rift event is largely hidden beneath the lake, but the highest elevation rocks remain exposed on the shores, particularly on the western half of the lake. Because the rocks are constantly weathered by the lake, visitors to the basalt cliffs and lava flows can find agates still tightly embedded in the rock and waiting for wind, waves and ice to free them. It is from this setting that the glaciers plucked agates and spread them all over the region.

The shores of northeastern Minnesota, northern Michigan's Keweenaw Peninsula and Isle Royale, and parts of southern Ontario are the original sources of virtually all amygdaloidal Lake Superior agates. These areas contain agate-bearing Midcontinent Rift rocks and were heavily worn by the glaciers. For example, locations like Paradise Beach in Minnesota and Brockway Mountain in Michigan are famous for their basalts and rhyolites that still contain whole agate nodules. But there are other agate-producing areas as well. Limestone deposits near Thunder Bay, Ontario, produce sedimentary vein agates that can weigh hundreds of pounds. Iron mines near Ishpeming, Michigan, have produced vein agates as well, which formed in the cracks within iron ores. And on the far eastern end of Lake Superior is Michipicoten Island, known for its large, but rare, purple agate amygdules still embedded in their matrix.

The glaciers swept up agates from locations like these, and when they finally receded 10,000 years ago, they deposited agates all over the Lake Superior region. In fact, the glaciers transported Lake Superior's agates as far south as Iowa and Nebraska. But it is the Mississippi River that has transported agates the greatest distance; it has been reported that Lake Superior agates have been found in the river as far south as Arkansas and Louisiana.

## THE PATH OF THE GLACIERS

During the last ice age, the glaciers advanced and retreated many times. The final glaciation is referred to as the Wisconsinan Glaciation, and it was responsible for the most widespread distribution of agates. It also deposited immense amounts of glacial till throughout the Lake Superior region. Various extensions of the glacier, called glacial lobes, descended from Canada in different directions, pushing agates along and determining the locations where we find them today. This is illustrated in Figure 42. Note the lobe protruding from the western tip of Lake Superior; this protrusion is known as the Superior Lobe and is one of the most important glaciers in

**FIGURE 40**

**FIGURE 40**
Thanks to the glaciers, beautiful agates like this polished specimen can be found all over the Lake Superior region, and even as far south as southern Minnesota and Iowa. Approx. 2" x 1.5" (5cm x 3.8cm)

the history of Lake Superior and Lake Superior agates. As the Superior Lobe advanced in a southwesterly direction, it passed directly over the rocks of the Midcontinent Rift, particularly those along the northeastern shoreline of Minnesota. In the process, it lifted and transported the agates that formed within the rocks. When the climate warmed and the glaciers began to recede, the Superior Lobe retreated back the way it came, depositing the agates contained within it. When the glaciers initially moved through the region, they removed the soft sedimentary material covering rocks of the Midcontinent Rift. This created a basin. As the Wisconsinan glacier melted, its water began to fill in this depression, thereby forming Lake Superior.

Because of the routes taken by the Superior Lobe (and others) of the Wisconsinan glacier, agates can be found immediately surrounding the lake in a wide path that trends southwest and extends from the westernmost tip of the lake. This distribution is illustrated in Figure 41; the dark red portions represent areas where agates originated and pale red represents the usual range of agates that have been transported by the glaciers and deposited as glacial till. Due to the maximum extent of the Superior Lobe, high concentrations of agates are found in the gravel pits southwest of the lake's westernmost tip, as shown in Figure 41.

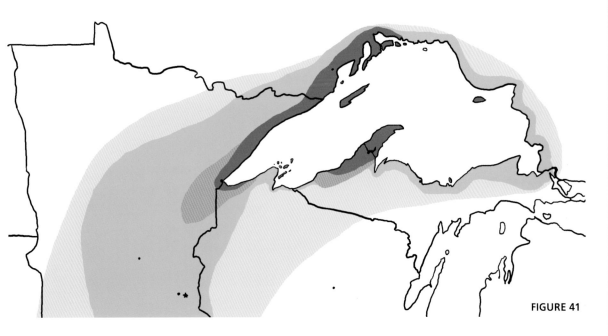

FIGURE 41

**FIGURE 41**
A generalized illustration of the usual range of Lake Superior agates. The darkest red coloration represents the areas in which the agates actually formed. Darker red colorations represent the areas of glacial till that bear agates. Lighter-colored areas generally yield fewer agates than darker colored areas.

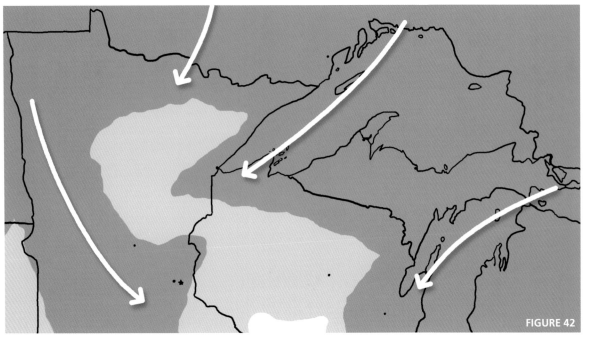

FIGURE 42

**FIGURE 42**
A generalized illustration of the past glaciations in the Lake Superior region. Dark brown shading illustrates the extent of the Wisconsinan Glaciation, and the arrows show the direction of each glacial lobe. Pale brown shading illustrates the extent of earlier glaciers.

# The Many Agates of Lake Superior

FIGURE 43 This map of Lake Superior shows a sampling of agates and where they were found around the big lake.

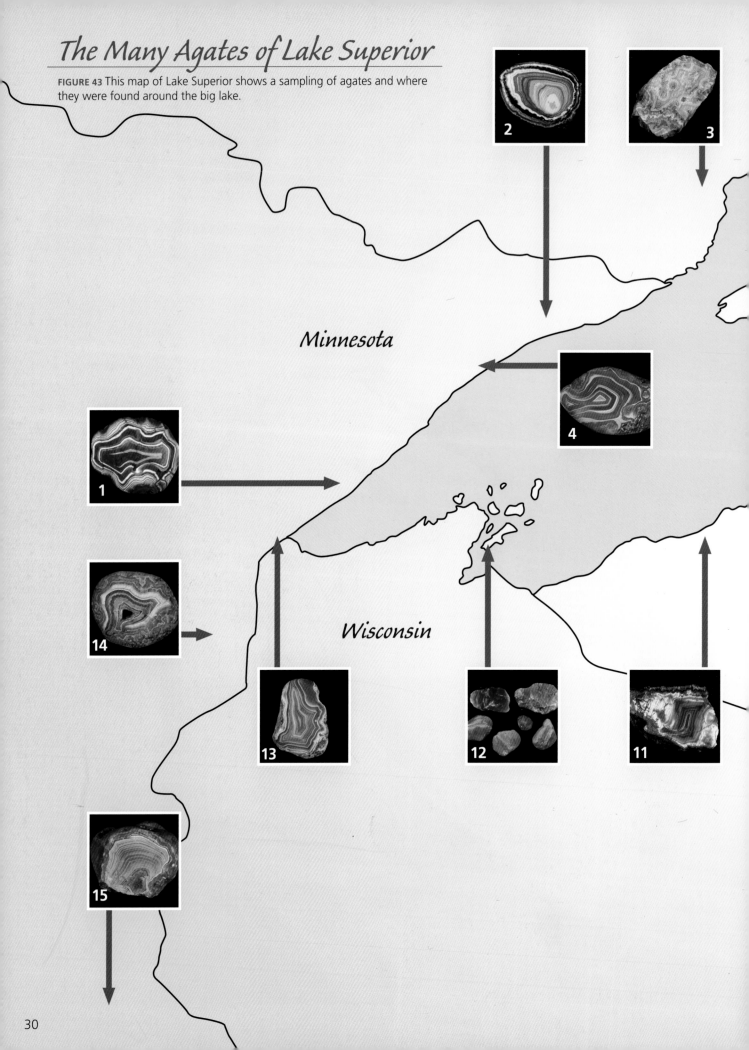

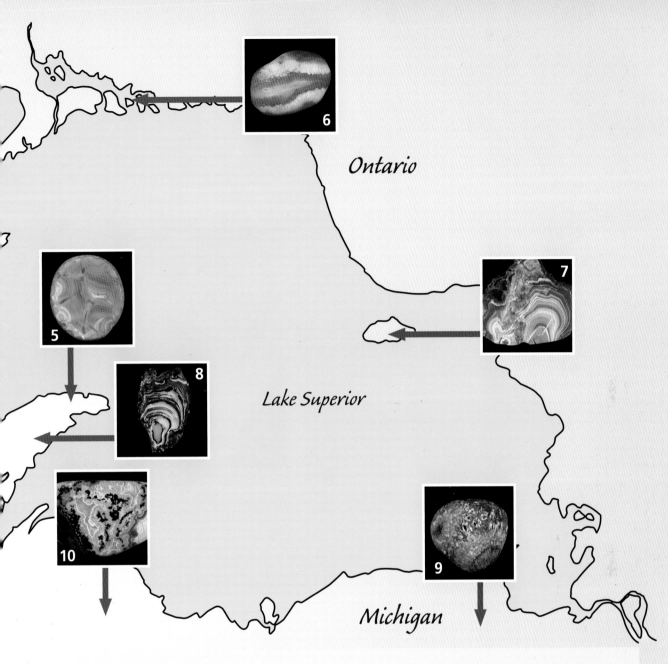

Ontario

Lake Superior

Michigan

# Location Key

1. Adhesional banded agate, near Two Harbors, Minnesota
2. Rare colored agate, near Grand Marais, Minnesota (Specimen courtesy of Christopher Cordes)
3. Vein agate, Thunder Bay, Ontario
4. Paint agate, Paradise Beach, Minnesota
5. Paint agate, Brockway Mountain, Michigan
6. Water-washed agate, Wilson Island, Ontario (Specimen courtesy of David Gredzens)
7. Adhesional banded agate, Michipicoten Island, Ontario
8. Copper replacement agate, Kearsarge, Michigan
9. Skip-an-atom agate, near Sault Ste. Marie State Forest, Michigan (Specimen courtesy of Terry and Bobbi House)
10. Vein agate, Ishpeming, Michigan
11. Adhesional banded agate, near Ontonagon, Michigan
12. Carnelian fragments, Madeline Island, Wisconsin
13. Adhesional banded agate, Duluth, Minnesota
14. Agate geode, Cloquet, Minnesota
15. Paint agate, Zumbro River, Minnesota

## IDENTIFYING AGATES

Identifying an agate seems easy—just look for the bands, right? Unfortunately, it isn't quite that simple. If it were, agates would appear to be much more abundant than they are. Unfortunately, many amateur collectors lacking the skills to identify agates let their excitement get the best of them when they find a large stone with banding. Situations like this have led to many newspaper stories with headlines declaring that the "largest Lake Superior agate ever found" has just turned up in a gravel pit. In reality, all of these "100-pound agates" are banded jasper, chert, or, at most, a moss agate. The fact is, Lake Superior agates are rarely larger than an adult's fist. There certainly are exceptional examples that are the size of an adult's head and weigh many pounds, but these are incredibly uncommon. The majority of the time, collectors merely find small chips or shards of agate no larger than a thumbnail.

Of course, size has nothing to do with the identification of an agate. Instead, we look to the physical characteristics of the stone itself. To begin, because agates are made of quartz, they are extremely hard and very resistant to weathering. Generally speaking, harder stones can take a higher degree of polish than softer

FIGURE 44

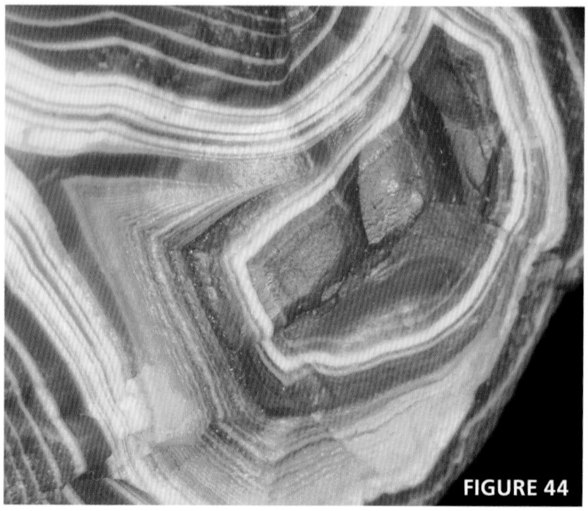

FIGURE 44
At this angle, the surface of the agate catches the light and reflects it similarly to the way wax reflects light. This is called a waxy luster, and is an identifying trait of agates.

stones. For this reason, beach-worn and glaciated agates have a waxy luster and texture, or a semi-shiny appearance and a smooth feel akin to wax. A freshly broken surface of an agate exhibits these wax-like traits as well. One caveat to bear in mind, however, is that whole, unbroken and unweathered agate nodules have a rough exterior with a dull appearance, making them easy to miss. Luckily, the vast majority of Lake Superior agates are well worn and smooth, and their waxy luster and texture will help set them apart from softer, duller rocks and minerals. Figure 44 and 48 show how the various surfaces of an agate can reflect light like wax does.

Agates are some of the hardest stones you'll find in the area; virtually anything else on the shore of Lake Superior or in glacial till deposits is softer than an agate. Pure quartz is the exception, and it is only slightly harder. An agate's many other telltale signs are generally enough to identify it, but if you wish to test its hardness, you can try scratching the specimen with a piece of hardened glass, porcelain or steel—none should be able to damage an agate.

Translucency is another very telling trait of an agate. When digging through a pile of gravel or walking along the lakeshore, few stones will

FIGURE 45
A one-inch moss agate sits as it was found on a beach full of basalt and rhyolite pebbles. Its translucency and texture set it apart from the other stones. Flood Bay, Two Harbors, Minnesota.

FIGURE 45

catch the sunlight like an agate will. Instead of simply bouncing off the surface of basalt or a similar opaque stone, some light actually penetrates an agate's surface, making it look like it's glowing in the sunlight. Nowhere is this more evident than in the tiny shards of carnelian that can be found by the handful on Lake Superior's

FIGURE 46

shores. Carnelian, pictured in Figure 46, is the ancient name given to bright reddish-orange chalcedony, and small fragments of this material are produced in the Lake Superior region when larger agates are broken down by weathering. Very opaque, impurity-rich agates are less translucent, but even these specimens will exhibit translucency at their edges or in thin portions of the agate.

Many minerals fracture in a specific way. This means that when struck or broken, the resulting damage will have a particular shape. Quartz and all of its forms, including agate, have a conchoidal fracture, which means that it breaks in rounded, semicircular shapes. With all of the weathering and glaciation Lake Superior agates have endured,

conchoidal fracturing is evident in nearly every Lake Superior agate found on the lakeshore or in glacial till. When in doubt of a stone's identity, looking for crescent-shaped cracks such as in Figure 47, or large, curved chips such as in Figure 48, will at least let you know if your specimen is a form of quartz or not.

When an agate forms, the vesicle is lined with growths of chlorite or celadonite; the agate grows around these minerals, and each protrusion of the soft mineral lining causes a pit to form in the surface of the agate. When Lake Superior agates retain their husk, the pits and dimples

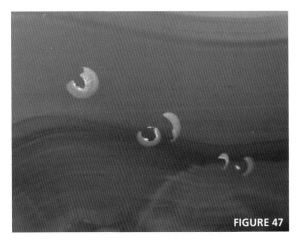

FIGURE 47

that remain on the surface of the specimen can be very telling when combined with the waxy appearance of the chalcedony. Figure 49 shows the characteristic pitted surface texture of a Lake Superior agate.

Finally, there is, of course, the banding. The vast majority of agates will have the characteristic concentric banding, which is your biggest clue. However, chert nodules can sometimes exhibit concentric banding as well. In the Lake Superior

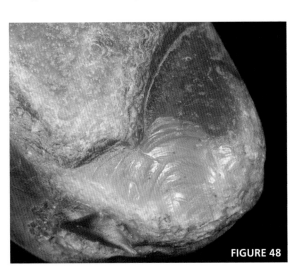

FIGURE 48

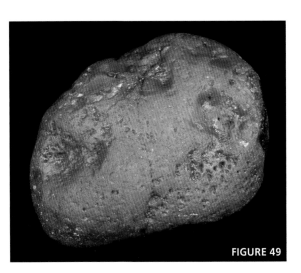

FIGURE 49

FIGURE 46
Common carnelian pebbles found on Lake Superior's shores catch the sunlight and can easily be spotted among the gray basalt. Largest specimen approximately 0.5" x 0.5" (1.3 cm x 1.3 cm)

FIGURE 47
Conchoidal fractures are very common on the surface of highly weathered agates. Look for the characteristic crescent or half-moon shape. 2x magnification

FIGURE 48
A large, conchoidal chip creates a stepped, shell-like appearance on the surface of this agate. Note the larger, curving fracture at the top of the photo that occurred earlier. Actual size

FIGURE 49
The dimpled, pitted surface of a whole agate nodule is a common identifying feature of Lake Superior agates. Approx. 2.5" x 2"

**FIGURE 50**
Small rounded
fragments are the most
common finds on Lake
Superior's shores.
Largest agate 1.5" x 1"
(3.8 cm x 2.5 cm)

region, chert is generally white to gray or black, and is often stained yellow or brown by iron, but is very opaque, which should help distinguish it from an agate. In addition, chert banding is generally very "fuzzy" and not as well defined as agate banding.

Generally speaking, these identifying features apply to fragmented agates, not whole agate nodules. After all, if the agate is whole, we cannot see the banding. Nevertheless, many unweathered nodules from Michigan and Minnesota can be obtained directly from the basalt in which they formed by carefully breaking the rock around them. These specimens retain the thin coating of greenish black chlorite or celadonite, causing them to appear opaque, dull and rough. However, bear in mind the shape of the vesicle in which they formed. Many whole agates exhibit the obvious amygdule shape and are rounded or almond-shaped, with one end wider than the other.

## HOW TO FIND AGATES

Visitors to Lake Superior often turn to experienced rock hounds for information on how to find agates, and they expect a revealing, tell-all answer. In reality, consistently finding agates comes only with practice and a well-trained eye. Part of the problem is that we can never tell when an agate will show up. Glacial till is randomly deposited, so you may not find a single agate in a day's worth of hunting in a gravel pit or on a riverbank. Then again, you could find a handful. You'll likely have better luck searching till deposits close to the areas around Lake Superior where agates originally formed, such as in the gravel beds of rivers flowing toward the lake.

For the amateur, walking the shores of Lake Superior searching for agates may seem a bit like looking for a needle in a haystack. But to an experienced "agate picker," an agate's translucent, reddish hues clearly stand out among the gray and brown igneous rocks. In the end, it all comes down to having experience and practice. More than anything else, learning to recognize and identify the many traits of agates (such as their waxy luster and conchoidal fracture) will help you find them.

Lake Superior agates are fairly widespread and can be found in a large area surrounding Lake Superior. As discussed earlier, areas of glacial till

**FIGURE 50**

are the most lucrative places to hunt for agates, but virtually anywhere in northeastern Minnesota, northern Wisconsin, the Upper Peninsula of Michigan, or southern Ontario will yield agates in riverbeds, lakeshores and areas with exposed gravel. Even farm fields in southern and central Minnesota produce many agates. Remember: anywhere the glaciers went, they potentially left agates behind.

The entire Lake Superior shoreline in Minnesota is a location of note. The beaches from Duluth, at the westernmost tip of the lake, to Grand Marais, near the Canadian border, regularly produce agates, albeit specimens that are highly weathered by the lake. Gravel pits consisting of glacial till deposits hundreds of feet deep can be found from Duluth, Minnesota, and extending southwest. The area around Cloquet, Minnesota, contains gravel pits that are particularly great hunting grounds for agates. But gravel pits are less accessible than other hunting grounds; they are privately owned and very dangerous, so rock hounds should not enter uninvited or unprepared.

In Wisconsin, beaches near Superior have produced agates, and in Michigan, agates can be found on the entire Keweenaw Peninsula, both on the beaches as well as in road cuts and on riverbanks. The Keweenaw Peninsula is also one of the only places where agates are found in mine dumps, which are piles of unwanted rock made during the days of Michigan copper mining. Finally, Ontario's southern shores are remote agate hunting grounds, which means that fewer visitors have collected the available agates, but be aware that some land is protected; it's your responsibility to know where it is illegal to collect. Though all of the locations discussed here are known for agates, there are no guarantees that you'll find anything.

It can be difficult to direct rock hounds to a location where agates will be found, since agate exposure relies on gravel erosion, which is dependent on the weather. For example, the best time to hunt for agates on Lake Superior's shores is after a windy storm that produced large waves. The strong currents push new rocks to shore, including agates. Similarly, heavy rain can cause rivers and streams to rise and rapidly remove dirt and gravel, possibly exposing agates that were buried just hours before.

## NON-AGATES

If you are familiar with the unique traits of agates, there are few other minerals that you could possibly confuse with them. However, newcomers to agate collecting frequently mistake several other forms of quartz for agates. Chert and jasper are the primary causes for confusion due to their similar coloration and because they are often banded. Chert and jasper also exhibit the waxy luster, high hardness and conchoidal fracture of agates, so it's easy mistake either for an agate.

Chert is a rock formed primarily from sediment accumulated at the bottom of ancient seas. Unlike fibrous chalcedony, it is formed of tiny, tightly compacted grains of quartz, which makes it opaque. Even though most chert formations are derived from sedimentary processes and therefore can contain banding, chert's opacity is the first clue that it is not an agate. In addition, magnification with even a low-powered loupe should allow you to see whether or not your specimen contains fibers. If it doesn't, it's not an agate.

Jasper, the impurity-rich form of chert, is easier to confuse with agates because of its red, brown or yellow coloration, which often resembles that of an agate. Jasper also occasionally exhibits

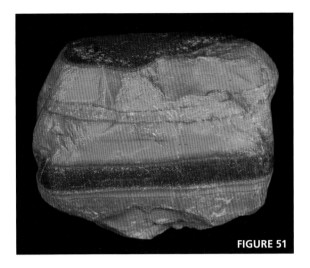

**FIGURE 51**
Jasper, seen here banded with black hematite, is the colorful, iron-rich form of chert. Approx. 3" x 2.5" (7.6 cm x 6.4 cm) Specimen courtesy of Dave Woerheide.

banding. Nevertheless, as a form of chert, it too consists of densely packed microgranular quartz, making it also appear very opaque compared to chalcedony and agates. In addition, when formations of jasper are banded, they nearly always contain parallel bands of red, iron-rich jasper and black, hematite-rich chert bands, not the concentric banding found in agates. Specimens of jasper that contain fossils of stromatolites

**FIGURE 52**
This specimen of jasper contains stromatolites, a fossil of ancient bacteria evident as banded swirls of color. Approx. 2" x 2" (5 cm x 5 cm)

(colonies of ancient bacteria) are the primary exception to this rule. Stromatolites in jasper appear as waving, rounded, layered shapes, though they are not concentrically banded. While they are not agates, jasper specimens containing stromatolites are highly collectible in their own right, as are other non-agate "look-alikes."

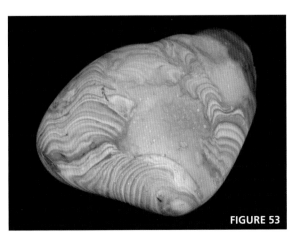

**FIGURE 53**

**FIGURE 53**
Gray or yellow chert, often with bands, as seen here, is a common find around Lake Superior. Approx. 3" x 3" (7.6 cm x 7.6 cm)

# Formation Theories

*There are many theories regarding agate formation, but all have their faults*

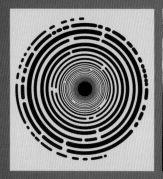

**LIESEGANG RINGS**

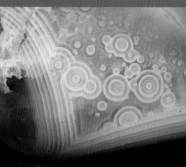

**AGATE EYES**

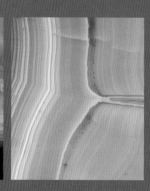

**INFILTRATION CHANNEL**

**INFILTRATION CHANNEL**

As frustrating as it may be, we simply do not know how agates form. For centuries, a few devoted researchers and scientists have tried to solve the riddles of agate formation, but no definite answer has ever presented itself. Instead, we only have numerous theories to account for agates and their beautiful bands, and each is more complicated than the last. But with each new theory proposed comes fresh ideas and recent findings that help bring us nearer to the elusive solution we seek. So while there is no answer yet, we are certainly getting close.

## DECODING AGATE FORMATION

For the amateur interested in agate formation, reading a research article in a scientific journal or a collection of studies is a daunting task, as the language, topics and terminology in such sources are nearly impenetrable for beginners. While these sources are a wealth of information, fully understanding them takes an enormous amount of background knowledge about quartz, chalcedony and igneous rocks, among many other topics. The previous discussions in this book cover much of this information. But there are other reasons why agate formation theories and studies are so complicated, some of which have already been mentioned—theorists must consider problematic agate characteristics such as the alternating fibrous and granular microcrystalline quartz bands present in many agates, or the mysterious absence of certain structures in particular agate varieties. Then there are even more difficult questions yet to be answered: What mechanism causes agate bands to form at all? And where does the large amount of silica necessary for agate formation come from? Attempting to answer these queries often requires a much broader knowledge of geology and chemistry, as well as seemingly unrelated sciences like physics and hydrodynamics.

There have been dozens of theories proposed since agate formation became a point of scientific discussion 300 years ago. Many of the earliest hypotheses were simple ideas based on observations of other rock and mineral formations. Today, theories are developed after years (or decades) of study to account for the many aspects of agate formation. Modern theories are much more elaborate, but also much more plausible, thanks to the ever-expanding body of geological research that theorists can draw from. As there are very few researchers who study agates exclusively, it is critical that theorists turn to the work of geologists and chemists to expand upon their ideas. After all, studying agates alone won't tell us much about the igneous rocks they form within or the silica colloid they may have developed from. By adapting and applying related research to the modern study of agates, many of the more improbable theories developed long ago have been refuted while allowing some of the feasible ideas to become the basis for more current studies. Today, most theories fall into one of two primary categories—accumulation theories and differentiation theories—each developed by expanding upon an established set of accepted aspects of agate formation. For example, we know that agates form when silica collects in vesicles, but opinions differ whether the silica begins in the form of a solution or a gel.

It is the nature of scientists to disagree and find flaws in others' hypotheses while defending their own, but the debate between agate formation theorists has actually greatly advanced the science of agates. Along with the invention of new research equipment and techniques, the desire for "better" theories has driven scientists to generate hypotheses that are better supported by experiments and observations than preceding theories. So while the concepts and ideas presented in research papers become more and more complex, each new theory brings us closer to understanding agate genesis while at the same time adding another chapter to the rich history of agate formation theories. But before discussing agate formation, we must first have a better knowledge of chalcedony and its properties.

## CHALCEDONY FORMATION THEORIES

Chalcedony is a very puzzling form of quartz. While we have an idea of how it grows and of the conditions in which it forms, it is still largely misunderstood, especially in agates. The fact that we don't know exactly how it forms complicates agate formation theories, but several theorists have developed ideas to explain how chalcedony may have developed in conditions specific to vesicles deep within basalt and rhyolite flows. One of the oldest theories regarding chalcedony crystallization is that it precipitates directly from a silica solution; this means that as the water in the solution dries up, the silica is left behind as the fibrous microcrystals we call chalcedony. However, it is generally accepted that this theory cannot be the answer. If simple chemical precipitation is responsible for chalcedony's formation, laboratory tests should be able to easily reproduce the process. But even under perfect conditions, lab tests are not able to produce the microscopic plate-like crystals of chalcedony. Instead, this results in granular microcrystalline quartz (quartz consisting of microscopic grains).

**FIGURE 54**

Today, it is generally believed that chalcedony forms from a silica colloid, not from a simple silica solution. A colloid is a substance consisting of particles of one material suspended within another material. Unlike a solution, the two materials in a colloid cannot be separated by standard methods. In addition, the particles of each material do not naturally separate by settling, as they do in a solution. There are several kinds of colloids—emulsions, aerosols and foams, to name a few—but a silica colloid is a gel, not unlike common gelatin. The idea of colloidal silica being the precursor to chalcedony was first developed in 1915 by Liesegang, and this theory has recently been supported by laboratory tests by Moxon in 1996, who found that a very rich solution of silicic acid, the acidic combination of silica and water believed to be a precursor to agate formation, will naturally flocculate, or clump up, into gelatinous masses of colloidal silica when given enough time. In theory, a cavity filled with silicic acid could therefore transform

into a body of silica gel. Earlier laboratory tests by Oehler in 1976 showed that chalcedony can actually be grown directly from a silica gel, though at temperatures higher than the estimated 100 degrees Celsius believed to have been present when agates formed. Still, the results seemingly support the precipitation theory mentioned above. However, problems arise from this hypothesis when one considers that silica gel is much less dense than chalcedony. When silica gel fills a cavity, it takes up more space than solid chalcedony does; therefore, if a single body of silica gel was responsible for the formation of an agate, the agate would be incomplete and remain hollow. Because the majority of agates are not hollow, this hypothesis is necessarily incomplete and must be developed further.

A second theory proposes a much more complicated process. As chalcedony requires very large amounts of silica to form, even a huge amount of silicic acid or colloidal silica does not contain enough silica to create a silica growth as large as an agate. Nevertheless, multiple flows of silicic acid over a long period of time could provide the necessary material. This theory developed over many years as a result of the combined research of many scientists, including Oehler, Masuda, Landmesser, and Moxon, among others. They propose that the first influx of a silica solution into a cavity produces a silica colloid. This colloid then begins to form opal, another form of silica. Opal is amorphous, which means that it has a disorganized crystal structure and is therefore not a true mineral. But opal forms under a wider range of conditions and requires less silica than chalcedony does. Specimens of opal are often white and opaque with no defined structure or shape. Later, secondary inflows of silica solutions are thought to interact with the existing body of opal by dissolving it back into a gel form, thereby enriching it with more silica, which is redepositing as the solution once again dries out. This can be thought of as the opal "ripening," or incorporating the new silica by reorganizing its crystal structure. The result would be yet another form of silica called cristobalite, which has a more organized crystal structure than opal. Finally, the future addition of more silica theoretically causes the cristobalite to "ripen" as well and evolve into the tiny quartz crystals that comprise chalcedony. This entire process is hypothesized to take a very long time. While this explanation is greatly simplified, the

**FIGURE 54**
Chalcedony fibers visible within a white agate band.
60x magnification

development of silicic acid into a silica colloid has been shown in lab studies by Moxon in 1996, and the slow maturation of opal to quartz has been observed in nature, particularly around hot springs, though this has not yet been observed in agates. In support of this theory are findings by Moxon that show that very young agates actually do contain some opal, but older agates do not, signifying that older agates are "riper" than younger agates. This theory provides a viable, yet unproven, link to the formation of chalcedony by proposing that it results from a series of incremental changes from silica gel to chalcedony itself. But again, silica gel is less dense than solid chalcedony and a single body of gel would not produce a complete agate, so adjustments need to be made to this theory.

## CHALCEDONY AND OPAL

The possible link between chalcedony and opal presented is not a new concept. A relationship between the two forms of silica has been thought to exist for a long time. Over the past 300 years of agate and chalcedony research and discussion, it was apparent to scientists that chalcedony possessed unique properties. Around the turn of the twentieth century, it was assumed that chalcedony's peculiar formation was actually a mixture of microcrystalline quartz and opal. Researchers believed this combination to be the reason for the fact that white bands within an agate are opaque, like many opals, while other bands are translucent or transparent. The theory was challenged in the 1930s by Jessop and later disproved in 1951 by Midgley when it was observed that a mixture of quartz and opal should exhibit a combination of the individual qualities of each mineral, yet chalcedony seemingly displayed only the properties of quartz. While the theory of chalcedony forming as a mixture of different forms of silica was disproved at the time, later discoveries would revive the concept.

## A THIRD THEORY

A third theory, first presented in 1990 by researchers Wang and Merino, states that the presence of impurities is essential for the formation of chalcedony. We know that many mineral impurities are present in chalcedony simply by observing a specimen's coloration— shades of brown or red, for example, are caused by tiny amounts of iron—but there is some evidence that these impurities actually initiate the crystallization of chalcedony and the formation of agate bands. According to this theory, inclusions of microscopic aluminum particles act as a catalyst for chalcedony growth by linking silica molecules of a similar charge. In chemistry, molecules all possess an electrical charge that is negative, positive or neutral. Silica generally has a negative charge whereas aluminum's is positive. Molecules possessing the same charge are not attracted to each other, but with the addition of another substance with the opposite charge, the molecules will then begin to bond. Chalcedony forms as a result of a chemical reaction between the aluminum atoms and the silica molecules; this causes the silica to begin bonding, thereby crystallizing into chalcedony. This theory also posits that a body of silica colloid, or gel, exists as the precursor to chalcedony crystallization, but it has also been found that this process could take place in a silica solution. Because this theory accounts for the fact that silica molecules share the same electrical charge and are resistant to bonding, this explanation of chalcedony formation is gaining favor.

## RECENT FINDINGS

Today, we know that chalcedony often contains more than just quartz, making the problem of chalcedony's formation even more complicated. While minute traces of opal are present in many agates, inclusions of another silicate (a silica-based mineral) called mogánite are more common. Discovered in 1976 in the Canary Islands, mogánite caused a stir among agate researchers when it was found in samples of chalcedony. Mogánite was quickly recognized as an important mineral, as subsequent studies revealed that it was present in nearly all agates from around the world. Even though it consists of silica, mogánite's unique crystal structure means that it is not a variety of quartz, but another mineral entirely. It forms as tiny, needle-like crystals intergrown among the fibrous structure of chalcedony; it is virtually indistinguishable from quartz, thereby making its presence determinable only in a lab and not by observations through a microscope. Since its discovery, we've learned that less than 25% of a typical agate's total weight consists of mogánite, but later studies by Moxon have found that very old agates, such as Lake Superior's, actually contain less mogánite than younger ones, and sometimes none at all. Meanwhile, much younger agates, such as those from Brazil, are often comprised of approximately 20% mogánite or more. It is thought that mogánite forms at the same time and in the same manner as the fibrous quartz microcrystals, but actually begins to transform into quartz as time passes due to an interaction with the trace amounts of water within an agate along with the possible later addition of heat. Similarly, the tiny quartz fibers of chalcedony also increase in size as an agate ages, providing evidence that some crystal growth continues to take place long after an agate finishes forming. There is a high probability that as the agate ages, its mogánite content is slowly changed and its silica is contributed to the further growth of chalcedony. The existence of mogánite intergrown with chalcedony may make explaining chalcedony's formation even more difficult, but mogánite's presence seems to correlate directly with the age of an agate, as does the size of the chalcedony fibers. Though these findings will undoubtedly play a part in understanding agate formation, we do not yet know exactly how.

There is no doubt that chalcedony is a complex form of quartz derived from an even more complex process of formation. But the details of that process and how it contributes to agate formation have eluded us. The many previously proposed theories have their own merits, but none have shown to be conclusive. In addition, because "ripening" chalcedony has been observed in nature and chalcedony has been produced in a lab from silica gel, it would appear that there might be more than one way chalcedony can form.

While we may not fully understand chalcedony in agates, we do not need to know the full details of this process in order to start formulating theories of agate formation, and for centuries theorists have done so. However, solving the agate enigma would no doubt be made easier by better understanding chalcedony and how it forms in vesicles. Nevertheless, we now have some knowledge of chalcedony and its most prominent formation theories. With this information, we can look at agate formation theories with an appreciation for both the chemistry and beauty at work in each and every agate.

## A HISTORY OF AGATE FORMATION THEORIES

It was once believed that the formation of agates was not all that complicated; after all, rocks like shale and sandstone have layers that form due to

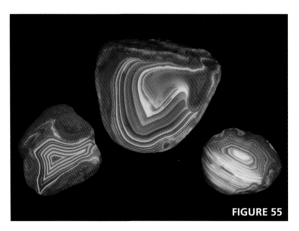

FIGURE 55
An assortment of beautiful polished Lake Superior agates. Largest agate 3" x 2.5" (7.6 cm x 6.4 cm)

repeated deposition of material by water, so it was thought that agates must have formed the same way. It didn't take long, however, for scientists and scholars to realize how unique agates are and that their formation cannot be so easily dismissed. In 1761, J. F. Hoffman suggested that agates formed after a silica solution trickled into a vesicle through tiny holes on its perimeter, and the first scientific agate formation theory was born.

The full history of agate research and formation theories is extensive and well documented. A few individuals, however, have been extremely influential and important in helping to piece together the story of agates throughout the past three centuries. One of the earliest known works that detailed various aspects of agate formation, especially the presence of color-causing mineral impurities, was written in 1776 by C. A. Collini. His work was the first published document that attempted to interpret agates rather than simply describe them. A natural historian and colleague of the French philosopher Voltaire, Collini was the first known author to suggest that iron minerals and compounds were responsible for the shades of red, brown and green found in agates, and that specific colors were derived from particular iron minerals. He also knew that basalt contains a large amount of iron and therefore was the origin of the iron in agates. Perhaps most interesting, however, is that he also had the idea that agates were not always hard, solid objects, but were at one time soft and easily affected by the iron-bearing minerals—a concept still utilized today.

## HAIDINGER AND NÖGGERATH

Though the next 70 years were not devoid of writings or research on agates, the next major publication regarding agate formation wasn't released until 1849. Austrian geologist Wilhelm

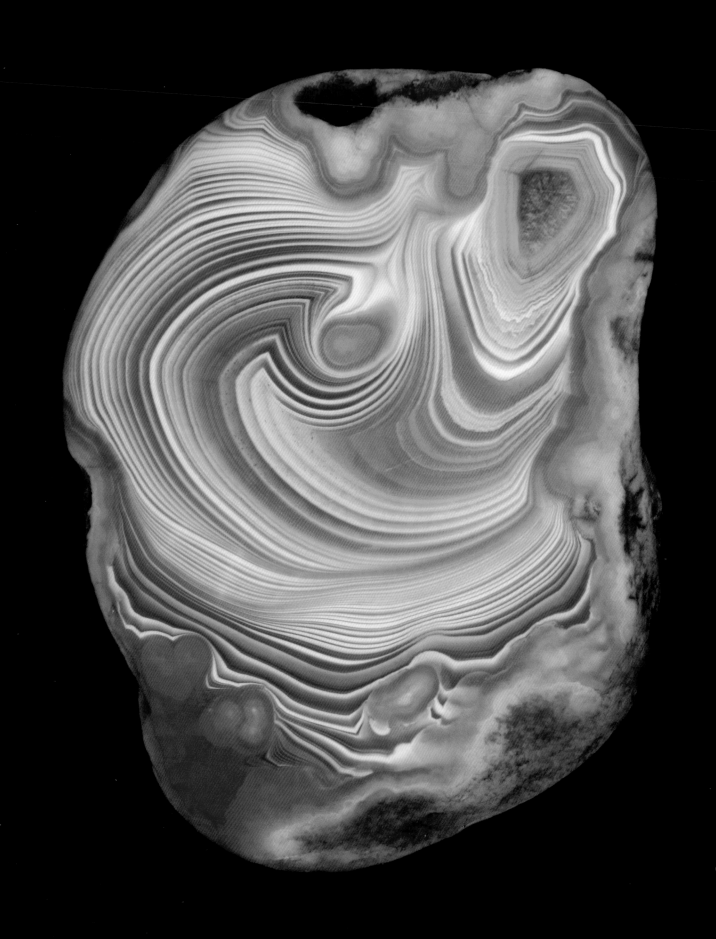

FIGURE 56

von Haidinger and German mineralogist Johann Nöggerath published a series of letters in which they discussed their ideas of agate formation. Though they opposed each other on most topics, they both agreed on the method by which silica entered the vesicle. They felt that the source was groundwater percolating through the tiny pores in the rock. Their hypothesis stated that as the water seeped through the pores, it dissolved silica from the minerals in the rock, forming a silica solution which then collected in a vesicle. However, they disagreed on the manner in which the silica was deposited. Haidinger felt that each layer was deposited in a solid state, but Nöggerath could not see how silica could penetrate a solid chalcedony layer. Gustav Kenngott, another German mineralogist, agreed with Nöggerath, insisting that each band was deposited first as a soft layer through which more silica could pass. He felt that if the outer layers, which formed first, were solid, the inner layers would not have been able to form. The writings of Haidinger, Nöggerath, and Kenngott were very influential contributions to agate research at the time, and many of their concepts formed the basis of today's theories.

## THE TWENTIETH CENTURY

By the turn of the twentieth century, the rate of agate research had accelerated, and scientists were beginning to expand their ideas of agate genesis by incorporating many chemistry studies into their theories. In 1901, M. Bauer proposed that hot springs (naturally heated, mineral-rich water) rose upwards through the rock and filled vesicles. As the water receded, it left a coating of silica-rich water on the inside of the vesicle, which later dried out and hardened into a band. The repetition of this process, he believed, would create agate banding. Though this theory may seem unlikely upon first glance, we must remember that hot springs are much more common in volcanic areas, such as those that created agate-bearing formations of basalt and rhyolite. That same year, M. F. Heddle suggested an entirely new mechanism for agate formation. He believed that the first layer of chalcedony, or the husk, acts as a semi-permeable membrane by which the process of osmosis can begin. Osmosis is the action of water moving from an area with a low concentration of a dissolved substance (a solute) to an area with a high concentration of that same substance. In this case, the solute is silica, which, in Heddle's theory, was already present and abundant inside the vesicle but not in the surrounding rock. Through osmosis,

water was drawn into the vesicle and toward the silica equally from all sides, which he believed was the reason why the banding in agates is evenly spaced and not often affected by gravity. Bauer's hot spring theory still has some bearing today, and Heddle's theory of osmosis in agates has proven very important, and has since appeared in more modern theories.

## RAPHAEL LIESEGANG

In 1915, German chemist Raphael Liesegang published *Die Achate* (The Agates), in which he proposed an agate formation theory that would become one of the most important and well known for decades to come. But his work didn't begin with agates. He was a colloid chemist and developed a level of fame performing experiments with gels. In 1896, Liesegang changed the history of chemistry when he discovered a phenomenon known today as "Liesegang rings." He began by placing a drop of a metallic salt compound (a combination of a metallic element with an acid) onto a solidified gel containing another salt. The metallic salt diffused into the gel and began a chemical reaction with the other salt. As the two salts combined and reacted, they produced a third chemical that formed a hard ring surrounding the original point of contact between the two salts. As the reaction continued and the metallic salt spread further throughout the gel, another ring formed, separated from the first by a ring of clear gel. He noted that the rhythmically (highly ordered) banded formation of the peculiar concentric rings looked remarkably like those of an agate. Later, Liesegang rings were noted throughout the natural world, where they are evident in fungal colonies, iron stains in sandstone and even in the human body.

It made sense for Liesegang to apply his laboratory findings to agate formation, as the theory that posited that agates began as a single soft body of silica, namely a silica gel, was already growing in popularity. In addition, it had long been known that basalt and similar agate-bearing igneous rocks are high in iron content. Liesegang believed that the iron salts found in agates, such as hematite and goethite, were introduced to the silica gel by the surrounding rock, thereby initiating the chemical reaction and producing Liesegang rings. He then suggested that the gel crystallized first into opal, which later transformed into quartz. Initial reaction to his hypothesis was positive; his theory was elegantly simple and

FIGURE 56
This Lake Superior agate shows how wild and contorted the banded patterns can be.
Approx. 3" x 2"
(7.6 cm x 5m)

quickly became a readily accepted solution to the problem of agate genesis.

While Liesegang's theory was accepted for some time, not everyone believed it. In 1917, O. M. Reis was the first to publish a description of the uniquely different structure of the husk, or outermost layer of chalcedony. He suggested that since

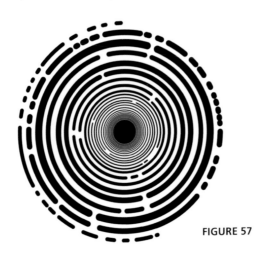

FIGURE 57

it was formed of spheres of chalcedony and thus differed from the internal bands, it must have formed separately from the rest of the agate. This was in direct conflict with Liesegang's theory, which required the vesicle to be completely filled with a silica gel before formation could take place. Reis also suggested that impurities, such as iron minerals, did not enter the vesicle after the gel, but simultaneously.

In 1930, researchers G. Linck and H. Heinz attempted to determine why agate bands often alternate colors and microcrystalline forms. They adapted Haidinger and Nöggerath's theory in an attempt to create a hypothesis more complete than Liesegang's. They believed that the banding is a result of alternating wet and dry seasons in the environment. Wet seasons would cause large amounts of water to percolate downward through the rock, dissolving silica on its way and carrying it to a vesicle. Dry seasons would cause groundwater to rise out of the ground and evaporate, passing vesicles and depositing silica on its way. They thought that these different sources of water could produce an even alternating banding pattern. However, researcher Knoll pointed out that such a system would be highly dependent on gravity and would produce only gravitationally banded agates, a variety of agate with flat, straight, parallel bands; these agates are less common than the classic, concentrically banded agate.

By this time, most researchers agreed that agates likely developed from a silica colloid, but in 1930, Jessop expanded upon these gel-oriented ideas. He proposed that all of the impurities found in an agate (including iron minerals and dissolved gases) were present at the same time the gel was deposited. He pioneered the concept of a "crystallization front," in which pure quartz or chalcedony crystallizes inward, pushing impurities along its front surfaces until the impurities accumulate enough and deposit as a colored band. This happens because quartz prefers to grow from pure silica, so it rejects impurities by pushing them out of the developing crystals. Eventually, there are too many impurities built up in front of the crystallization front and the chalcedony is forced to form an impure band that incorporates the impurities. That same year, Jessop also challenged the prevailing theory that white, opaque chalcedony was a mixture of quartz and opal.

## DISPROVING LIESEGANG

Other aspects of Liesegang's theory were under fire too. His claim that iron salts reacting in a silica gel were what produced the agate's characteristic banding saw its first major criticism in 1934 when P. P. Pilipenko presented several problems with Liesegang's theory. Three of his observations are the most damning. First, Pilipenko observed that Liesegang rings are not entirely solid, but very often contain splits or breaks, features rarely seen in agate banding. He also noted that there are many agate geodes (agates with a hollow center), and if Liesegang's theory were true, it failed to account for the existence of such agates. Finally, Pilipenko felt that Liesegang's theory failed to explain how many different colored bands can be present throughout an agate and how several colors can be present even within the same band. But perhaps the biggest flaw in Liesegang's theory was presented in 1939 by T. Isemura. His research showed that even a very rich silica gel is primarily water and only contains 5% silica by volume. Therefore, Liesegang's theory, which assumes that the vesicle is entirely filled with a silica gel, could only result in the formation of a thin chalcedony coating, if one at all. Liesegang published some papers in response to his critics, but he failed to sufficiently defend his theory. He later conceded that multiple fillings of silica gel would be required for the formation of an agate.

In 1948, R. Nacken published results of his experiments involving silica glass. Glass is a semisolid with no organized crystal structure, and glasses comprised of silica can be found in nature. Nacken's experiments showed that with great heat and steam, silica glass will actually recrystallize into quartz. Nacken therefore proposed a theory that droplets or orbs of molten silica are present in a basalt flow that then crystallize into chalcedony upon cooling. According to his theory, the agate banding is formed during the cooling process in a manner similar to the way molten sulfur will produce a band-like effect when cooled rapidly.

## CONTEMPORARY AGATE RESEARCH

Nacken's ideas didn't survive long. In 1954, W. Fischer found several key flaws in Nacken's theory, the most prominent of which was that basalt lava and silica have two very different melting points, and therefore could not exist together as fluids. Basalt's melting point is around 1,100 degrees Celsius (about 2,000 degrees Fahrenheit) while silica does not melt until it reaches 1,600 degrees Celsius (almost 3,000 degrees Fahrenheit). Fischer also sought to further disprove Liesegang's hypothesis, stating that Liesegang clearly had not applied his laboratory findings to enough natural observations. Fischer felt that if Liesegang had compared his results to many more natural agates, he would have seen more of the flaws with his theory and not been so certain of his ideas. Today, it is clear that Liesegang's theory lacked a sufficient amount of supporting evidence and it has been all but disproved. Perhaps Liesegang's primary shortcoming was that he based his hypothesis entirely on lab experiments and few real-world observations —this is the opposite problem most theorists have. When applied to observations of real agates, Liesegang's theory is unable to explain many of the different varieties of agates and the structures within them, especially gravitationally banded agates. Liesegang rings were certainly a significant discovery and have proven useful in biology as well as other areas of geology, but they are an insufficient formation theory for agates.

The second half of the twentieth century saw a boom in agate research, partly as a result of the invention of new instruments and lab equipment, which aided in observations. In 1963, researchers Keith and Padden developed a theory of spherulitic chalcedony growth. While we now know that the outermost layer of chalcedony is made of spherulites, Keith and Padden suggested many years earlier that every band of chalcedony is comprised of tiny quartz spheres with "fingers," or fibers, that grow inward toward a fresh supply of silica gel at the center of the agate. The fibers of chalcedony form a crystallization front, pushing impurities into their own bands, as in Jessop's theory. They also proposed that impurities of certain non-silicate minerals, such as calcite and barite, enter the vesicle alongside the silica and later interact with the iron-bearing minerals in the surrounding rock, drawing in the color-causing impurities.

A few years later in 1976, Sunagawa and Ohta revived the theory that a silica solution, not a gel, entered the vesicle via tiny pores in the rock as well as in the extant hard layers of chalcedony. They were primarily interested in the idea of silica polymers, or groupings of silica molecules suspended in a fluid. They felt that silica polymers would easily coagulate, or build up, on the inner wall of the vesicle, and begin building upon each other, forming long fibers of silica that would later harden to form chalcedony. They believed this was the key to chalcedony development because single silica molecules, called monomers, do not bond easily with each other to form quartz. Elements of Sunagawa and Ohta's theory have seen acceptance and were later incorporated into other theories, and their ideas seem particularly relevant in explaining gravitationally banded agates.

In 1984, M. Landmesser, one of the most prominent agate researchers working in recent years, expanded upon the research of Keith and Padden by way of many microscope observations. He presented definitive visual evidence that the outermost layer of chalcedony was indeed composed of chalcedony spherulites and that the inner bands were made of tiny parallel fibers. Landmesser also promoted the "gel theory," or the idea that a silica gel organized itself into bands via chemical reactions within the gel itself. The prevailing self-organizing gel theory was further supported in 1989 by H. G. Macpherson who suggested that a chemical reaction caused the silica gel to separate into hydrous, or water-rich, chalcedony layers and anhydrous, or water-poor, microgranular quartz layers, resulting in distinctly separated bands.

In 1990, Y. Wang and E. Merino introduced their theory that aluminum impurities, which are abundant in agates, acted as a catalyst for chalcedony growth. They published an elaborate model for agate formation based on the idea that aluminum speeds up the crystallization process until eventually all the nearby silica is depleted. Crystallization would then slow drastically until more silica was available, at which point the rapid crystallization could once again occur. Wang and Merino felt that this hypothesis explained the bands, especially those of alternating thicknesses, better than any previous theory.

Landmesser published another article in 1992 where he added more aspects to the existing gel theory of agate formation. He proposed that the silica was transported through the basalt and into the vesicle in the form of silicic acid. This idea proved to be important and is widely accepted today. He also acknowledged that the silica necessary for agate formation must come into the vesicle from an external source.

## CHEMICAL REACTIONS IN AGATES

Expanding upon their own research from 1991, R. K. Pabian and A. Zarins published one of the most complete agate formation theories to date in 1994, which included an entirely new mechanism for the creation of agate banding. Utilizing the 1987 studies performed by Madore and Freeman, Pabian and Zarins attributed agate banding to a peculiar chemical reaction known as the Belousov-Zhabotinskii reaction, or "BZ reaction," for short. This reaction occurs when a vesicle filled with silica gel also contains water that bears alkaline (basic) elements such as potassium, calcium and barium, which are incompatible with silicic acid due to similar electrical charges. In the Belousov-Zhabotinskii reaction, incompatible compounds generate an electrical imbalance in the silica gel, causing them to separate in an orderly, rhythmic fashion that can produce evenly spaced bands of alternating colors. The result is similar to the repeating circular waves formed when a stone is dropped into water, and laboratory examples of the BZ reaction have produced startlingly agate-like patterns of concentric rings. Pabian and Zarins also attribute the BZ reaction to the initiation of the crystallization of chalcedony spherulites. Expanding upon Keith and Padden's theory of spherulitic chalcedony growth, Pabian and Zarins suggested that the chalcedony tries to expel the incompatible alkaline compounds from its structure by pushing them inward and away from the crystallizing band by a crystallization front. When a large enough layer of the impurities

accumulates in front of a developing chalcedony band, they too are deposited as a band. While Pabian and Zarins' model may seem complicated on first glance, it is actually a fairly simple set of principles that could explain a large number of the different varieties of agates.

Terry Moxon, one of the foremost authorities on agate genesis, published *Agate: Microstructure and Possible Origin* in 1996, an important book in which he challenges many past theories and analyzes the many variables that must contribute to the formation of an agate. Moxon determined that due to the extremely organized nature of agate structures, crystallization of chalcedony simply cannot begin until the vesicle is entirely filled with silica. Supporting the spherulitic chalcedony growth theory, he also attempted to discredit theories involving repeated inflows of a liquid silica solution by proposing that in order for enough silica to be deposited, so much water must pass through the rock that the vesicles themselves would have eroded and lost their regular amygdaloid shapes. Since agates often have these distinct rounded shapes, and since we can observe agate amygdules still embedded in their matrix, we know such erosion didn't take place.

In 2001, Götze and his colleagues published an interesting study that seemingly proves that agates form as a result of several processes, not a single chemical reaction. Their study looked at tiny trace amounts of rare elements present within agates. In particular, they were interested in the different isotopes (elemental forms) of oxygen and hydrogen, including deuterium, a rare form of hydrogen that naturally occurs in water. They found that in many agates, the amount of deuterium changes from band to band. They found similar results when testing for different isotopes of oxygen, which also differed between bands in the same agate. Such distinct variations in these isotopes can only mean that agates did not form from a single body of silica, and that each band developed separately from one another, which Götze believes could be a result of an initial deposit of opal or by interrupted flows of silica.

In 2004, Landmesser published yet another article in which he established a new agate formation theory based on ideas presented in past theories. First, he suggested that the pores within the basalt surrounding the vesicle must be saturated with silicic acid, thus providing a source of silica for the vesicle to draw from during the formation of an agate. He then proposed the "ripening silica" theory discussed earlier as the mechanism by which chalcedony forms from silicic acid. Silica glass or opal is first deposited as spherulites, then, due to the addition of more silicic acid, the non-crystalline silica turns into cristobalite, and

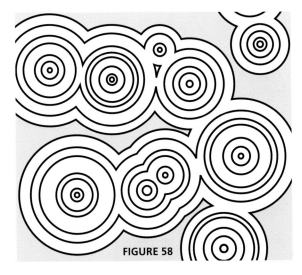

FIGURE 58

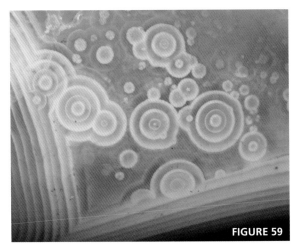

FIGURE 59

finally into chalcedony, or fibrous quartz. This theory was essentially a modification of Keith and Padden's spherulitic chalcedony growth hypothesis. Landmesser's work with gel theories has gained significant popularity in recent years.

## ECKART WALGER

In 2009, Eckart Walger published an excellent article, which was submitted posthumously on his behalf by his colleagues. In it he discussed the many problems of the popular agate formation theories of the past, including Landmesser's, while also proposing a complex but rather complete agate formation theory that takes into consideration many of the conditions both inside and outside of the vesicle. In essence, he incorpo-

rated many of the findings of previous theorists to generate his own theory, which combines many aspects of the gel theory as well as theories that posit multiple inflows of silica. His theory also utilized the principles of osmosis and diffusion. While the details of his theory will be discussed later, Walger provides one of the most thorough examinations of the many aspects of agate formation. However, his theory is not without its criticisms as well.

While the most recent theories are also the most relevant, it is important to consider the full history of agate formation theories and the scientists who created them. As with any science, by looking at what theories have already been proposed and the criticisms that arose from those theories, we can better determine avenues for further study. Each new theory adds to our understanding of agate formation and contributes ideas that can be employed by future theorists. Liesegang's theory, for example, has been largely disproved, but Liesegang's notion that agates start as a silica gel is believed by virtually every theorist today. Even theories that have been disproved are useful because they show us what areas of research are no longer worth pursuing. While even a brief overview of the history of agate research may seem long and somewhat confusing, it is important to our understanding of agates because many of the concepts formed decades ago, such as chalcedony crystallization fronts, spherulitic chalcedony growth, and chemical reactions such as the Belousov-Zhabotinskii reaction, are key elements of today's theories. And from this rich history of agate research and our accumulated knowledge of what may or may not have taken place during agate genesis come the two branches of modern agate study—the accumulation theory, which builds upon the earliest ideas of agate formation—and the differentiation theory, which incorporates many of the newest findings from recent years. Whether or not either of these theories will explain agate formation remains to be seen, but researchers from both sides have made significant advancements in recent years.

## ACCUMULATION THEORY

The accumulation theory, known colloquially as the inflow theory, is based upon the idea that agates are formed by the accumulation of layers that have been individually deposited over time by multiple inflows of silica. At the core of the

FIGURE 58
A generalized illustration of the rings produced in a Belousov-Zhabotnikii reaction.

FIGURE 59
Rings in an agate that look surprisingly similar to those produced by the Belousov-Zhabotnikii reaction. 3x magnification

accumulation theory is the idea that agate bands form and are well ordered due to external processes. For example, the amount of available water and the climate at the time of an agate's formation are two external forces considered by inflow theorists.

The highly organized concentric structure of the layers within an agate clearly signifies that a unique natural rhythm governed their orderly formation. Proponents of the accumulation theory attribute the agate's internal order to the repetition of certain events happening outside the vesicle. Most of the oldest theories, such as Haidinger and Nöggerath's influential work, fall into this category simply because it was the most logical theory up until the twentieth century. However, accumulation theories quickly fell out of favor after Liesegang published his theory involving colloidal silica, which seemed to offer a better explanation of agate banding.

Linck and Heinz's accumulation theory from 1930 is of particular interest because it was one of the first to focus on climate changes as a key role in banding formation. They suggested that periods of a very wet climate would cause large amounts of meteoric water (water derived from the atmosphere) to percolate downward through the rock, which could bring dissolved silica down into the vesicles. During dry seasons, heat and evaporation would cause groundwater to rise up out of the earth, filtering through vesicles on its way and depositing a new layer of silica. To Linck and Heinz, this theory resolved several issues. Primarily, it described the mechanism that causes even, orderly agate banding, but the theory also explained coloration of agate bands. Silica coming from two different sources—the rocks above and below the vesicle—would likely provide different amounts of impurities, and produce bands with different colorations. But this theory is governed too much by gravity and if it were true, it would take a very long time to produce an agate. In addition, as Moxon pointed out in 1996, such a large amount of water passing through the vesicle would likely erode it before the agate could successfully form. Still, Linck and Heinz's theory considered elements of agate genesis that few had taken into consideration before.

The accumulation theory saw more support in 1976 with Sunagawa and Ohta's theory of silica polymers. A single molecule is known as a monomer, and an example is a single silica molecule. A polymer, on the other hand, is composed of many identical monomers that have bonded together in a larger unit. (A polymer can therefore be considered as a large molecule.) One of the most interesting aspects of polymers is their long, thin, chain-like structure. Sunagawa and Ohta believed that strands of polymerized silica began to accumulate on the walls of the vesicle, which later hardened to form the fibers visible in chalcedony. They also suggested that the silica polymers were transported within a liquid solution, not suspended in a gel, which would allow them to easily seep into the tiny pores within basalt and chalcedony. Supporting this theory is the fact that silica polymerizes easily under acidic conditions, which we now know could be present due to our current knowledge of silicic acid. Further studies regarding silica gel were published in the 1980s which diminished the importance of silica polymers, but certain aspects of Sunagawa and Ohta's theory persist today, especially in regards to some of the less common varieties of agate.

It is Eckart Walger's 2009 article that provides the most recent, complete and viable accumulation theory. By building off of many previous theories, Walger put together a hypothesis that combines elements of the accumulation theory with elements from (the theories concerning silica gel).

Walger's theory, like Landmesser's 2004 gel theory, begins by suggesting that both the vesicle as well as the tiny pores within the rock surrounding the vesicle must be filled and saturated with silicic acid before formation can take place. The large amount of silicic acid within the vesicle flocculates (clumps) and develops into a colloid (a gel), which then begins to nucleate, or attach, to various points along the inside of the vesicle wall. This begins the development of chalcedony spherulites which continue to accumulate silica and grow larger until they contact each other. When the first gel layer, comprised of spherulites, is allowed to dry out and crystallize, the outermost layer, or husk, is formed. Walger believed that the husk was critical to the formation of the rest of the agate because it helps create an area of lower pressure within the vesicle, which then changes how the vesicle interacts with the surrounding rock and the silicic acid.

We know that chalcedony contains micropores, or tiny openings, within its fibrous crystal structure, which is why agates can be artificially dyed. Walger felt that the silicic acid saturating the surrounding rock could move through the first layer of chalcedony and into the vesicle through the tiny pores by means of diffusion. Diffusion is the action of particles spreading from areas of high concentration to areas of low concentration simply due to the random movement of the particles. According to Walger, after the outermost layer of chalcedony has formed and solidified, the interior of the vesicle contains water with a very low silica concentration, as much of the silica is removed during the formation of the husk. The pores within the surrounding rock, however, still contain a high concentration of silica in the form of silicic acid. The silica molecules naturally move from "crowded" areas outside the vesicle to inside the vesicle, where there is more room; this occurs because the area of lower pressure within the vesicle draws the liquid inward, and because of the random motion of the silica molecules in the acid. This supplies the interior of the vesicle with a fresh supply of silica.

## WALGER'S THEORY

Walger believed that the layers of chalcedony that formed after the outermost layer grew in an entirely different manner. As silicic acid diffused into the vesicle, its silica was deposited on the inner wall of the husk as a gel, leaving the bulk of the vesicle filled with water. In his article, Walger describes the manner in which a layer of soft silica gel acts as a semi-permeable membrane, which initiates the process of osmosis. While he surprisingly doesn't reference Heddle's theory of osmosis in agates, Walger describes a similar process. Semi-permeable membranes allow water to pass through them in order to move from areas of low solute concentration to areas of high solute concentration. The solute, in this case, is, of course, silica. Because the silicic acid within the vesicle deposits its silica into the forming gel layer, the leftover water is naturally drawn out of the vesicle and back into an area with a higher concentration of silica. The water therefore moves through the developing gel layer, then through the porous solidified husk, and finally back into the surrounding rock where it begins to collect more silica. This process of diffusion and osmosis continues until one of two conditions are met: if the inflow of silicic acid is uninterrupted and continues for a long period of time, then the accreting gel layer can eventually become too thick and prevent the further inflow of silica, or the external source of water can be temporarily interrupted, causing the cessation of the inflow.

Once the process has stopped via one or both of the conditions, the gel layer then dries out and crystallizes to form chalcedony.

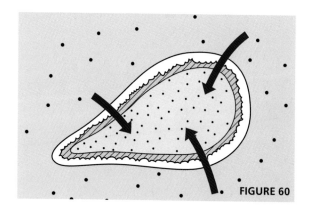

FIGURE 60

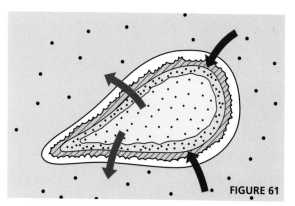

FIGURE 61

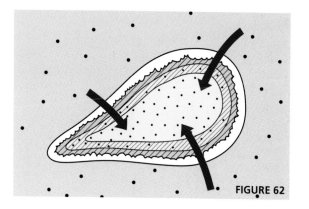

FIGURE 62

**FIGURE 60**
Walger's theory begins with silicic acid entering the vesicle via diffusion and accumulating in the center of the vesicle.

**FIGURE 61**
As the vesicle fills with the silica solution, a thin coating of gel begins to accumulate on the inner walls of the vesicle. As this gel layer thickens, it stops the inflow of silicic acid. After the water deposits its silica on the walls, it is pulled out of the vesicle via osmosis.

**FIGURE 62**
Once the newly deposited gel layer hardens, porosity is returned and silicic acid can once again diffuse into the vesicle.

According to Walger's theory, after the gel solidifies, the micropores within the new layer of chalcedony open to allow new inflows of silicic acid to enter the vesicle. The entire diffusion-osmosis process can begin to form the third layer of the agate, and so on. However, if at any time during the agate's formation there is no silicic acid remaining in the surrounding rock due to a prolonged interruption in the external water source, the agate will remain incomplete and hollow. This is known as an agate geode. Alternatively, if water returns to the rock, possibly due to a wet season, the process can initiate once again. Eventually, there may not be enough silica for chalcedony growth. A silica-poor solution would not flocculate (clump) and form a gel, instead precipitating directly into macrocrystalline quartz. Since a large number of agates contain a macrocrystalline quartz center, Walger suggests that the previously formed chalcedony used the bulk of the available silica, not leaving enough remaining silica for continued chalcedony growth, instead resulting in a center filled with macrocrystalline quartz.

## BENEFITS AND CRITICISMS

One of the benefits of Walger's theory is that it accounts for the fact that igneous rocks, particularly basalt, retain very little water. With Walger's theory, what little water is available is "recycled" via the processes of osmosis and diffusion. Walger's theory could also be combined with Linck and Heinz's theory of wet and dry seasons or Bauer's hot spring hypothesis to provide a broader source of the water and silica required for agate formation. In fact, most accumulation theorists tend to be much more concerned with the source of the silicic acid than gel theorists are.

Walger's article discusses how this method of agate formation can account for many of the varieties of agate, including gravitationally banded agates, eye agates and more. But his theory is not without its problems. He suggests that iron-based, color-causing impurities weather out of the rock and enter the vesicle within the silicic acid, which is accepted by most theorists; however, it is extremely unlikely that the process described in his article could result in the red-and-white alternating bands seen in many Lake Superior agates. After all, if the water continually exits and re-enters the vesicle via the same body of rock, the impurities produced by that rock should be the same with each repeated inflow. Perhaps this would be more likely if we considered two sources of water, such as in Linck and Heinz's theory, but the production of such organized, alternating colors by external forces would still be improbable. Gel theorists, on the other hand, attribute the organized coloration of agates to an internal mechanism governing the distribution of impurities.

Another complaint with Walger's theory is that if silicic acid bearing impurities continually filters through the older layers of chalcedony in order to get to the center of the vesicle, the outermost layers of an agate should theoretically be stained very dark due to the prolonged contact with impurities. This would create a color gradient within agates, causing the outer bands to be much darker than the inner bands. However, this is a trait we do not often see in agates.

Then there is the criticism brought up by many researchers throughout the years that a single piece of basalt can contain two agate nodules in very close proximity to each other, sometimes just millimeters apart. Yet both of these agates can contain completely different patterns and color-causing impurities. If the same flow of silicic acid supplied both agates with silica, it is easy to believe that the resulting agates would be very similar, but we know that this is not always the case. Accumulation theories have largely failed to reconcile this fact.

Finally, researcher T. Moxon points out in his 2009 publication that there is no reason why silicic acid would diffuse into the vesicle when it seems much more likely that it would continue its unimpeded downward percolation through the pores in the basalt. Walger states that his theory does require the rock surrounding the basalt to be saturated with silicic acid for the process of agate development to begin, which could keep silicic acid in contact with the vesicles for the process to complete, but even with the lower pressure within the vesicle drawing silica inward, some question the likelihood of a prolonged saturation of such a large formation of rock.

## PROS AND CONS OF THE INFLOW THEORY

Accumulation theories, or inflow theories, receive a lot of criticism because of their dependency on seemingly random external events, such as climate change and availability of water. On the other hand, inflow theories provide a definite, easily understood orderly mechanism for the development of banding. Walger's theory may not be perfect, but it is forward-thinking in that it incorporates (and even depends on) sciences other than geology, as it places considerable emphasis on hydrodynamics (the study of liquids and fluids). Some of the positive and negative aspects of the accumulation theory can be summarized as follows.

Pros:
- Provides a logical mechanism for production of banding
- Takes into account the several possible sources of silica and water

- Accounts for the formation of some varieties of agates other than those with concentric banding, including agate geodes

- Considers that the problem of agate formation is not for geology alone to solve and applies other sciences

Cons:
- Silicic acid would not likely diffuse into the vesicle when it could more easily bypass it altogether

- The process of agate formation would likely take an extremely long time when recent evidence suggests otherwise

- Repeated inflow of water would likely erode the vesicle before completion of the agate

- The formation of bands of alternating colors is highly unlikely, even if the silica comes from multiple sources

- Neighboring agate amygdules can have different impurities

- Accumulation theories don't often take into account the transparent, colorless microgranular quartz bands present in most agates

## DIFFERENTIATION THEORY

Contemporary differentiation theory, commonly known as the gel theory, developed largely as an offshoot of Liesegang's original colloid-based theory. Whereas the accumulation theory argues that agate banding is caused by external processes, the differentiation theory focuses on the idea that agate banding is a result of internal chemical or physical changes in a silica gel. This hypothesis is therefore dependent upon a closed system, one where a vesicle filled with a silica gel is self-organizing and banding occurs independent of external factors. This theory has gained significant support in recent years, and many studies have in fact corroborated the theory. Traditionally, the differentiation theory is concerned with a single, one-time filling of a vesicle with a silica colloid that then separates into orderly bands via a rhythmic, internal chemical reaction. Some more recent theories vary somewhat, but the core principles remain the same.

Liesegang's contribution of the gel theory advanced the study of agates possibly more than any other researcher in the last 100 years, but it was the differentiation theorists who came after him that provided some of the most researched

and viable ideas. Keith and Padden's theory of spherulitic chalcedony growth, in which chalcedony begins as tiny quartz spheres which then grow outward by extending fibers deeper into the agate and toward a supply of fresh silica, has seen support in recent years. The same is true for Macpherson's suggestion that chemical reactions, such as Pabian and Zarins' consideration of the BZ reaction, cause the gel to separate into hydrous and anhydrous layers, which later harden to form distinct agate bands. But there are inherent difficulties associated with differentiation theories, as the theory relies on complex, and often poorly understood, chemical reactions and many of the concepts presented in differentiation theories are difficult to understand without a sufficient background in chemistry and physics.

The theory of chalcedony growth from a silica gel developed by M. Landmesser in 1984 saw initial support which has only grown as he has modified his theory several times in years since. Today, Landmesser's theory centers on the idea of "ripening" silica. He believes that silicic acid first saturates the pores within the basalt, including the vesicle itself. Eventually, the concentration of silica-rich solution within the vesicle converts to a silica gel. Silica molecules within the gel then begin to accumulate into larger particles which adhere to various points along the inner wall of the vesicle, forming sites at which more silica will nucleate. As the accumulation of silica continues along the inner wall of the vesicle, a band of silica gel is formed. Landmesser assumes that the body of silica gel within the vesicle contains numerous variables, such as silica particle size and differing impurities, which he believes causes the gel to organize itself into layers of varying composition. Therefore, he claims that the banded structure of an agate has already been determined long before the silica turns to chalcedony.

As the banded silica gel begins to harden, it turns into silica glass or opal, which contain much less silica than does chalcedony. Landmesser's theory then states that because silica can attract more silica, particularly in the presence of other elements, diffusion will draw more silicic acid from the surrounding rock into the vesicle. The incoming silicic acid "ripens" the existing mass of solidified silica by partially dissolving and then subsequently enriching each of the layers. There are many forms of solidified silica, including glass, opal, cristobalite and quartz or chalcedony, as well as some rarer intermediate stages, each of which requires increasing amounts of silica to form. Therefore, Landmesser states that, due to the slow diffusion process, each band may be in a different stage of silica growth or "ripeness," further distinguishing the bands from each other. After each layer of an agate has eventually been enriched with enough silica for it to recrystallize into chalcedony, the agate is complete.

## PROBLEMS WITH THE THEORY

The "ripening" transformation of silica from one form to another has been observed in nature, and Landmesser feels comfortable applying this principle to agate formation. But there are several problems with Landmesser's theory, few of which are addressed in his papers. One of the criticisms of his theory involves the density of various forms of silica. Because silica gel is generally over 90% water, it is much less dense than solid opal. Opal, which is generally comprised of approximately 10–15% water, will therefore take up much less space than the silica gel it formed from. Similarly, chalcedony is considerably more dense than opal because it contains less water and consists of more tightly packed, well-organized crystal fibers. Therefore, the transition from a silica gel to opal to cristobalite and finally to chalcedony results in an increase in density, but should also result in a significant decrease in the size of the formation, as each subsequent variety of solid silica has a more compact structure. Because the silica gel clings to the inner walls of the vesicle as it dries out, the agate resulting from this lengthy process would also be formed only along the interior of the vesicle and contain a hollow center, also called a geode. Landmesser's original theory would therefore only result in agate geodes, which in reality are not very common. Landmesser later addressed the concerns of silica density by amending his theory with the concept of pores within the crystalline structure of chalcedony. He proposed that microscopic openings can collect excess silica diffusing into the agate, further enriching the chalcedony, increasing its density and retaining enough size to fill the vesicle entirely.

But not all of the criticisms of his theory are so easily dismissed. As Walger pointed out in his 2009 article, many odd structures within agates cannot be explained by Landmesser's theory. Landmesser attributes many of the strangest and wildest patterning found in agates to deformation. Many differentiation theorists believe that agates not only form in a soft gel state, but that they also remain in a semisolid state for a very long time. In that time, Landmesser suggests that any number of internal causes, such as increased pressure inside the vesicle created by the crystallizing chalcedony, or external actions, such as the basalt shifting, could cause the semisolid agate to be deformed, pulling, smearing, or pushing the banded pattern within. Walger, however, successfully shows that many of these "deformation structures" are far too organized and are so similar from agate to agate that they could not possibly have been a result of random deformation of the gel.

## PABIAN AND ZARINS

In 1994, R. K. Pabian and A. Zarins published their differentiation theory involving the Belousov-Zhabotinskii reaction, which was later published again and amended in Pabian's 2006 book. While their theory is decidedly complex, it offers an attractive alternative to Landmesser's gel theory because it better considers the conditions outside of the vesicle and the events that took place in order for an agate to begin forming. Pabian and Zarins begin by supposing that a newly formed basalt flow is later buried by rhyolite ash. Rhyolite lava contains many volatile gases which can result in the molten rock being blown apart by violent explosions, pulverizing rock and causing ash and dust to bury the landscape. The heat of the ash causes it to melt or weld together, forming the clastic igneous rock called tuff.

According to Pabian and Zarins' theory, as the tuff formation weathers, lakes form in the resulting depressions, collecting minerals and elements decomposing from the rock. Rhyolite, its ash, and tuff are all rich with silica as well as minerals containing alkaline elements, such as calcium, sodium, potassium and barium, all of which are present in the water of these "alkaline lakes." Alkaline elements, which have the opposite properties of acids and are incompatible with silica as they both possess similar electrical charges, are believed to be necessary in order for silica to combine with the water in the lakes to form silicic acid. A rich solution of silicic acid will then transform into silica gel, which is later transported downward into the tuff when the alkaline solutions percolate through the rock. Finally, after traveling further downward and into the underlying basalt, the mixture of alkaline solutions and silica gel accumulates in the vesicles.

As the silica gel is incompatible with the alkaline solutions (as well as with many of the compounds entering the vesicle from the weathering basalt), this begins the BZ reaction, which forms a wave front, or "ripple effect," within the gel that separates the incompatible compounds into concentric rings. During the reaction, Pabian and Zarins believe that the silica gel will begin to develop chalcedony spherulites and separate into hydrous and anhydrous layers. As the BZ reaction continues, the layers of spherulites develop fibers that reach out radially in all directions in search of fresh silica while simultaneously pushing impurities out of their way. The impurities begin accumulating into their own bands or into the spaces between chalcedony fibers, as in Keith and Padden's theory of spherulitic chalcedony growth. As the spherulites and their fibrous extensions contact each other, a common growth direction is established. In other words, when two fibers growing in different directions contact each other, the one growing in the most preferential direction—directly outward and towards a fresh silica supply—then determines the direction of both fibers. As the fibers continue to contact, the parallel nature of the fibers seen under a microscope becomes more prominent. After the reaction slows, the agate remains in a soft, semi-solid state for some time, allowing deformation to further alter the shape of the banding before the agate finally dries out and hardens.

This theory is supported by the properties of immiscible gels. Like oil and water, gels that are immiscible will not mix to form a homogeneous substance. In this case, silica gel will not willingly mix with alkaline solutions or gels, which could initiate the BZ reaction. But Pabian and Zarins' theory is not without its problems. In both their 1994 publication as well as Pabian's 2006 book, they suggest, as does Landmesser, that there is an increase in pressure within the vesicle as the gel crystallizes into chalcedony. It is unclear how the increased pressure is generated, but in his 2006 publication, Pabian attributes it to the "internal forces of crystallization." This is problematic as we know that both pure chalcedony and agates are much more dense than a silica gel, and they therefore take up less space than the silica gel from which they formed. In addition, Pabian and Zarins consider the increased internal pressure the cause of many "deformation structures," primarily the "exit channels" that appear as banded "bulbs" at the edges of an agate. In their theory, the high pressure is relieved by squeezing soft gel out through various points of weakness around the agate's perimeter, resulting in "exit channels." However, as with Landmesser's theory, Walger shows that if the so-called "exit channels" were caused by pressure forcing material outward, it is easy to imagine a high degree of randomness governing their shape. Instead, these structures are very regular in shape and exhibit specific features that can be seen in many different agate specimens. Finally, as Pabian and Zarins' theory considers that the increased pressures inside an agate are a result of the crystallizing chalcedony, then all agates should exhibit "exit channels," but in reality only some agates contain these structures. (These so-called "exit channels" will be discussed in more detail later.)

## CRITICISMS

Another issue with Pabian and Zarins' theory is the very specific volcanic events required for agate growth. While the earth has seen periods of drastically increased volcanic activity, particularly during the formation of Lake Superior's agates, not all volcanic eruptions were violent enough to produce ash. As Moxon explains in his 2009 book, there are basalt formations in India, South America and Scotland that were formed by "quiet" eruptions, producing very little or no ash, yet these areas still yield agates. While Pabian and Zarins' idea of decomposing silica-rich tuff is a novel approach to determining the source of silica, it cannot be a prerequisite for all agate-bearing basalts. Similarly, if decomposing ash or tuff formations were the source of silica for all agates, thousands, if not millions, of years would pass before enough of the rock was weathered to produce a silica solution rich enough to develop into a gel. Moxon's studies on the age of agates in relation to their host rock, however, shows that this is not the case. By developing a system to determine the age of an agate and comparing the findings to the known age of the rock in which it was found, he has ascertained that virtually all agates form relatively shortly after their host rock, except in a few exceptional locations.

Finally, most basalt flows do not bear agates in their uppermost vesicles. As can be observed around Lake Superior, the upper portion of basalt flows generally contains amygdules of soft minerals like chlorite, celadonite, calcite, zeolites, or clays, as well as some harder minerals, such as feldspars and macrocrystalline quartz. Other vesicles high in the basalt are still completely

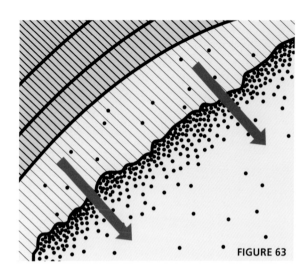

FIGURE 63

**FIGURE 63**
This figure illustrates how a chalcedony crystallization front will push the impurities contained in the vesicle inward. Some impurities are incorporated into the chalcedony.

empty or contain only a thin lining of chlorite. Agates, on the other hand, are generally not encountered until the upper-middle portion of a basalt formation is reached, where vesicles are fewer. In 2009, Moxon used this knowledge to pose another problem for Pabian and Zarins' theory, as well as any other theory relying on the downward transportation of silica—if silica-bearing water percolates downward from the surface, why aren't agates found in the upper portion of basalt flows? Why should the silica-rich water "bypass" empty vesicles higher in the rock in order to collect in much deeper vesicles? These theories cannot yet answer this question.

There is little question that differentiation theories are complicated, but they remain popular explanations for agate formation. Countless observations seemingly prove that agate banding could have only formed by some sort of chemical reaction or other internal mechanism. For example, in 1990, Wang and Merino published an article regarding "twisted" chalcedony fibers that provides a strong argument for their differentiation theory. Wang and Merino's research with aluminum impurities in chalcedony led them to develop the hypothesis of aluminum acting as a catalyst for chalcedony growth. However, they also used these findings as the basis for their own theory of the development of agate banding. They believe that the presence of aluminum, which has a different electrical charge than silica, is necessary to promote the bonding of silica molecules. When this condition is met, rapid chalcedony growth occurs, which then proceeds as a crystallization front. Chalcedony fibers grow inward, pushing aluminum and other impurities in front of the chalcedony. As the layer of aluminum impurities thickens, it actually speeds up the growth of the chalcedony behind it. But as the chalcedony band grows wider, it uses the available nearby silica gel too quickly to continue its current rate of growth. Crystallization then slows drastically, which stops pushing the impurities and allows the aluminum impurities to diffuse back into the gel, subsequently allowing fresh silica to once again contact the crystallizing chalcedony. During this slow phase of crystallization, the chalcedony only grows by using the purest silica it can reach, rejecting all impurities. When enough time has passed, the rapid crystallization once again continues, forming a new crystallization front that pushes more aluminum impurities inward as they fuel the process. The repetition of rapid and slow crystallization phases

results in the agate's banding and continues until the agate is complete.

Certain elements can substitute for each other in compounds due to similar elemental properties. For example, atoms of aluminum can substitute for a minute amount of the silicon in the crystal structure of quartz. During the rapid crystallization stage of Wang and Merino's theory, aluminum is so prevalent at the crystallization front that some is incorporated within the crystal structure of the chalcedony fibers. However, aluminum atoms are larger than silicon atoms, which causes the chalcedony fibers to turn, or twist, as they grow. In contrast, during the slow chalcedony growth phase, the fibers can only continue to grow by using the purest available silica, so the fibers in the "slow growth" layers are short, straight and contain no aluminum. The distinction between twisted and non-twisted chalcedony fibers also provide Wang and Merino with a method by which the bands derive their colors. The twisted, impure chalcedony fibers allow more room for impurities to collect between them, while the short, purer fibers are more densely packed, containing only microscopic bubbles as impurities. Therefore, according to Wang and Merino's theory, the translucent colored bands in an agate are composed of twisted, impure fibers, while the white or opaque gray bands, which are characteristically thinner and more ribbon-like, are composed of tightly packed, purer fibers. All of these ideas are supported by analyses of the two types of bands; thicker, colored bands have increased aluminum content while thin, white bands have little to no aluminum content.

This theory suffers from some of the problems previously described in the other differentiation

FIGURE 64

form an agate must be present from the start. The difficulty with this idea is that silica gels are much less dense than agates, so when the gel loses its water content, the resulting agate would take up less space than the gel. Landmesser suggests that additional incoming silica fills the pores within the agate, increasing the volume of the agate, but other theorists propose less satisfactory ideas. In addition, differentiation theories rely too much on random deformation events creating some of the odd patterns and structures within agates, when in reality, many of these structures seem anything but random.

## PROS AND CONS OF THE GEL THEORY

The differentiation theory offers some distinct advantages over accumulation theory, but as popular as theories like Landmesser's are, they are far from perfect. Research over the past 50 years or more has greatly emphasized the importance of differentiation theories, leading many researchers to work exclusively with differentiation concepts. Perhaps in another 50 years, the research will have advanced to the point where we better understand lesser-known aspects of agate formation such as ripening silica and the pressures that may (or may not) be at work inside the vesicle. Some of the positive and negative aspects of the differentiation theory are as follows.

Pros:
- Provides a reasonable explanation of band production that doesn't rely on random external events
- Crystallization fronts provide a viable mechanism for impurity separation
- Provides a feasible method of impurity distribution, thereby explaining bands with perfectly alternating colors
- Could explain many of the strangely well-organized internal structures, such as fiber twisting

Cons:
- Chemical reactions thought to be responsible for separating bands are difficult to apply to agate formation when we don't yet fully understand the conditions under which agates formed
- Many theories fail to reconcile the fact that silica gel contains primarily water and very little silica, and therefore a single body of gel could not produce a whole agate

theories. However, Wang and Merino also provide some evidence beneficial to all differentiation theories. Particularly, they looked at the arrangement of the twisted fibers in relation to each other. Under scientific lighting and high magnification, they noted that the twisted fibers reflect light differently along their length, resulting in alternating dark and light reflections along the same crystal. When viewed next to many other twisted fibers, a peculiar pattern was observed. The areas of dark reflections are in nearly the same position on every fiber, but differ slightly. The tiny differences in the locations of the dark reflections creates the appearance of a chevron, or zig-zag, pattern across the fibers. Wang and Merino suggested that such an organized arrangement across so many crystals cannot be a result of repeated inflows of silica and individually deposited silica molecules, but instead must be formed by internal reactions "communicating" among all chalcedony fibers. This assumption is hard to disprove.

A large part of Wang and Merino's theory depends on experiments conducted in 1976 by Oehler, who produced chalcedony directly from a silica gel without any of the intermediate silica phases described in Landmesser's theory, such as opal and cristobalite. The experiments involved higher temperatures and pressures than those believed present when agates formed, but Oehler's results are still very important to agate formation theorists. Wang and Merino see this as evidence that agates begin to form at higher temperatures than popularly believed.

These are just a few of the most recent differentiation theories. All differentiation theories are subject to one criticism: If the vesicle was only filled once, then all the material necessary to

**FIGURE 65**
The most puzzling agate in the authors' collection is this small nodule which appears to be missing some of its bands. Approx. 0.5" x 1" (1.3 cm x 2.5 cm)

- Most "deformation structures" are too specific in shape to result from random deformation of a gel
- Many theories fail to fully explain why the husk is of a structurally different composition
- Some theories fail to take into account the many varieties of agate, especially gravitationally banded agates and geodes

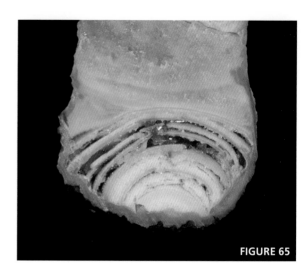

**FIGURE 65**

## DIFFICULTIES WITH BOTH THEORIES

Neither the accumulation theory nor the differentiation theory can explain all the many varieties of agate. After looking at some of the most prevalent past and present theories, it is obvious that we are still missing important pieces of information. With each new theory, we approach a more feasible hypothesis for the development of agate banding, but there are some fundamental problems with these ideas. First, observations in nature and lab tests have shown that chalcedony can develop in multiple ways, so we cannot know the exact mechanism of chalcedony growth in agates until we have determined the exact conditions that must be present within the vesicle, including temperature, pressure, acidity, impurities and so on. Then there is the question of the conditions leading up to agate formation, such as volcanic activity, the earth's climate at the time of formation, the availability of water and a host of other circumstances that can all vary from one agate locality to another. While agates are defined by their characteristic banding, there are other more basic problems to resolve before we can attempt to deduce how banding develops. Too often theorists are more concerned with an agate's bands than with the vesicle's surroundings. Nevertheless, such a focus on banding is understandable, since agate banding continues to be the most alluring aspect of agate formation research. As the most interesting and beautiful element of an agate, any agate theorist would be proud to be the first to propose the "correct answer."

So far, that answer has been elusive. There are many concentrically banded structures found throughout the natural world, including everything from colonies of fungi and tumors to other rocks and minerals. While the mechanisms that form these concentric structures have been explained in many cases, agates remain a mystery. Perhaps we could already have a satisfactory explanation if agates contained coloration that

was less even or banding that wasn't so well defined, but the perfect alternation of bands and sharply delineated colors suggests that an efficient—yet unknown—method of organization is at work.

Perhaps the biggest difficulty with all the previously proposed theories has yet to be discussed: Where does the silica come from? Certainly this is one of the most important aspects of agate formation, yet many theories consider this problem only briefly, while others don't at all. Accumulation theorists have historically been more concerned with the source of silica, but the entire topic has been overshadowed in recent years by theories of band development. At the heart of the problem is the fact that silica does not dissolve easily, and a huge amount of silica and water must be in the presence of alkaline elements to make even a very dilute solution of silicic acid. Also troublesome is the great concentration of silicic acid needed to develop into a silica gel. Pabian and Zarins' recent theory establishes a model involving "alkaline lakes" that formed atop decomposing tuff as a method of providing the vesicle with silica. While it does satisfy the aforementioned conditions, this explanation is too specific; agates are found in a number of different geological environments, not all of which have tuff, so this explanation can't pertain to all of the world's agates. With so many agate-bearing rocks worldwide, it seems more likely that the silica develops through one of several possible processes.

As with any aspect of science, there are always exceptions to the rules. New discoveries will always make us take another look at our past ideas and challenge what we think we understand. Take the agate pictured in Figure 65 for example, which was found on the Keweenaw Peninsula of northern Michigan by the authors in 2008. The agate nodule was found whole, within the dense, greenish basalt in which it had been entombed for the past billion years. After carefully sawing through the one-inch nodule, the internal pattern was revealed, as were peculiar "missing" bands. Indeed, in this specimen, agate banding appears to alternate with band-shaped cavities that are lined with tiny macrocrystalline quartz crystals. How does this agate fit into either of the two primary theories? The missing bands are most likely the result of very impure layers that once contained soft and easily dissolved minerals, such as calcite, which were later weathered and washed away by acidic water. But this idea could possibly apply to either the accumulation or the differentiation theory. The closer we inspect the odd details present in many agates, the more we must challenge the prevailing theories. Without questioning what we think we know about agates, we will never truly determine their origins.

## ACCEPTED ASPECTS OF AGATE GENESIS

The past 300 years of studying, researching and writing about agates have not yielded a definitive theory of agate formation, but they have resulted in a significantly expanded knowledge of our favorite banded stones. There are many aspects of agates and agate formation that are generally undisputed and accepted among all agate theorists. These agreed-upon ideas represent the accumulated findings of researchers over the centuries, and often form the basis of new theories. The following is a list of what we know about agates; these are the many important aspects of agates and their formation that are generally accepted as fact.

### Geological setting:
- Amygdaloidal agates form primarily in basalt, but are also prevalent in rhyolite as well as other volcanic rocks, such as andesite, which is rare in the Lake Superior region
- Agates do not form in the uppermost or lowermost vesicles of a basalt flow, instead forming only in vesicles near the upper-middle portion
- Vesicles are nearly always lined with chlorite or celadonite prior to filling with agate
- Agates are believed to form in temperatures around 100 degrees celsius (212 degrees fahrenheit), but some evidence supports slightly higher temperatures

- Agates form under relatively low pressures, but pressure is believed to be more important to agate formation than temperature

### Silica:
- Silica is very resistant to being dissolved
- Silica is incompatible with alkaline elements due to similar electrical charges
- The presence of alkaline elements will cause silica and water to form silicic acid
- Silicic acid is believed to be the silica solution that initially fills the vesicle
- Silicic acid contains very little silica
- Silicic acid will naturally flocculate into a gel if given enough time
- Silica gel typically consists of over 90% water
- Very dilute silica solutions will produce quartz, but not chalcedony
- Silica polymerizes easily in acidic conditions
- Possible sources of silica are largely unknown

### Chalcedony:
- Chalcedony is quartz; specifically, it is composed of flat, plate-like microscopic crystals of quartz arranged into stacks that appear fibrous
- Chalcedony forms in the cracks and cavities within rocks, particularly basalt
- Theoretically, chalcedony can form in multiple ways
- Chalcedony requires considerably more silica to form than macrocrystalline quartz or microgranular quartz do
- Chalcedony is colorless or pale translucent gray when pure
- Colored chalcedony contains very few impurities despite its rich coloration
- Chalcedony in agates frequently contains ample amounts of mogánite, unless the agates in question are very old

### Agate structure:
- Freshly exposed agates retain a thin coating of chlorite or celadonite, though this feature is absent on weathered agates
- Agate formation is believed to begin by silicic acid filling the vesicle
- Agate bands develop inward, starting with the outermost layer

FIGURE 66A
The complexities of agate formation are exemplified by the sweeping bands and odd pockets of macrocrystalline quartz seen in this beautiful polished paint agate. Approx. 2" x 3" (5cm x 7.6cm)

FIGURE 66
The accepted process of agate formation begins with a thin coating of vesicle-lining minerals, such as chlorite or celadonite, followed by the first generation of chalcedony growth (the outermost layer of an agate) which is composed of spherulitic chalcedony growths.

FIGURE 67
The development of agate banding then follows, but it is unclear how they form. If not enough silica is available, the banding will not fill the entire vesicle.

FIGURE 68
If a silica-poor solution is left over after the formation of banding, macrocrystalline quartz is formed at the center of the agate. Millions of years after development, weathering frees the agate from its host rock.

- Chalcedony fibers within agate bands form perpendicularly to the exterior surface of the agate

- Agate bands are very sharply defined and are evidence of an efficient organizational mechanism

- Outer layers generally closely follow the contours of the vesicle, but the banding appears smoother toward the center of the agate

- The outermost layer of an agate, or husk, consists of radial groupings of chalcedony, called spherulites; this is generally one of the most translucent layers

- Three distinctly textured types of bands can be present in agates; fibrous chalcedony is most common, but microgranular quartz and macrocrystalline quartz bands can occur as well, though they may be absent

- White bands consist of tightly packed chalcedony fibers, often with tiny inclusions of water bubbles

- Bluish gray bands consist of chalcedony that has very minute inclusions of bubbles; these bubbles scatter red light, making the band appear blue

- Translucent colored bands are made of fibrous chalcedony with impurities, while opaque colored bands consist of fibrous chalcedony with a large amount of unweathered impurities

- Colorless bands consist of microgranular quartz, sometimes with a few coarse chalcedony fibers

### Age in agates (from research by T. Moxon):

- Agates generally form within a few million years of their host rock; this is a relatively short amount of time, geologically speaking

- As agates age, chalcedony fibers and quartz microgranules increase in size, and the chalcedony fibers become better organized and more compact

- As time passes, the water content and mogánite content present in an agate decrease while quartz density increases; this signifies that the remaining water may react with mogánite to transform into quartz

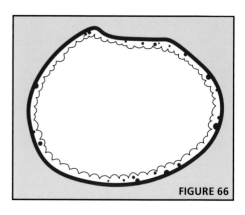

FIGURE 66

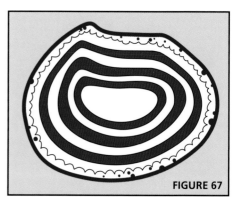

FIGURE 67

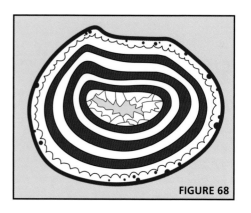

FIGURE 68

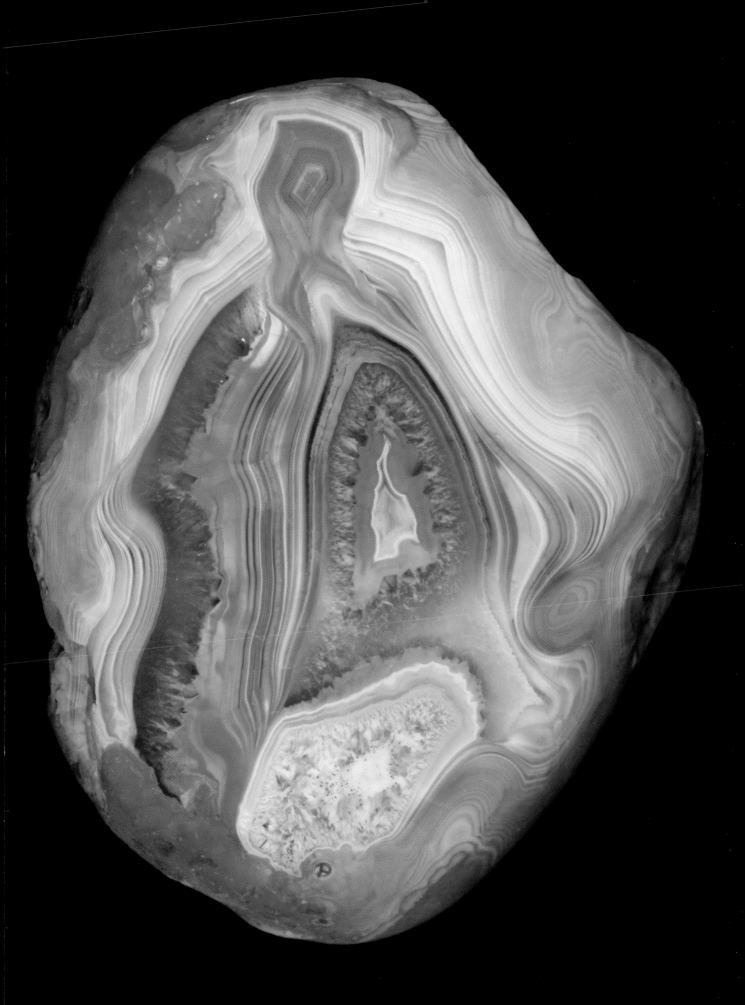

# Source of Silica

## THE ORIGIN OF THE SILICA

We know that even a small agate requires a large amount of silica to form. But even though silica is extremely common in the earth's crust, there are problems when trying to determine how vesicles were supplied with enough silica to form agates. Certainly the source of silica is a major component of agate formation, yet past theories have primarily focused on the mechanism that causes banding in agates, and recent theories continue to largely ignore the problems inherent to providing the vesicle with silica. The difficulties stem from several factors; first, even a large amount of silica solution actually contains very little silica. Secondly, agates do not form in the uppermost vesicles present in rocks; instead, they form in vesicles that occur lower in rocks. Finally, basalt, the primary environment for agates, does not contain much silica itself. There have been several theories throughout the years, but most revolve around a few key ideas.

## POSSIBLE SOURCES

Possibly the first researchers to publish discussions on the source of silica were Haidinger and Nöggerath in 1849; they presented a simple, logical method of silica delivery. They proposed that groundwater percolating through the basalt actually dissolved the silica from the basalt itself, then later deposited it into the vesicle. This theory was generally accepted for quite some time, and still has some relevance today; however, as Moxon points out in both his 1996 and 2009 publications, a very large amount of water would have to pass through the vesicle for this hypothesis to be true, which would likely erode the vesicle and change its shape long before an agate could form. In addition, basalt generally consists of less than 20% silica, and it is simply not a rich enough source of silica to supply a developing agate. Moxon's observations of agate-bearing basalt formations also show that the silica-rich mineral crystals in the basalt—primarily plagioclase feldspar and olivine—actually show very little signs of weathering or decomposition, even when such minerals occur in very close proximity to an agate nodule. It would seem that the basalt cannot provide the vesicle with the silica needed to form an agate. Rhyolite, although a less common host to amygdaloidal agates, contains much more silica, but still does not show the kind of mineral decomposition necessary to provide enough silica.

In 1901, Bauer presented a theory that posited that hot springs were an ideal source of both the silica and water necessary for agate formation. The water from hot springs naturally contains many minerals, including silica, which can deposit as opal, as has been observed around the world. Bauer's theory stated that spring water, heated by the earth, would rise into the basalt and fill the vesicles with a solution of silica. Considering that hot springs are a result of volcanic activity, it is very likely that there was enough hot spring activity throughout agate-bearing volcanic localities at the time of their formation to provide the vesicles with enough silica. As the heat of the volcanic activity dissipated, so did the hot springs, which is why we do not have hot springs around Lake Superior today.

Linck and Heinz's 1930 theory of two alternating sources of silica—meteoric water (rain) and groundwater due to changes in climate—proved to be a unique mechanism for producing the layers within an agate. However, contemporary theories suggest that agates generally form shortly after their host rock, which seems to disprove this idea, as changing climate would no doubt cause agates to take eons to form. Eighteen years later, Nacken provided an interesting hypothesis that suggested the silica was already present in the basalt lava at the time the rock cooled. He claimed that the silica was present as "drops" or "blobs" of melted silica that developed banding as they cooled and solidified. There are major problems with this theory, however, as silica melts at a much higher temperature than basalt.

Pabian and Zarins' 1994 theory of weathering volcanic ash or tuff as a source of silica is compelling. They believe that many basalt flows were later buried by more violent eruptions of rhyolite lava, which produced ash and tuff. The decomposition of the silica- and alkaline-rich tuff provided a source of silica as well as a mechanism by which the silica gel formed and was transported into the basalt below. Since it is known that alkaline elements can contribute to the development of silicic acid and silica gels, Pabian and Zarins' theory provides a plausible scenario where these substances would interact. Nevertheless, as Moxon notes, for agates to form in this manner, violent rhyolite eruptions must take place, and such conditions are not present in many agate-bearing basalts around the world, so this process cannot apply to all agate formation. In addition, the downward percolation of silica would produce agates in vesicles within the upper portion of basalt flows, but in reality, many of the upper vesicles remain empty.

Pabian and Zarins' theory does have some relation to Lake Superior, however. We know that the Lake Superior region was the site of intense volcanic activity over one billion years ago, which produced tons of basalt and rhyolite. While there is no tuff or ash to be found around Lake Superior today, thunder eggs, which are agates that only form within ash or tuff formations, can be found near Grand Marais, Minnesota, close to the shoreline of Lake Superior. Of course, this suggests that violent, ash-throwing eruptions of rhyolite did take place in the Lake Superior region, and that the soft ash and tuff has since been weathered away. If the process proposed by Pabian and Zarins has actually taken place, Lake Superior's agates may be a prime example of their theory. The formation of thunder eggs themselves cannot be compared to amygdaloidal agates because thunder eggs are a simpler matter and likely derived their silica from the silica-rich tuff in which they grew.

Today, our best hypotheses for the source of silica actually reflect Bauer's ideas from over a century ago. Moxon's 2009 publication poses many strong arguments that hot springs and hydrothermal waters are the source of silica in agates. Hot springs occur when groundwater is heated and driven upwards by rocks that are still warm from their formation. Hydrothermal waters result when steam in molten rock interacts with groundwater that has been affected by intense volcanic heat. Both methods produce something of the same effect: water is naturally heated, enriched with minerals and driven upward. Given the Lake Superior region's geological history, both of these sources are viable theories. Warm water rising from deep in the earth could easily explain why the upper vesicles of a basalt flow are virtually never filled with agate. In addition, Moxon reminds us that hydrothermal waters deposit metals and metal ores in rocks. While he notes that amygdaloidal agate associations with metal deposits are rare, he does refer to Michigan's Keweenaw Peninsula. The Keweenaw Peninsula is significant because it represents one of the world's largest and most important deposits of copper. Copper, like many precious metals, is deposited by hydrothermal waters passing through bodies of rock. Here, formations of basalt that house veins of copper can also contain agate amygdules by the hundreds. In several rare locations, copper has even been found within agates themselves. It would appear that if agates were supplied silica by hydrothermal waters, Michigan's "copper country" would be a perfect example of this process.

Finally, Moxon also points out the issues with the formation of Brazil's agates. He found that Brazilian agates are much younger than the basalt they formed within, and he concluded that a second, later volcanic event must have helped fill the vesicles from the first volcanic eruption. The second eruption would have brought heat and steam with it, reintroducing hydrothermal conditions to the older rock. Because the basalt is approximately 50 million years older than its agates, it can be deduced that over the course of all those many years, agate was not produced until a second volcanic event occurred. Therefore, hydrothermal waters are almost certainly the silica source in those agates.

## CONCLUSION

We do not know the exact source of the silica in all agates, but it appears that hot, volcanic waters are the most likely source. But the ideas of Pabian, Zarins, Linck and Heinz offer unique solutions that focus on specific aspects of agate formation. While somewhat problematic, these ideas can't be discounted entirely. As with many aspects of agate formation, there may not be one answer—agates likely derive silica from several sources.

# Infiltration Channels

## IN OR OUT?

To this point, there has been little mention of "infiltration channels"—the theorized channels through which a jet of silica solution entered a vesicle. Typically, infiltration channels are a narrow segment of banding that run more or less perpendicular to an agate's husk. The channels always begin at the outer edge of an agate and lead inward toward the central banding, intersecting the agate's regular banding along the way. And when the regular banding meets the edges of an infiltration channel, the bands are bent outward towards the entrance point of the channel while simultaneously tapering and growing dramatically thinner. The warping of the regular banding is what has led many theorists to believe these are actually exit channels, as it appears as if the bands were being pushed out of the agate.

Infiltration channels represent one of the most important, yet most debated, features within agates, ever since von Leonhard described them in 1823. In 1849, Nöggerath proposed that infiltration channels were the structure that delivered silica to the entire agate, and that they were essential to agate formation, but his colleague, Haidinger, disagreed. However, they did come to a consensus that these peculiar structures are important and possibly hold the key to agate formation. The disagreement has its origins in the structure of the infiltration channel itself, which to many appears as if the banding has been pushed outward from the center of an agate. For this reason, many theorists and collectors have referred to these as "exit channels" for years, yet few have offered theories as to their formation. While upon first glance they may appear to be "exit" channels, history has taught us that things are not always as they seem.

Today, infiltration channels are a point of contention among theorists and hobbyists alike. (In fact, just calling them "infiltration" channels is to take a stance on the argument.) By taking into consideration forces that have not been previously applied to the development of these structures, recent studies have supported the older idea that the channels were actually formed by silica entering, not exiting, the vesicle.

## STRUCTURE OF INFILTRATION CHANNELS

Infiltration channels, can be eye-catching in some agates while very subtle in others, but they have a consistent set of features from agate to agate. Often described as an "onion" or "bulb" shape, infiltration channels are generally rounded with a pinched or pointed end that is oriented towards the interior of the agate. Occasionally, the infiltration channels can also be smoother, skinnier and straighter, but many of the same characteristics are still present.

The interior of the "bulb" can be banded, but is more frequently filled with macrocrystalline quartz. Occasionally, the inside of an infiltration channel can also be hollow and lined with macrocrystalline quartz points, as seen in geodes. Since we know that macrocrystalline quartz forms from more dilute solutions of silica, we can deduce that there was a drop in the amount of available silica during the formation of many infiltration channels.

FIGURE 69
The large infiltration channel within this specimen is filled with macrocrystalline quartz. Note the regular agate banding thinning while following the contours of the channel. 10x magnification

FIGURE 70

FIGURE 70
A thin, slender infiltration channel. 2x magnification

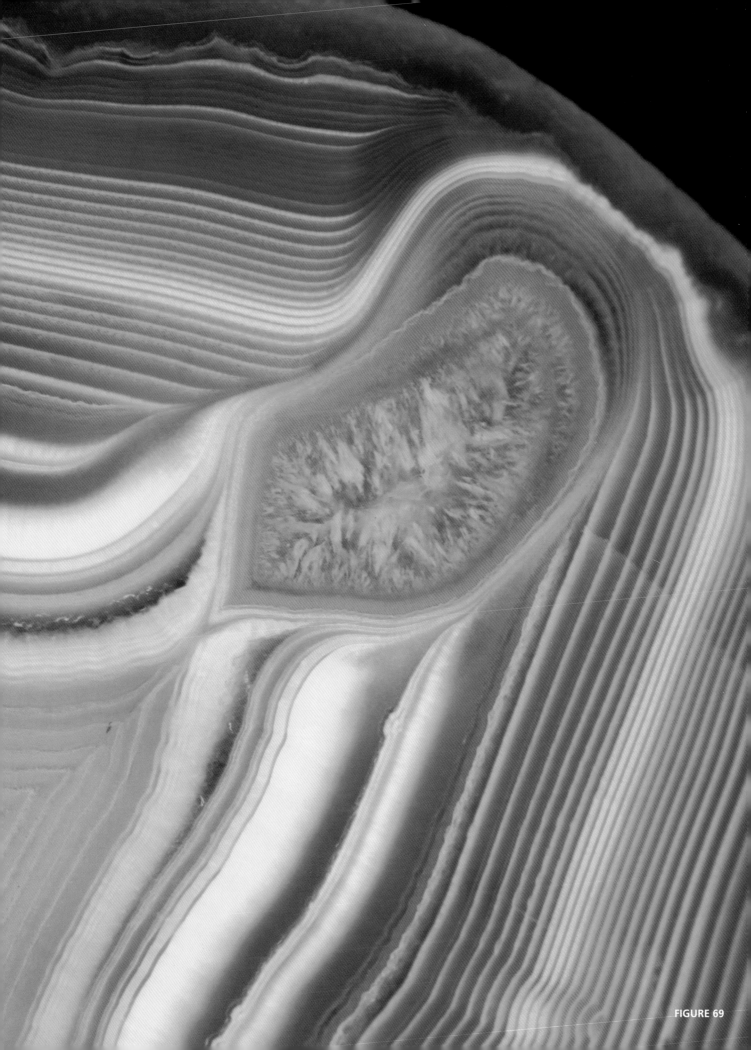

FIGURE 69

Some agates can contain several infiltration channels, and rare examples actually can exhibit dozens. On the other hand, some agate specimens contain no infiltration channels at all, signifying that these structures are common, but not crucial, to the formation of an agate.

## THEORIES OF CHANNEL FORMATION

With the advent of the differentiation theory, many theorists changed their thinking about infiltration channels, and this resulted in the recent concept of "exit channels." Admittedly, the warped banding makes it easy to see why researchers such as Shaub, Pabian and Zarins, and Landmesser would think these structures to be formed by material exiting, rather than entering, the agate, and this meshes well with the basic assumption of differentiation theory—that each vesicle filled with silica only once and the resulting agate was the result of chemical changes within that initial silica deposit.

Landmesser, in particular, was very critical of infiltration channel theories when he developed his ideas of agate growth in 1984. He declared "with certainty" that the channels were formed by the deformation of a semisoft agate, attributing the shape of the channels to "sliding" gel. Ten years later, Pabian and Zarins proposed that the crystallization of chalcedony caused an increase in pressure within the agate, forcing silica gel out of the vesicle through points of weakness. Other theorists argued that steam generated within the agate during formation was released rapidly and exited through the gel, creating the "exit channel" in the process.

Walger's 2009 article, which focused primarily on infiltration channels, provided the most up-to-date look at these unique structures while discrediting differentiation theorists' ideas at the same time. Walger was quick to point out the problem with Landmesser's ideas—in particular, random sliding or shifting of the gel couldn't possibly create the same specific shape seen in many agates. Similarly, the outward forces of pressure or steam would likely result in drastic variations in the shape of the channel or even complete destruction of localized banding, but observations show that this is not the case. In addition, if pressure or steam were produced in every agate, then every agate should exhibit "exit channels," but this is not the case, either. Dissatisfied with these ideas, Walger set out to develop a more viable scientific model that would generate the "onion" shape of the channels, which he believed was caused by incoming silica solution.

Walger's theory of agate formation revolves around the processes of diffusion and osmosis, which he believed caused water to enter and exit the vesicle through the previously formed layers of chalcedony. However, he suggested that if the first and outermost layer of chalcedony was broken or cracked (perhaps due to the basalt shifting) an agate would form in an entirely different manner. Contrary to Landmesser's theory, Walger believed that an area of low pressure existed within the vesicle; this low pressure area was the result of water moving through the vesicle due to osmosis and diffusion. Normally, diffusion of silicic acid back into the vesicle would take place, but if the outermost layer of chalcedony was cracked, the fissure would serve as a canal

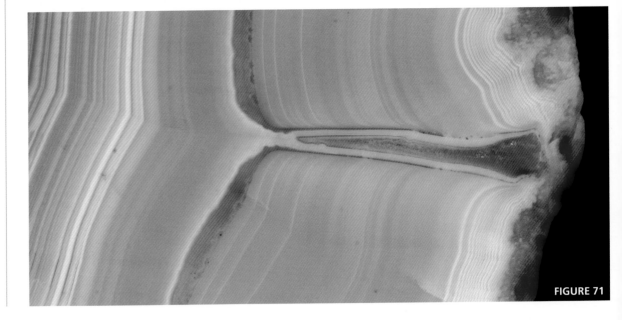

**FIGURE 71**
This long, slender infiltration channel was affected by red particles of hematite in the later stages of its formation. 5x magnification

**FIGURE 71**

for the incoming silica; the lower pressure within the vesicle would draw silica inward through the crack, which would be the path of least resistance. Because the vesicle is always filled with a liquid—either silicic acid or silica-poor water, depending on the current stage of development—the incoming silica solution would form a weak jet or current that would affect the rest of the banding. Walger designated this the "injection process."

One might think that an agate's banding would form in the same direction as the inflow of silica, but Walger argued that this wasn't the case. On the contrary, the regular banding in an agate tapers and points towards the entrance point of the channel—against the direction of the inflow jet—rather than inward towards the center of the agate. Walger's theory provides a detailed mechanism for this occurrence. By applying the principles of fluid dynamics, he determined that under the conditions in which agates form, and considering the stillness of the water within the vesicle, a weak inward jet of silicic acid would cause compensation currents to develop around the opening of the fissure. In other words, the incoming stream of silicic acid, driven by the low pressure within the vesicle, would cause the water near the opening to move towards the jet and join it.

An effect similar to this can be replicated at home in a bucket or sink filled with water. By running your fingertip through the surface of the still water, you will cause some of the water to move in the direction of your hand; however, nearby water will also swirl and be pulled into the current created by your finger, particularly where the motion was strongest. This principle is essentially the same in Walger's theory, but it affects agate band development because the compensation currents move too quickly for the silica contained within them to be fully deposited around the jet. Therefore, the banding directly surrounding the fissure and inflow jet remains very thin. As the banding develops normally in the rest of the agate, only the bands near the source of the jet would be affected by the compensation currents. Because the inflow jet is very weak to begin with, the friction of the liquid inside the vesicle would cause the jet to cease once it has flowed too far from its source, which Walger called the jet's "maximum penetration depth." Eventually, the "onion" shape would form due to the diminishing effect that the jet and its compensation currents would have on the encroaching nearby

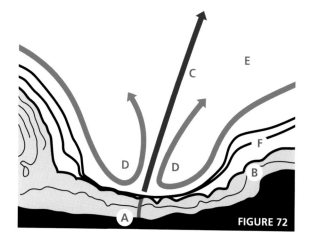

**FIGURE 72**
Walger's theory begins with a small fissure (A) in the outermost chalcedony layer (B). The pressure difference caused by the fissure creates an inflow jet (C). The interior of the agate is filled with silicic acid (E), and small compensation currents of the solution (D) are pulled towards the jet and then are directed back into the center of the agate. Banding (F) cannot accumulate around the jet due to the motion of the compensation currents.

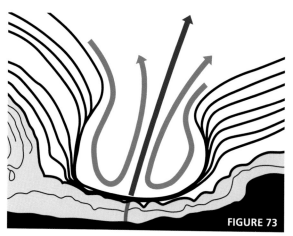

**FIGURE 73**
As the process continues, the banding begins to encroach on the inflow jet because the jet becomes weaker the farther it extends from its source ("maximum penetration depth").

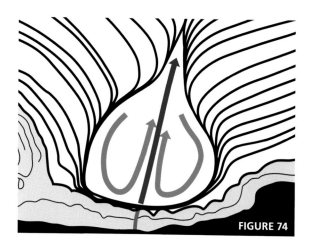

**FIGURE 74**
Eventually, the banding will accumulate beyond the maximum penetration depth and will therefore be able to connect and form regular agate banding. The "bulb" shape of the infiltration channel is formed when this happens.

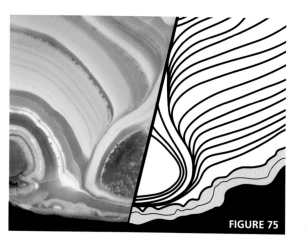

**FIGURE 75**
As the inflow jet diminishes, the silicic acid inside the "bulb" will turn into a gel and cause agate banding to form, giving the infiltration channel its own distinct pattern.

normal bands. As the agate's growth completes, the infiltration channel becomes banded, or is filled in with macrocrystalline quartz if there is little remaining silica.

## EXAMPLES FROM LAKE SUPERIOR

Infiltration channels are easier to understand once one has seen multiple examples. But while infiltration channels are common in Lake Superior agates, a billion years of weathering has obscured some of the details. Particularly, the outermost layers of chalcedony are often missing, which can change the appearance of infiltration channels. Another feature that is unfortunately almost never present in Lake Superior agates is the fissure or crack itself. Whole, complete agate nodules from various locations around the world can actually exhibit the tiny crack on their exterior that initiated the inflow jet, but this aspect is very rarely seen on Lake Superior agates. But the news isn't all bad; the harsh weathering Lake Superior's agates have endured has exposed some characteristics of infiltration channels that are rarely seen anywhere else.

Figure 69 is a quintessential example of an infiltration channel from Lake Superior. The regular agate bands clearly taper towards the source of the channel, while the channel itself remains filled with macrocrystalline quartz. In contrast, the channel pictured in Figure 70 is clearly much longer, thinner, smoother and lacks much of the "onion" or "bulb" structure, possibly resulting from a much stronger inflow jet. Similarly, Figure 71 shows an opaque gray agate with an elongated infiltration channel, but the infiltration channel and one of the last bands affected by the inflow jet are uniquely highlighted with red hematite impurities. Such a stark delineation of color that appears to have been "injected" by the infiltration channel may be an indicator that this agate saw multiple influxes of silica from differing sources.

While infiltration channels can be much easier to see when polished, some rough, untouched agates can provide equally impressive examples. Figure 76 shows an agate whose pattern is dominated by in infiltration channel on the right side. Interestingly, the infiltration channel itself is hollow and filled with a drusy coating of amethyst, or purple macrocrystalline quartz. Figure 77 also shows an unpolished infiltration channel, though it has been significantly weathered to reveal more of

the channel than we normally see. It is obvious that this infiltration channel appears longer than most. Compare this agate with that pictured in Figure 78, which also clearly exhibits a very long infiltration channel that was revealed during the polishing process. These two agates are illustrations of the fact that infiltration channels are a result of a crack or fissure forming in the agate's first layer, and sometimes that crack can be quite long. When looking at a polished agate, such as the one pictured in Figure 69, it can be easy to

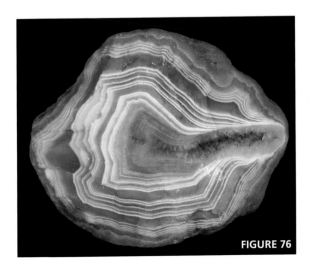

FIGURE 76

forget that the structures you see are actually in three dimensions and continue deeper within the agate. When the edge of an infiltration channel is polished (instead of just its face), it's clear that they are often much larger structures than commonly thought. If we sliced the agate pictured in Figure 78 into many pieces, like a loaf of bread, we would be able to see the common infiltration channel structure in each slice along the length of the channel shown in the photo.

To further illustrate the three-dimensional aspect of infiltration channels, Figure 80 gives us a

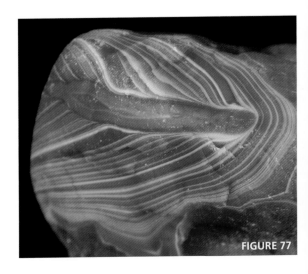

FIGURE 77

FIGURE 76
The agate shows a large infiltration channel that only partially filled with microcrystalline quartz. The interior of the channel is hollow. Approx. 3" x 2.5" (7.6 cm x 6.4 cm)

FIGURE 77
This beautiful red-and-white banded agate contains an elongated infiltration channel, exposed by weathering. 3x magnification

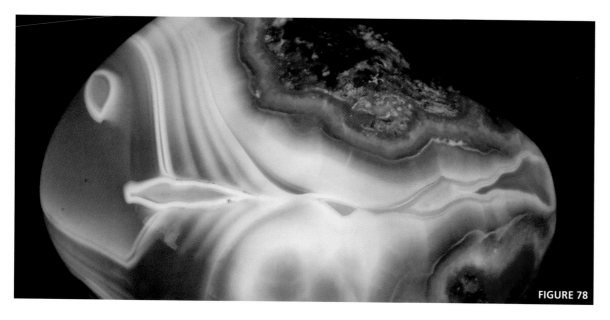

**FIGURE 78**
Polishing this agate revealed a long infiltration channel that extends along the entire side of the specimen. Approx. 4" x 3" (10.2 cm x 7.6 cm)

unique and beautiful view that is rarely seen. The bulk of this infiltration channel is composed of macrocrystalline quartz except for a small area of banded chalcedony at its center. The red chalcedony of the channel continues deeper within the agate, below the clear quartz, until it disappears behind the triangular banded pattern at the center. At the top of the photo, where the channel meets the surface of the agate, we can see the entire diameter of the channel, giving us evidence that the fissure that initiated this channel was quite small. This is in contrast with the long fissure that created the channel in Figure 78. Finally, in perhaps the authors' best example of a three-dimensional view of an infiltration channel, Figure 79 shows the highly weathered surface of a peeled agate. "Peelers," as they are commonly called by collectors, exhibit layers that have been separated by weathering, (particularly freezing and thawing), creating the appearance

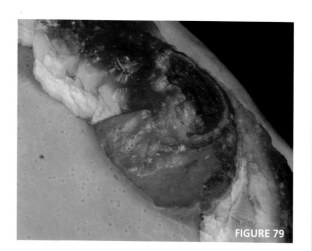

**FIGURE 79**
Due to the weathering of the agate, this infiltration channel stands above the surface of the specimen, illustrating that it is a three-dimensional structure. 2x magnification

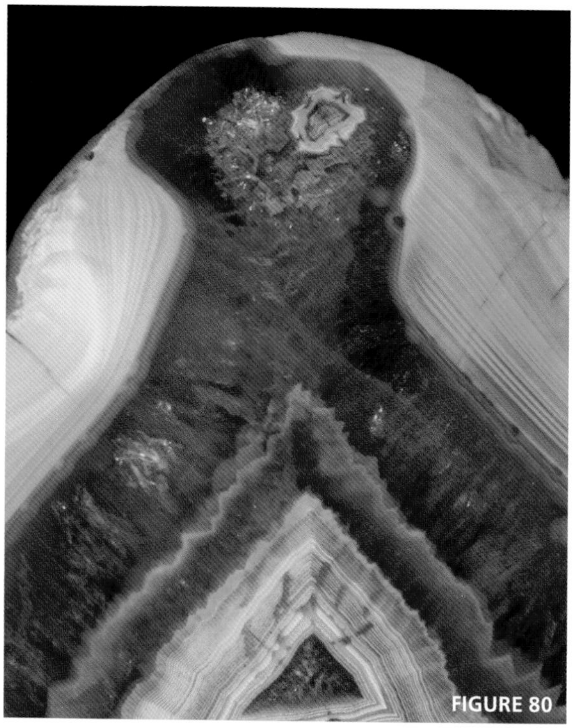

that upper layers have been "peeled" off of lower layers. This photo shows a reddish cone-shaped protrusion rising above the surface of the peeled layer. Normally, such a structure may go unnoticed, but close inspection reveals that the nearby banding exhibits the characteristic tapering and thinning of an infiltration channel. The upper portion of the cone also shows that it is filled with macrocrystalline quartz, which, as we know, is a common characteristic of infiltration channels. Were we to saw this agate in half directly through the cone-shaped structure, we would see the infiltration channel continued within the agate.

It should be mentioned that many infiltration channels can be observed differently depending on the way an agate is cut and polished. Collec-

**FIGURE 80**
This infiltration channel is surrounded by transparent macrocrystalline quartz, allowing you to see the channel as it descends into the agate. 4x magnification

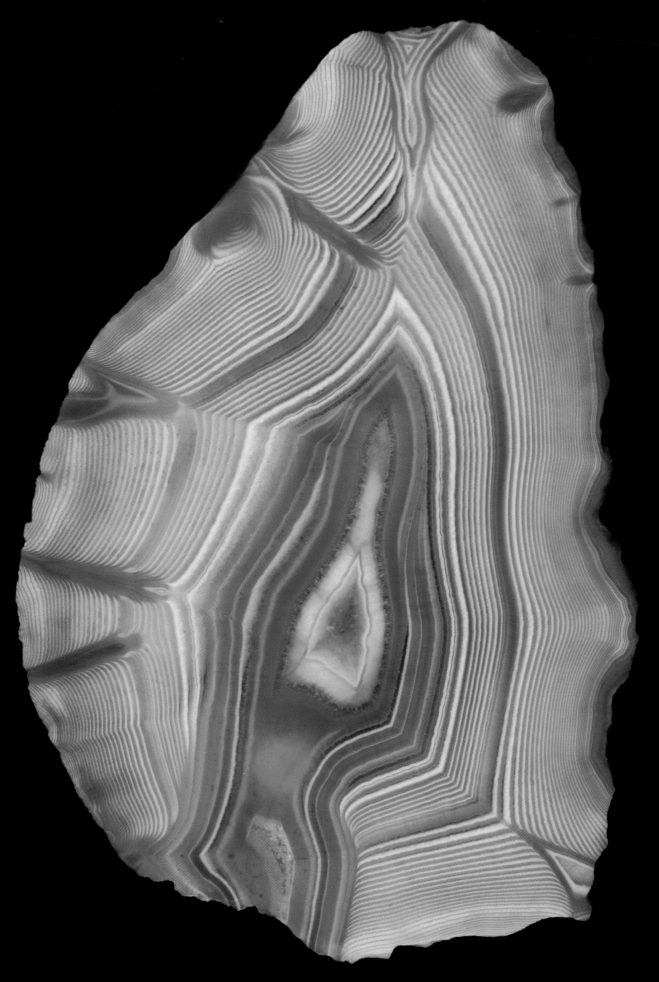

FIGURE 82

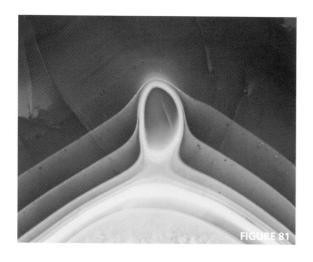

FIGURE 81
The way in which this infiltration channel was cut and polished makes it appear as a tube.
6x magnification

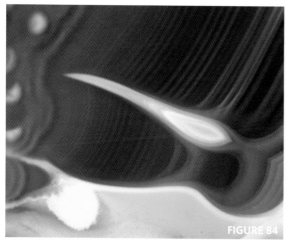

## SUMMARY

When you've learned to look for them, infiltration channels can be found in a huge number of agates. After hundreds of years of wondering what may have caused these unique structures, we may finally have an answer. In turn, this may teach us more about the formation of agates in general. Walger's injection process may seem complicated at first, but careful inspection of his ideas shows that his theory is rather complete and was well thought-out. While it still may appear as if the banding around an infiltration channel has been pushed outward, Walger shows us that the formation of these structures is more complex than meets the eye. His theory also sufficiently explains why infiltration structures are relatively uniform in shape across many agate specimens. And, because not every agate suffered cracks during the formation of its first chalcedony layer, his theory also provides a reason why infiltration channels are not seen in every agate. By applying knowledge from other sciences, particularly hydrodynamics, Walger was able to provide a new theory, complete with aspects of channel formation that other theorists had not yet considered. While the "injection process" theory of infiltration channel formation is sure to attract criticisms, it will be hard to disprove Walger's well-supported ideas.

FIGURE 82
This beautifully banded agate contains several infiltration channels, all extending to various depths within the agate.
Approx. 2" x 3.5" (5 cm x 8.9 cm)

FIGURE 83
A floating "teardrop" infiltration channel that was created due to the way the agate was cut and polished.
5x magnification

tors and hobbyists frequently alter their stones in order to help them show all the beauty they have to offer, but infiltration channels can be revealed in any orientation. For example, the common "bulb" or "onion" shape is not seen in the agate in Figure 81 because of the way the agate was cut. Instead, the channel takes the appearance of a tube or tunnel, and the slight translucency of the grayish bands reveals that the structure continues deeper into the agate. This was caused because the cut intersects with the channel deep within the agate and at a diagonal angle. Similarly, infiltration channels are often seen as pictured in Figure 83 and Figure 84, where the angle of the cut only reveals a small, angled cross-section of the channel. The result are teardrop shapes that appear to be "floating" among the regular banding. These examples show us that it is important to remember that if an agate has been cut, polished or worn down by weathering, many of the structures contained within it will not be complete and can be misleading.

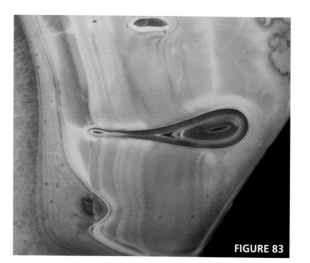

FIGURE 83

FIGURE 84
The long, wisp-like appearance of this infiltration channel was caused by the angle at which the agate was cut and polished.
5x magnification

# Concluding Agate Formation

## A DEPOLARIZATION OF THEORIES

There's a reason why after 300 years we still don't have a definite answer for the question of agate formation. Almost nothing about their formation or structures is simple and easy to understand. But after looking at many of the most current and prevalent agate formation theories, there seems to be evidence in favor of both the accumulation theory as well as the differentiation theory. Since these theories generally contradict one another, how can we conclude agate formation? Quite simply, we can't. As complex as the current theories are, they do not adequately explain the essential processes that lead to agate formation. And there may be variables that we don't know exist yet.

But perhaps the two theories need not be so polarized. In his 2009 article, Eckart Walger described his agate formation theory as a combination of both the accumulation and differentiation theories, stating, "The agate structure is primarily an accumulation structure, but was formed by an internally controlled process." Because his theory considered that inflowing silica was stopped by the thickening of gel layers which later dried out and crystallized to form chalcedony bands, it can indeed be found to include aspects of both accumulation and differentiation ideas. By utilizing aspects of both theories while expanding his research to other sciences at the same time, Walger created a theory of agate formation that is perhaps more complete than any that has come before. This melding of ideas is a practice that should continue to be applied by theorists as we delve deeper into agate research.

## THE AUTHORS' APPROACH

Once one has learned some of the history of agate research and pondered many of the leading theories, it can be easy to come up with one's own ideas. The authors believe, as Walger did, that the answer to agate formation is a combination of elements from many of the leading theories. While the authors admittedly are proponents of Walger's theory, they also believe that there is considerable value in Wang and Merino's theory, as well as Keith and Padden's utilization of Jessop's crystallization front. By combining attributes of these theories, the authors have developed their own ideas of agate formation.

The authors assume that agate formation begins by a vesicle filled with silicic acid. Silica polymers formed within the acidic conditions would initiate spherulitic chalcedony growths which would then form the outermost chalcedony layer, as in Walger's theory. Later, diffusion brings a new filling of silicic acid, which begins to form the second layer by first collecting as a coating of silica gel. Thus, the banding process begins. As Walger argued, each band of differing color and impurity level is created by incoming silica from multiple inflows of silicic acid. The authors, however, agree with Moxon's comments and see this as an unlikely process for the development of bands of alternating color. Instead, the authors believe that each gel layer is likely separated into various colored bands by a differentiation process, particularly a crystallization front moving through a gel layer.

In his 2006 publication, Pabian suggests that each time the banding process occurs, two bands are

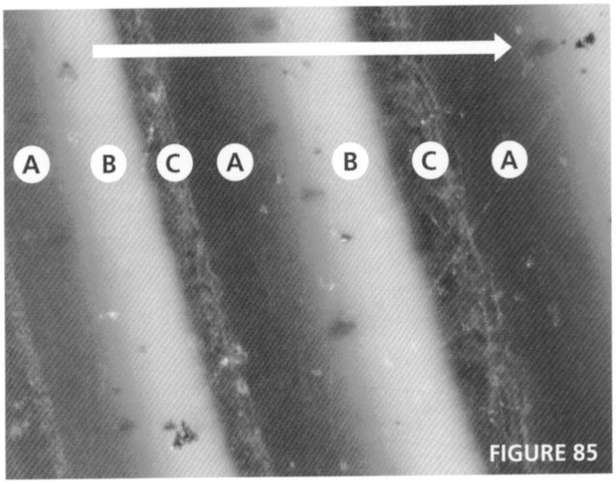

FIGURE 85
Agate layers showing the multiple stages formed during the banding process. "A" signifies colored chalcedony. "B" signifies white, dense chalcedony. "C" signifies clear microgranular bands. The arrow points to the center of the agate and signifies the direction of growth. 65x magnification

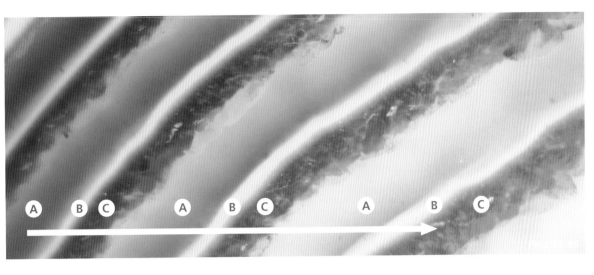

FIGURE 86
Agate layers showing the multiple stages formed during the banding process. "A" signifies colored chalcedony. "B" signifies white, dense chalcedony. "C" signifies clear microgranular bands. Arrow points to center of agate and signifies direction of growth. 30x magnification

formed at one time—a purer band of chalcedony in addition to an impure colored band. The authors subscribe to this theory, but after many observations, they argue that a single banding event can deposit a set of either two or three bands.

For example, observe the agate banding pictured in Figure 85 and Figure 86. In these specimens, the formation of each band clearly occurred in separate stages. The authors propose that Wang and Merino's theory of chalcedony growth may have been at work, but not within a large body of gel as they described. Instead, the authors apply Wang and Merino's ideas only to Walger's idea of a thin coating of silica gel lining the inner wall of the vesicle. Crystallization of each banding event began with the colored bands—the brownish translucent bands in Figure 85 and the cloudy, gray-blue bands in Figure 86 (labelled "A")—as aluminum catalyzed its growth. As the crystallization front moved inward, pushing impurities along its face, the process was slowed by the thickening impurity layer. As crystallization temporarily stopped, the impurity layer diffused back into the rest of the liquid-filled vesicle, allowing fresh silica to once again slowly come into contact with the chalcedony. During this phase, the chalcedony struggled to continue crystallizing, seeking out the purest silica solution possible, rejecting impurities and resulting in the thin, dense, opaque white bands (labelled "B"). The development of the colored bands and the white bands may have used most of the available silica, leaving only a silica-poor solution incapable of forming chalcedony, but which could produce granular quartz. The silica-poor water then formed the transparent, colorless microgranular bands (labelled "C"), which are evident as bands of a distinctly different texture that follow the white chalcedony bands. Finally, thin bands

composed of small "blobs" of red hematite are found collected at the front of the microgranular bands, suggesting that another crystallization front occurred as the microgranular quartz bands developed. These three types of bands—the cloudy gray or colored bands, the white bands and the transparent granular bands—should therefore be viewed as a set, or three parts of the same layer. And, clearly, three stages of the same banding process occurred.

The authors' observations show that Lake Superior agates with the type of banding shown in Figure 86 are very common; however, specimens with banding comparable to that in Figure 87 are also abundant. In Figure 87, the agate banding is more in line with Pabian's ideas and exhibits only two distinct parts to each layer, seemingly missing the microgranular quartz stage. This style of agate banding may indicate that the chalcedony

FIGURE 87

FIGURE 87
Colored bands and an opaque white band in an agate. The microgranular quartz bands are seemingly missing. 25x magnification

growth depleted the silica content so completely that the microgranular quartz band could not form, or could only form a microscopically thin layer.

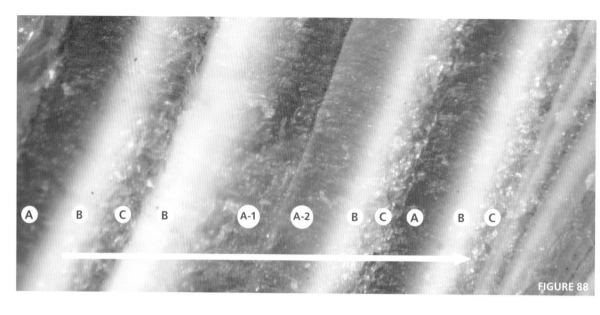

**FIGURE 88**
Agate layers showing the multiple stages formed during the banding process. "A" signifies colored chalcedony. "B" signifies white, dense chalcedony. "C" signifies clear microgranular bands. Note the interrupted banding pattern. Arrow points to center of agate and signifies direction of growth. 45x magnification

Differentiation theorists may argue that layers forming in neatly divided sets are additional evidence of a self-organizing formation process within a large body of silica gel. However, there are counterexamples that indicate an accumulation process took place over time; for instance, the agate pictured in Figure 88 clearly shows that the pattern of the banding sets was interrupted. The agate appears to be the result of a three-part banding process, except for a discrepancy in the bands at the center of the photo. In the image, impure, translucent chalcedony bands are labelled "A"; dense, opaque white chalcedony bands are labelled "B"; and transparent microgranular bands are labelled "C." Therefore, the ideal pattern would be "A-B-C." But notice how two impure, colored bands, labelled "A-1" and "A-2," meet at a distinct boundary and disrupt the pattern. This could be evidence that varying amounts of silica can be present within the vesicle at different times, pursuant to Walger's theory. For example, "A-1" could have used all of the silica available at the time of its formation, preventing the expected white and colorless bands from forming.

After the silica within the vesicle was used in forming a layer and its various bands, silica-free or very silica-poor water incapable of producing any further growth would be left in the vesicle. According to Walger's theory, osmosis would pull this water from the vesicle back into the surrounding silicic acid-saturated rock where it could collect more silica and re-enter the vesicle by diffusion. Once the vesicle was filled with silicic acid again, the multi-stage banding process could begin once more.

The authors' observations of peeled agates seem to support the idea of a multi-stage banding process. If agate banding developed in a single, self-organizing process, as in Pabian and Zarins' differentiation theory, it is easy to conceive that a strong adhesion between layers would exist. However, "peelers" show us that freeze and thaw

**FIGURE 89**
The authors' theory begins with the vesicle being filled with silicic acid (A), which accumulates as a gel layer (B and C) on top of any pre-existing bands, such as a microgranular layer (D), compact fibrous chalcedony layer (E), and/or an impure colored chalcedony layer (F). Impurities within the gel layer are pushed by a chalcedony crystallization front (C). The colored translucent bands result.

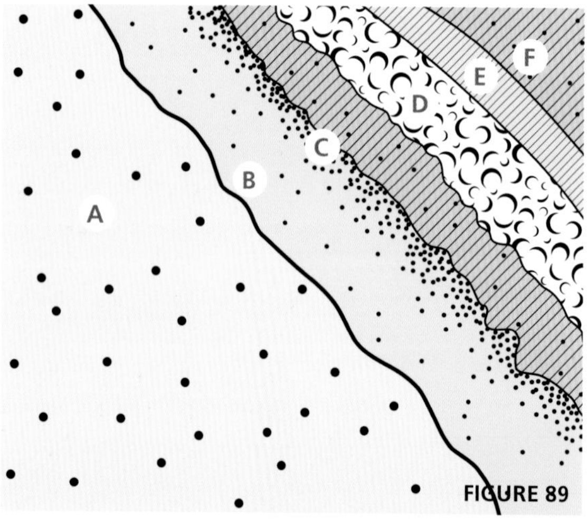

**FIGURE 90**
After the colored band (E) forms on top of the previous bands (F, G and H), a slow-growing, dense, white chalcedony band forms (D) which rejects impurities. The remaining gel (B) is low in silica, so it can only produce a granular quartz layer (C). The body of fluid at the center of the agate (A) now has little to no silica.

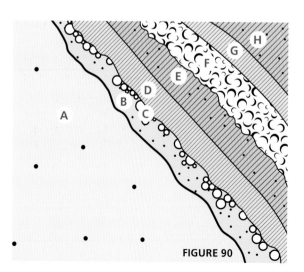

72

cycles can easily cause agate bands to separate between their layers. Agates in the authors' collection show that agate layers tend to peel in between the sets of bands, signifying that the two or three bands in a set are cohesive and formed together in each individual banding event.

As with any ideas of a mechanism for banding, there remains the question of the silica source. Assuming that amygdaloidal agates do form relatively quickly after their host rock (as modern research suggests) we can then also assume that the rock still retains quite a lot of heat as agate formation initiates. This volcanic heat generates

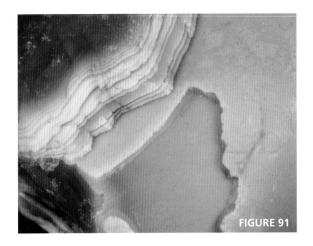

FIGURE 91

hydrothermal waters, which likely caused mineral-rich water to rise through the basalt and up to the vesicles. Therefore, the authors believe, as do many theorists, that agates can be thought of as a product of hydrothermal activity. And since hydrothermal waters bring with them metallic elements, it is easy to determine the source of Wang and Merino's aluminum catalyst as well as the many metallic impurities that can be found in Lake Superior's agates. In addition, Oehler's 1976 experiments showed that chalcedony can form directly from a silica gel, skipping the intermediate forms of silica, such as opal and cristobalite, as presented in Landmesser's theory. Oehler did perform his experiments at slightly higher temperatures than those generally believed present during agate formation, but such temperatures could easily be produced in a hydrothermal environment. Research presented by Götze in 2001 corroborates Oehler's experiments with chalcedony growth. By studying the aluminum content of agates, Götze and his colleagues were able to determine that agates could form in a temperature range of 50 to 200 degrees Celsius (122 to 392 degrees Fahrenheit), which would easily be produced in hydrothermal conditions.

In summary, the authors propose that because a silica solution contains very little silica, a single infusion of silica-rich water could not produce a vesicle-filling mass of silica gel, but rather only a thin coating of gel along the inside of the vesicle, as discussed by Walger. Therefore, the gel necessary to form a single layer within an agate is deposited by an accumulation process, but the gel layer itself is later governed by a differentiation process that divides the coating of gel into two or three distinctly colored bands. Because of this differentiation process, we see many of the highly organized structures within agate, such as the odd chevron or zig-zag pattern observed by Wang and Merino within the twisted, aluminum-rich chalcedony fibers. The accumulation aspects of this theory also account for changes in band thickness, band patterning and infiltration channels. By adapting Walger's theory and combining it with aspects of Keith and Padden's crystallization front, Wang and Merino's ideas of chalcedony growth, Pabian's thoughts on multiple-step banding, Götze's research, and their own observations, the authors have put together an amalgamation of ideas that they believe could form an agate.

## TOWARD A DEFINITIVE THEORY

It is obvious that our knowledge of agates and their possible formation has expanded greatly over the past century, but it clearly is not conclusive. At the time of this writing, there is no possible way to conclude the formation of agates. None of the existing theories are necessarily "correct" or "incorrect," but beginning to combine the more viable aspects of each of the theories (as the authors have) will likely lead to better ideas in the future.

Of course, each of the theories discussed here primarily pertain to the formation of the common concentrically banded agate. There are many different types of agate, many of which do not fit into the pre-existing theories. It has been said that a sufficient explanation of agate formation would take all of these different varieties into account—but should it? Perhaps the reason why we see such vast differences from one agate to another is because there isn't just one method of formation, but several.

FIGURE 91
Peeled agates often separate at the boundaries of each set of bands. 2.5x magnification

# Post Formation

## ENTOMBED IN ROCK

We don't know exactly how agates form, but we do know that they spend a long time embedded in their host rock before being brought to light. Many differentiation theorists believe that an agate remains in a semisoft gel state for many years after its bands finish developing. It is during this time that they argue infiltration channels and other strange, sweeping shapes form as a result of gravity or other forces deforming the still-soft agate. Accumulation theorists, on the other hand, assume that the chalcedony crystallized and hardened band-by-band; they therefore assume that an agate is solid at the time of its completion. In either case, agates invariably spend millions of years within their matrix, and a lot can happen in that time.

While still in the rock, it is evident that a number of events occur that can alter an agate. Iron-bearing groundwater can stain the banding, shifting rock can crack or crush agates, and it has been theorized that reheating can drastically change and recrystallize agates. Figure 92, for example, shows an agate that was crushed when it was only partially formed. Note how the banded segments of agate seem to float within a body of broken rock and quartz particles that later "healed" the agate back together. A specimen like this would seem to support the accumulation theorists' ideas, but we cannot know for certain what state an agate is in immediately after formation until one in such a state is observed directly, which is unlikely to ever happen, or until much more telling evidence is discovered.

What happens after agate formation may not be entirely a mystery, however, as Moxon's research indicates that significant changes occur in an agate's internal structure the longer it remains in its matrix. His observations suggest that an agate's mogánite content and water content decrease with age. In addition, he noted that older agates, including those of Lake Superior, appear to have coarser, more organized chalcedony fibers and larger quartz microgranules. Since studies have shown that mogánite is slightly more soluble than quartz, Moxon suggests that the trace amounts of water trapped within agates after formation, along with possible reheating, may actually slowly dissolve the mogánite and contribute its silica to the further growth of quartz as time passes. His observations corroborate this idea, as very young agates, such as those from Brazil, contain abundant mogánite and trace water while Lake Superior's ancient agates show virtually none, instead exhibiting larger quartz microgranules.

Whatever the state of agates after their formation, they are fated to remain entombed in rock until wind, waves and ice free them, or until they are destroyed in the depths of the earth. Fortunately for us, millions of agates experience the former outcome, and because they are made of quartz, they are hard and resistant enough to withstand weathering while their host rock wears away. Still, they did not survive unscathed, and the glaciers fractured and pulverized many. The tiny, rounded shards of agate found on Lake Superior's shores are evidence of that. But while a huge number of Lake Superior agates are scattered around the region, countless more are no doubt still embedded deep in the many basalt formations, but it will take another few thousand years of weathering to expose them.

**FIGURE 93**
This beautiful agate specimen is exceptional in that it formed within a crack in a large mass of reddish brown jasper instead of basalt or rhyolite. Approx. 4" x 5" (10.2 cm x 12.7 cm) Specimen courtesy of Christopher Cordes.

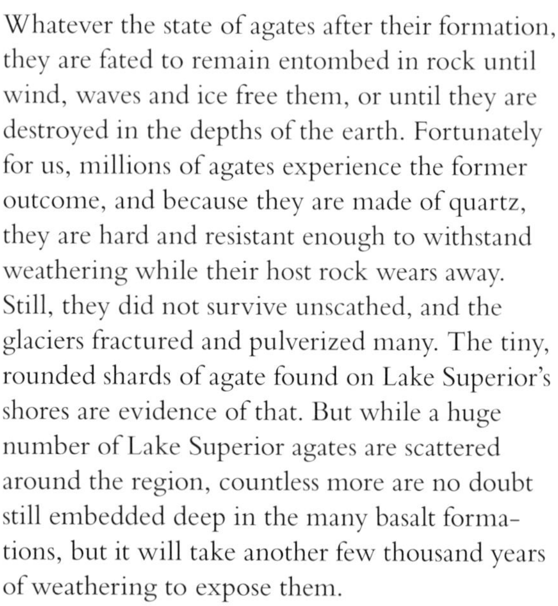

**FIGURE 92**
This agate was crushed during formation, evident by the segments of bands "floating" in a body of rock and quartz. Approx. 3" x 2.5" (7.6 cm x 6.4 cm) Specimen courtesy of David Gredzens.

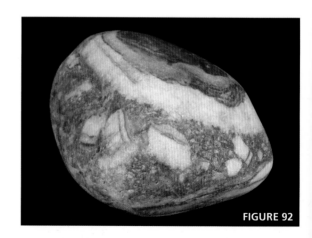

**FIGURE 92**

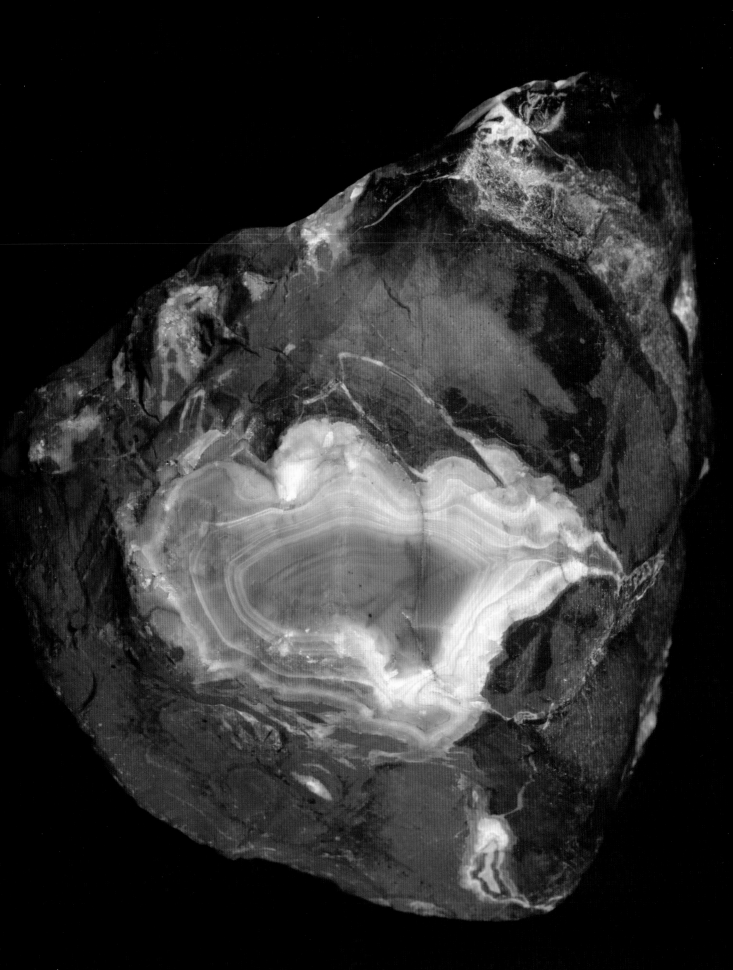

FIGURE 93

# Agate Varieties

*Lake Superior agates exhibit dozens of strange and beautiful variations*

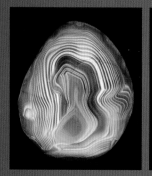

**ADHESIONAL BANDED AGATE**

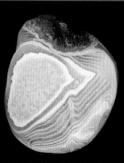

**BANDED QUARTZ AGATE**

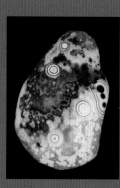

**EYE AGATE**

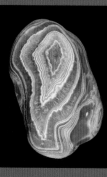

**FLOATER AGATE**

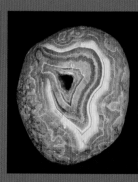

**AGATE GEODE**

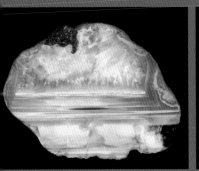

**GRAVITATIONALLY BANDED AGATE**

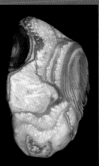

**SKIP-AN-ATOM AGATE**

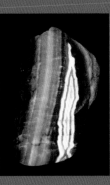

**VEIN AGATE**

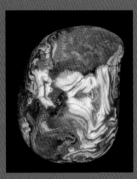

**WHORL AGATE**

If one thing can prove that agates form under highly variable conditions, it's the existence of the many varieties of agates found in the Lake Superior region. In fact, one of the things that make Lake Superior agates so unique and distinguishable from agates from most other agate-producing regions around the world is the incredible amount of variation from agate to agate. The many agate varieties are the result of many factors, the most important of which is the structural variation determined by the way an agate's bands formed. There are nine primary types of banding found in Lake Superior agates, and each variety is considered a distinct type of agate. Most importantly, every Lake Superior agate can be classified as one of the following nine types.

## WHY VARIETIES?

There are dozens of different appearances an agate can take, and many are considered different varieties of agate. There isn't a firm set of guidelines to determine what constitutes an agate "variety," but it basically comes down to the abundance of a particular trait along with its popularity and its identifiability. Adhesional banded agates (more commonly known by collectors as fortification agates) are the classic, concentrically banded gems we've come to know, and they are also the most common agate variety. Adhesional banded agates are considered the "truest" agates and are the primary focus of all scientific studies. But there are dozens of other varieties—eye agates, moss agates and gravitationally banded agates—just to name a few. And some agate varieties are so drastically different from each other that it would appear that the only common thread between them is that they all consist of chalcedony. It is because of these vast differences that we classify agates into categories.

There are four primary reasons that different varieties of agates form: differences in agate structure; inclusions and replacements within the agate; impurities that cause color variations; and changes due to various forms of weathering.

Collectors often classify agates that exhibit structural variations as specific agate varieties. These changes, which occurred during the agate's formation itself, can result in variations in banding and patterning. In contrast, agates that feature inclusions or replacements aren't defined by the banded structures they exhibit, but by other minerals that interacted with the agate during its formation. Sagenitic agates, for example, formed when crystals of zeolite minerals grew in the vesicle before the agate. The agate then later filled in around the crystals, often replacing them with chalcedony. Collectors often prize agate varieties with impurities that cause unique or rare color combinations. While Mexican, Brazilian and German agates display wide ranges of color, Lake Superior agates tend to remain in shades of red, brown and dark yellow, making bright greens, canary yellows and purples very sought after. Weathering can improve an agate's desirability (or ruin it altogether) so these different appearances are classified as specific agate types as well.

## PROBLEMS WITH DEFINITIONS

According to the traditional contemporary definition, an agate is a concentrically banded variety of chalcedony. But there's a problem with this

**FIGURE 94**
Eye agates, such as this rare-colored orange and green agate, are a popular and valuable variety. Approx. 1" x 1.5" (2.5 cm x 3.8 cm) Specimen courtesy of Christopher Cordes.

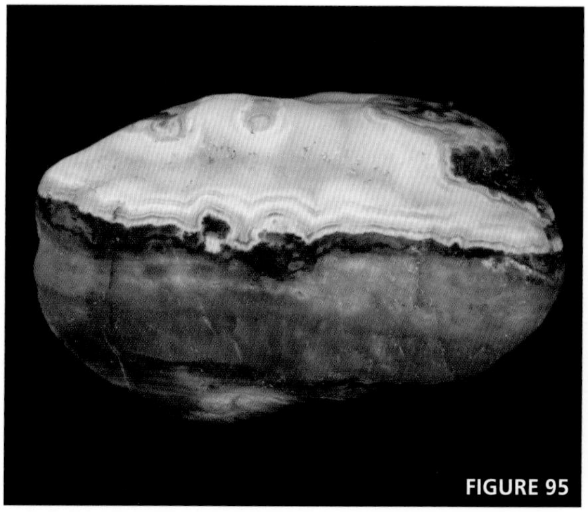

**FIGURE 95**
Black and white vein agates from northern Minnesota are a unique, iron-rich agate variety. Approx. 2.5" x 1.5" (6.4 cm x 3.8 cm)

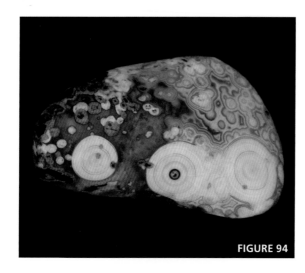

FIGURE 94

FIGURE 95

definition: not all agates have concentric bands, and some agates have no banding at all! For example, a moss agate is a mass of chalcedony containing moss- or tree-like growths of iron minerals, and moss agate specimens only occasionally exhibit bands. So why do we classify moss agates as agates? Though the definition of an agate has been updated by numerous writers and theorists over the years, the technical description of what an agate exactly is remains vague. A possible reason for some of the confusion can be traced back to the ancient Greek writings in which agates were first described. In the year 77, Pliny the Younger wrote about the primary types of agates known at the time. This account included indefinite descriptions of various patterns and colors seen in the stones. Though some of the varieties he described differed greatly from what we would consider an agate today, he obviously recognized that despite their differences, they were all composed of the same material and shared the same traits. Clearly, the ancient Greek definition of an agate wasn't limited to banded chalcedony, but all chalcedony. The idea that any compact nodule of chalcedony can be considered an agate, no matter its appearance, has been carried throughout the centuries and persists today. So moss agates, even without banding, are agates because antiquity and tradition defines them as such. Some collectors, however, would beg to differ; to many, the only "real" agates are those with distinct, well-formed bands. Technically, they are correct.

## "FAKES" AND POLISHING ARTIFACTS

The way an agate is cut or polished can create the appearance of unique structures or patterns that really aren't unique at all. Because the authors are lapidaries who have cut and polished countless agates, they are very familiar with the sometimes peculiar results of working them. Figure 96, for instance, shows a polished agate with a strange crescent shaped formation. Despite the fact that this rounded shape creates an interesting focal point on the face of the agate, close inspection reveals that it was a rounded, bubble-like feature on the surface of the agate that was later coated with limonite, an iron deposit that frequently forms on the surface of agates. The polishing process then removed the top of the bubble as well as much of the limonite coating, but not from around the feature's perimeter. This is an example of a polishing artifact, or an incidental "feature" created when the agate was being worked, similar to the "floating" infiltration

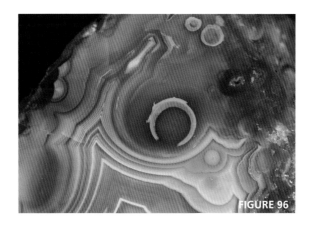

FIGURE 96

channels discussed earlier. Polishing can also result in "fakes"—polished agates that replicate other agate varieties, albeit generally unintentionally. An example is Figure 97, which illustrates how clever polishing can cause common banding to appear as an agate eye. Rotating the stone (as in Figure 98) reveals that this was merely a shard of a larger agate polished in such a way that an agate "eye" was formed. True agate eyes are hemispheres that typically formed on the outer surfaces of an agate. When viewing polished agates, it is important to bear the alterations in mind; having a trained eye helps tell an agate's native structures from those that are created during the polishing process.

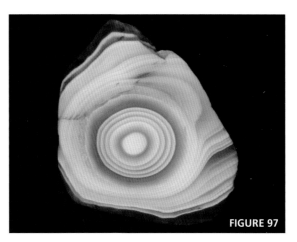

FIGURE 97

FIGURE 98

FIGURE 96
Polishing over a limonite-coated bubble-like structure created this unique, ¼" crescent shape.

FIGURE 97
From this angle, this agate would appear to contain a large agate eye.

FIGURE 98
This angle reveals that the agate "eye" is simply common agate banding polished in such a way that it appears to be an eye when viewed from above. 1.5" x 1" (3.8 cm x 2.5 cm)

79

# Adhesional Banded AGATE

*Classic, concentric banding and alternating colors make this the most popular agate variety*

**CHARACTERISTICS:** Exhibits classic agate appearance; layers within layers create multiple bands of colors and fill the vesicle entirely, though sometimes such agates have a central core of macrocrystalline quartz

**SYNONYMS:** Fortification agate, wall-lining agate, common agate, classic agate, fort agate, zonally concentric banding

**DISTRIBUTION:** Adhesional banded agates are found anywhere in the Lake Superior agate's usual range

**RARITY:** Adhesional banded agates are one of the most common agate types

................................................................

## DESCRIPTION

Adhesional banded agates are the quintessential agate. They are the primary concern of formation theorists and researchers, and are what most collectors think of when the word "agate" is mentioned. Because they consist entirely of agate banding, they are also often considered the "true"

agates, and learning the secrets of their formation will likely result in an understanding of nearly all other agate varieties.

As adhesional banded agates are the most common variety of agate, they therefore have dozens of names from all over the world. These agates are undoubtedly better known as fortification agates, a name they received because their banding often resembles the interior walls of a fortress. In 2004, Petránek suggested that they be referred to as adhesional banded agates in order to resolve much of the confusion resulting from their many names. This term better reflects how these agates formed and the way in which each band uniformly adheres to the interior wall of the previous band. Calling them adhesional banded agates also contrasts them greatly with gravitationally banded agates, which exhibit non-concentric, parallel banding that clearly was formed by a process very different than that which led to the formation of virtually all other agate types.

Adhesional banded agates consist of fibrous chalcedony and microgranular quartz layers arranged into the common band-within-a-band pattern, and are organized in a more or less spherical arrangement and often contain a core of macrocrystalline quartz. These repeated changes

**FIGURE 99**
Nicknamed "the King," this large, valuable agate shows the classic fortification pattern as well as a large infiltration channel on the lower left side. Approx. 4.5" x 5.5" (11.4 cm x 14 cm)

**FIGURE 100**
Alternating red and white colored bands repeat tightly as they fill the agate nodule completely. Approx. 3" x 2.5" (7.6 cm x 6.4 cm)

**FIGURE 101**
Bluish gray tones contrast with orange bands in this well-formed example. Approx. 2.5" x 2.0" (6.4 cm x 5 cm)

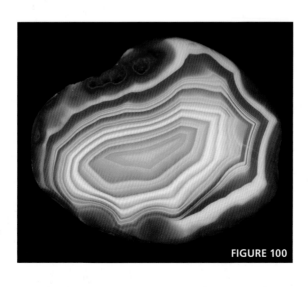

FIGURE 100

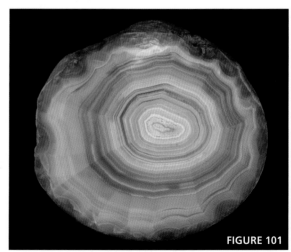

FIGURE 101

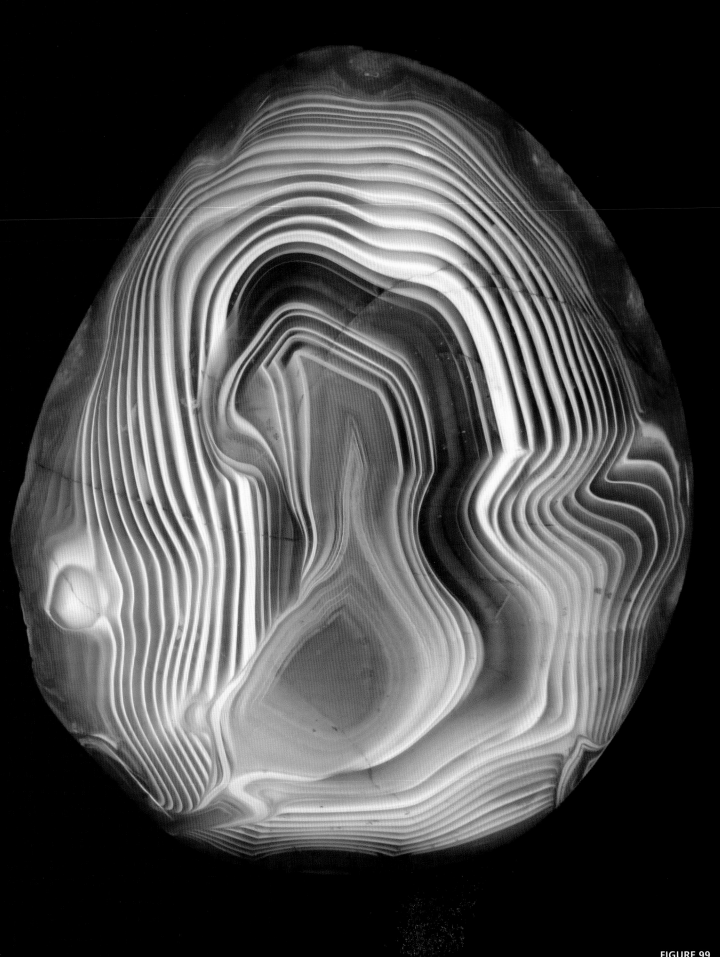

FIGURE 99

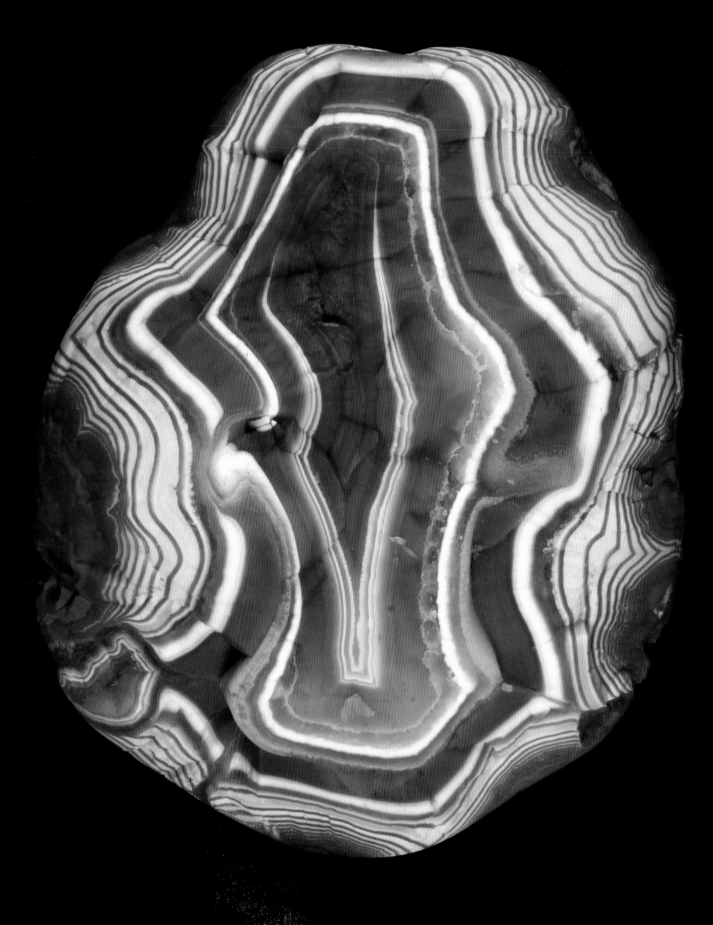

FIGURE 104

in band crystallization are often not visible to the naked eye and require a microscope to distinguish, but nearly every Lake Superior agate exhibits them upon close observation. Adhesional banded agates also frequently contain infiltration channels, causing beautiful swirls and bends in the banding patterns.

Lake Superior's adhesional banded agates provide great examples of the manner in which agate banding develops. The agate in Figure 103, for example, shows how the outermost bands closely match the contours of the agate's outer surface. As the banding approaches the center of the

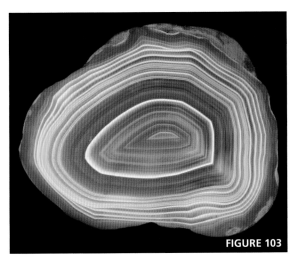

FIGURE 103

agate, however, these details are gradually smoothed and flattened, resulting in the center-most banding replicating the general shape of the entire agate, but lacking many of the details present in the outer bands.

The alternating banding within adhesional banded agates can create beautiful patterns of color and variations in opacity from band to band. Translucent chalcedony bands are frequently gray to dark grayish blue when fairly pure, but Lake Superior agates are most often stained red, brown or yellow by iron-rich impurities, such as hematite or goethite. Opaque white bands often occur in between colored bands and consist of tightly packed chalcedony fibers. Changes in color from one band to another are common, and signify changes in the amount of impurities present during each band's formation. In addition, the overall color of an entire agate can sometimes gradually change in hue from the outer to inner bands, suggesting that the amount of available impurities progressively increased or decreased during formation.

## FORMATION

While we don't know exactly how agates form, adhesional banded agates are obviously the result of an uninterrupted formation process. Since these agates are the primary focus of research, both the accumulation theory and differentiation

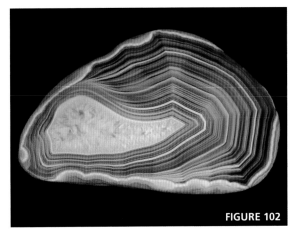

FIGURE 102

theory offer explanations for their formation that rely on orderly forces from either outside of the agate or within. A combination of the two theories can more easily make sense of such agates. Whatever the cause for agate banding, adhesional banded agates were allowed enough time and silica to fully form while remaining mostly free of disruptive mineral inclusions.

We know that chalcedony requires more silica to form than microgranular and macrocrystalline quartz do. When all three of these forms of quartz are present in an agate, there were significant repeated changes in the amount of available silica during the agate's formation. The uniform, alternating bands of fibrous chalcedony and microgranular quartz seem to suggest that some form of internal differentiation was at work,

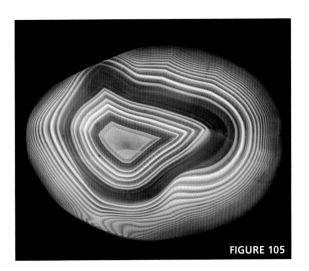

FIGURE 105

FIGURE 102
This adhesional banded agate proves that an agate doesn't have to be large to be gorgeous. Approx. 1.5" x 1" (3.8 cm x 2.5 cm)

FIGURE 103
An adhesional banded agate with nearly flawless banding. Approx. 2.5" x 2" (6.4 cm x 5 cm)

FIGURE 104
A large, red and white adhesional banded agate is easily the most desirable kind of Lake Superior agate. Approx. 4.5" x 5.5" (11.4 cm x 14 cm)

FIGURE 105
A quintessential adhesional banded agate. Approx. 3" x 2.5" (7.6 cm x 6.4 cm)

**FIGURE 106**
Tight, intricate banding.
Approx. 2.5" x 2"
(6.4 cm x 5 cm)

**FIGURE 107**
Very fine banding.
Approx. 3" x 3"
(7.6 cm x 7.6 cm)

**FIGURE 108**
Multicolored banding
arranged in a "herring-
bone" pattern, in
which the bands slope
away from a central
bend in the pattern.
Approx. 3" x 4.5"
(7.6 cm x 11.4 cm)

**FIGURE 109**
Natural, unpolished
adhesional
banded agate.
Approx. 3.5" x 2"
(8.9 cm x 5 cm)

either in a large mass of silica gel or in just a thin gel layer, because an accumulation mechanism alone would not likely result in bands of perfectly alternating colors and textures, as seen in many agates, such as that pictured in Figure 104. A macrocrystalline quartz center, seen in many adhesional banded agates, signifies that there was

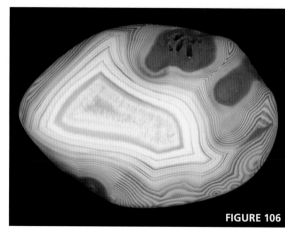

**FIGURE 106**

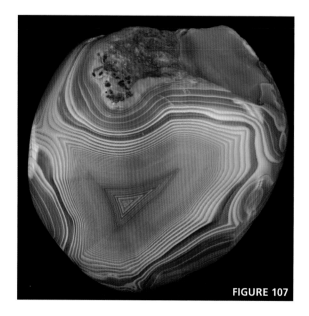

**FIGURE 107**

a silica shortage within the vesicle, likely due to depletion of the silica source during the formation of the chalcedony layers.

Infiltration channels are more common in adhesional banded agates than in most other varieties, suggesting that the specific conditions within the vesicle were different than those for other, less common, varieties of agate. For example, gravitationally banded agates from

Lake Superior rarely, if ever, display infiltration channels, signifying that their unique features resulted from conditions not conducive to the formation of infiltration channels. If Walger's model for infiltration channel development is assumed correct, this would mean that the area of lower pressure within the vesicle that is responsible for the infiltration channel can be absent or drastically diminished in other types of agates. Because adhesional banded agates are the most abundant and best-formed variety of agate, they are the model to which all other agate varieties are compared, and the conditions that resulted in their formation, as well as the development of any features contained within them, are considered the ideal circumstances under which an agate can form.

## COLLECTIBILITY

When it comes to Lake Superior agates, adhesional banded agates are the "stars of the show."

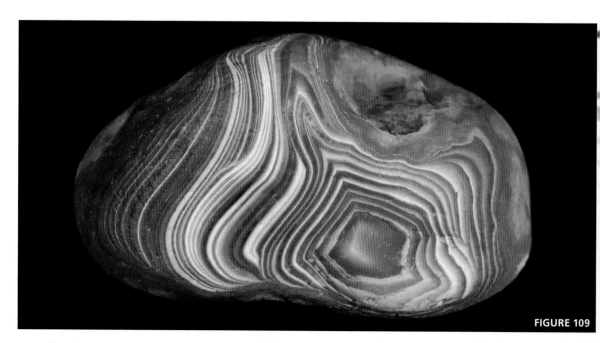

**FIGURE 109**

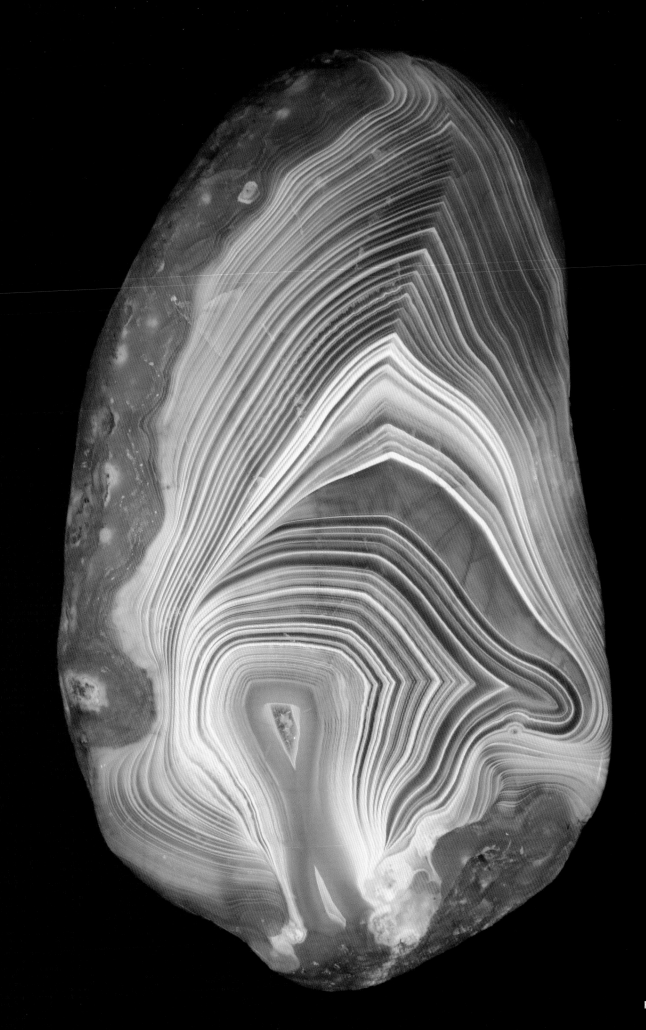

FIGURE 108

Despite being the most common variety, no other type of agate is as collectible or can be as valuable. But because of their abundance, experienced collectors are very discerning and carefully scrutinize every specimen in order to determine which agates are exceptional and which are merely above average.

Hobbyists new to agate collecting often ask why certain agates are valued so much more than others. While each agate is vastly different, there are several factors that experienced collectors take into consideration when assessing an agate's value—especially that of an adhesional banded agate. While size and weight are considered, there are more important factors, including coloration, contrast between bands, patterning, inclusions, macrocrystalline quartz content, damage and overall aesthetics. In other words, quality is more significant than quantity. Taking these many details into consideration may seem difficult, but it's really very simple once you've learned what to look for. Agates with vividly colored bands that contrast well (Figure 99), specimens with intricate, detailed patterning (Figure 110), or agates with a unique color combination (Figure 111) are all hallmarks of a highly collectible agate. There are also certain in-demand color combinations, such as "red, white and blue agates," which can be extremely valuable.

Three primary factors can make an adhesional banded agate less desirable (and less sought after by collectors): the presence of fractures, too much macrocrystalline quartz, or bland, lackluster coloration. Lake Superior agates almost always

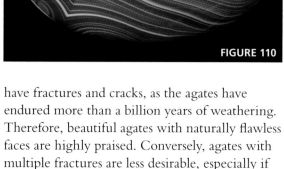

FIGURE 110
Very finely banded agate. Approx. 2.5" x 2" (6.4 cm x 5 cm)

have fractures and cracks, as the agates have endured more than a billion years of weathering. Therefore, beautiful agates with naturally flawless faces are highly praised. Conversely, agates with multiple fractures are less desirable, especially if the cracks are stained by other minerals, which

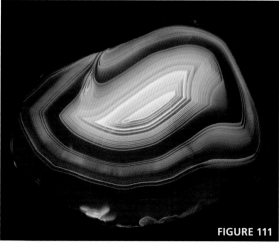

FIGURE 111

FIGURE 111
A dark, black and white agate with an infiltration channel. Approx. 3" x 2" (7.6 cm x 5 cm)

makes them darker and even more distracting. Macrocrystalline quartz, though a natural part of some agates' formation, is also unwanted by many collectors.

Serious collectors typically only seek what they refer to as "solid" agates, which contain only banded chalcedony. The presence of macrocrystalline quartz at the center of an agate is tolerated if in a small quantity, but agates with too much quartz are considered "quartz balls," causing a drastic drop in the value of such specimens. Finally, the more contrast an agate has in its coloration, the more desirable it becomes. But many agates are found in varying shades of gray or brown, with little variation between bands. Even with amazing patterns, dull coloration makes an agate much less appealing.

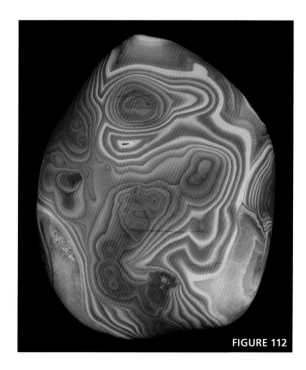

FIGURE 112

FIGURE 112
This beautiful agate got its wild patterns when it was polished parallel to its surfaces, rather than perpendicularly, as in most polished agates. Approx. 3" x 4" (7.6 cm x 10.2 cm)

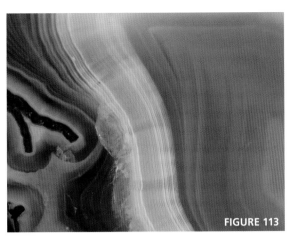
FIGURE 113

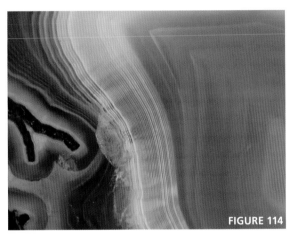
FIGURE 114

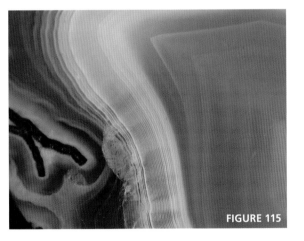
FIGURE 115

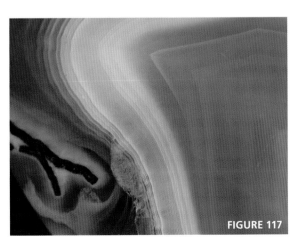
FIGURE 117

## NOTABLE VARIATIONS

The "shadow effect" is a particular phenomenon that can be seen in many types of agate, but which is particularly common in adhesional banded agates. When the pattern in an agate is particularly fine, and the specimen has very thin alternating bands of colored chalcedony and transparent microgranular bands, a shadow effect can be produced by slowly moving the agate under a bright light. Called "shadow agates" by collectors, this phenomenon is simply caused when the bands cast a shadow onto each other. Because the microgranular bands are mostly colorless and transparent, shadows cast by the surrounding chalcedony bands can be seen through them. This effect is similar to parting the pages of a book slightly so that just a small space exists between each page. As you change the positioning of the book, a dark band of shadow is produced. Figure 116 illustrates a shadow appearing in agate banding and the characteristic way that agate shadows tend to be isolated in small, curving ribbons. For collectors, one of the most exciting aspects of shadow agates is that the shadows appear to "dance" as the agate is moved. This effect is illustrated in Figures 113 through 115, in which an agate was slowly tilted to produce shadows in Figure 113, which then appear to move down the banding in Figures 114 and 115 before finally disappearing in Figure 117. Though this specimen is polished and makes the shadow quite apparent, the shadow agate phenomenon can easily be seen in some rough agates as well, especially when freshly broken across their bands.

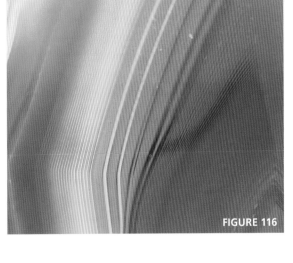
FIGURE 116

# *Banded Quartz* AGATE

*Agates with bands consisting of macrocrystalline or granular quartz, rather than fibrous chalcedony*

**CHARACTERISTICS:** Agates containing large bodies of macro- or microcrystalline quartz arranged into banded layers, often with little or no chalcedony in between them

**SYNONYMS:** Quartz ball, quartzy agate

**DISTRIBUTION:** Banded quartz agates are found anywhere in the usual range of Lake Superior agates

**RARITY:** Banded quartz agates are fairly common and are among the most abundant types of agate

......................................................................

## DESCRIPTION

Informally known as "quartz balls" by collectors, banded quartz agates primarily consist of layers of micro- or macrocrystalline quartz. Each band is created by individual growths of quartz, just as the banding in adhesional banded agate consists of individual chalcedony bands. Unlike chalcedony bands, quartz bands are typically quite jagged, irregular and often poorly delineated. The uneven, spiky appearance of the bands is caused by the pointed tips of individual quartz crystals. Because they often contain very little chalcedony (and are less desirable than other agates), banded quartz agates are seldom written about, but it's important to distinguish them from other varieties because of their distinct features and abundance.

Lake Superior banded quartz agates frequently have a thin outer shell of colored chalcedony banding, as in a typical agate, but this quickly turns into masses of coarse quartz growths. Opaque white chalcedony bands can further divide the quartz layers and provide more visual interest, but the interiors of banded quartz agates are generally nearly colorless, containing only very pale shades of gray, white and occasionally brown. This lack of color occurs because the quartz crystals and dense white chalcedony bands lack the impurity-catching pores found in the translucent colored bands of other agate varieties. These pores easily capture impurities within their twisted fibers, providing such agates with their varied colors.

## FORMATION

Banded quartz agates clearly differ from most other agate varieties because of the very large amount of coarsely crystallized quartz they contain. Because we know that microgranular

**FIGURE 118**
Multiple layers of granular quartz form most of the bands in this specimen. Note the tubular structure that the bands formed around. Approx. 2.5" x 3" (6.4 cm x 7.6 cm)

**FIGURE 119**
This agate consists mostly of layered macrocrystalline quartz growths. Approx. 2.5" x 2.5" (6.4 cm x 6.4 cm)

**FIGURE 120**
A large specimen with several quartz bands. Approx. 4" x 3" (10.2 cm x 7.6 cm)

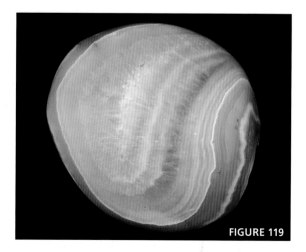

FIGURE 119

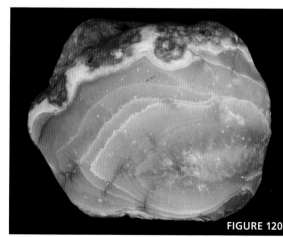

FIGURE 120

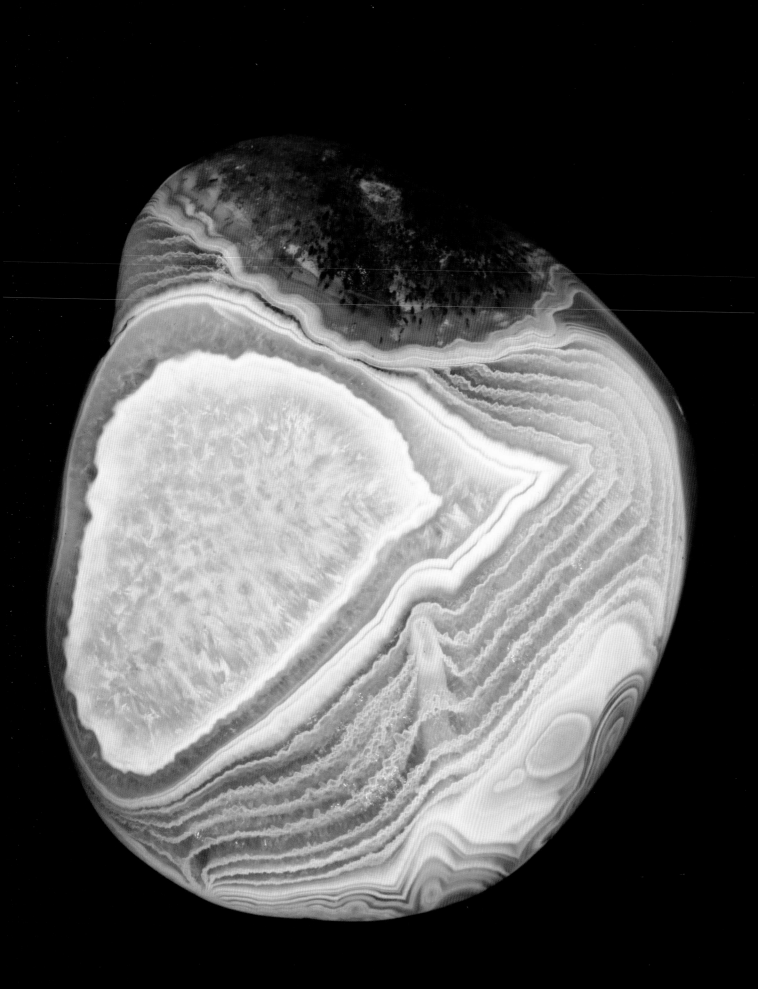

FIGURE 118

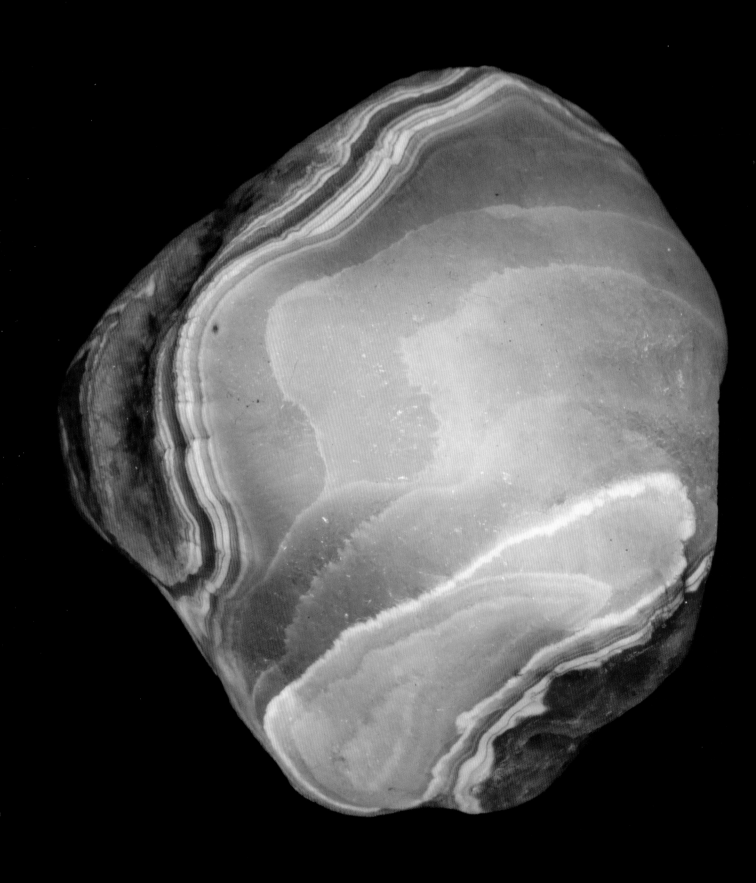

FIGURE 122

and macrocrystalline quartz require less silica to form than chalcedony, banded quartz agates likely developed in silica-deficient environments that were incapable of providing the silica necessary for continued chalcedony growth. There must have initially been ample silica, evident by the outermost chalcedony bands, but the silica source was quickly depleted. Repeated inflows of silica-poor water caused new layers of macrocrystalline quartz to form within the older layers, resulting in the banded appearance of the quartz. As shown by agates such as those in Figures 118 and 123, silica-rich solutions or gels may once again return to the vesicle, leading to the formation of interior chalcedony bands sandwiched between quartz layers. Coincidentally, these agates, which are often ignored by collectors and theorists alike, may provide some insight into agate formation. The differentiation theory states that macrocrystalline quartz centers in agates form when the remaining solution within the vesicle is silica-deficient, but does not take into account banded quartz centers or why such bands would form within macrocrystalline quartz. On the other hand, the accumulation theory, with its ideas of multiple inflows of silica from external

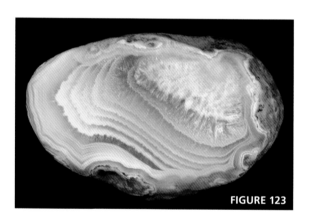

**FIGURE 123**

sources, could easily explain the banded quartz agates and the chalcedony bands that can sometimes be observed deeper within the agate.

Interestingly, some of the largest Lake Superior agate nodules found are banded quartz agates. In the event of very large banded quartz agates, such as the specimen in Figure 120, it is assumed that the vesicle was simply too large for the amount of silica present. In these situations, the amount of silica required to develop a single band may have been enough to form an entire agate in a smaller vesicle. Therefore, the silica was quickly depleted, leaving only silica-poor solutions and forming macrocrystalline quartz.

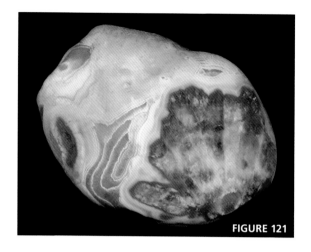

**FIGURE 121**

## COLLECTIBILITY

Banded quartz agates generally hold little value unless they are particularly interesting or well formed. Even very large specimens are not highly desired by most collectors. Discerning Lake Superior agate collectors seek out "solid" agates, or agates containing little macrocrystalline quartz, and typically show little interest in banded quartz agates. Some collectors do, however, appreciate the transparency displayed by some of the quartz layers, which allows one to see deeper into the agate.

## NOTABLE VARIATIONS

While it technically doesn't consist of banded quartz, a related variety of quartz growth can be found in Lake Superior agates. Large, well-developed radial groupings of macrocrystalline quartz crystals can be occasionally found in agates. These quartz "sprays" (see Figures 121 and 124) are clusters of quartz crystals that grew within the vesicle before the agate formed, causing the chalcedony to conform to their shape.

**FIGURE 124**

**FIGURE 121**
A large radial quartz formation dominates this specimen. Approx. 4.5" x 3" (11.4 cm x 7.6 cm)

**FIGURE 122**
The very definition of a "quartz ball." Approx. 2.5" x 2.5" (6.4 cm x 6.4 cm)

**FIGURE 123**
This banded quartz agate has more white chalcedony than most. Approx. 2" x 1" (5 cm x 2.5 cm)

**FIGURE 124**
A large, radial quartz formation sits below agate banding. Approx. 3" x 2" (7.6 cm x 5 cm)

# *Eye* AGATE

*Agates containing circular eye-like formations, particularly on the surface of the agate*

**CHARACTERISTICS:** Perfectly round, banded structures on the outer layers of small agates

**SYNONYMS:** Fish-eye agate, bull's-eye agate, hemisphere agate

**DISTRIBUTION:** Eye agates can be found anywhere in the usual range of Lake Superior agates, but are more common on Minnesota's northern shores and Michigan's Keweenaw Peninsula

**RARITY:** Eye agates aren't particularly rare; however, most eyes on agates are small and easily overlooked, making eye agates seemingly uncommon

## DESCRIPTION

When a newcomer to Lake Superior agates begins building a collection, eye agates are almost always one of the first varieties they add to their shelf. Eye agates have always been favored by collectors, perhaps because each specimen seems to have a personality, or because their perfectly circular formations are as fascinating as they are beautiful. Whatever the reasons for their popularity, the source of their name is obvious: the circular formations seen on the surface of these agates clearly resemble eyes. Many agate eyes, or "fish eyes," as some collectors call them, are banded with delicate rings, while others are a solid color. Eyes with large centers of solid coloration are also common, as seen in the specimens in Figures 126 and 127.

One of the most compelling and easily observable attributes of agate eyes is that they are very shallow features originating from the outer surface of the agate. This is a trait that is more obvious in specimens that have been cut or broken to reveal the agate's interior, but when viewing an agate that displays eyes, take note of where you are seeing them—they will be part of the outermost layers of chalcedony. This is because agate eyes stem from the spherulitic chalcedony growth that occurs in the very first chalcedony layer, or husk. But as with any variety of agate, the rules can sometimes be broken, and very occasionally eyes can be found deeper within an agate, forming just on the surface of another band.

**FIGURE 125**
Several banded eyes dot the surface of this small agate nodule with a rare coloration. Approx. 0.5" x 1.5" (1.3 cm x 3.8 cm) Specimen courtesy of Christopher Cordes.

**FIGURE 126**
A single large eye is surrounded by dozens of smaller, non-banded eyes. Approx. 1" x 1" (2.5 cm x 2.5 cm)

**FIGURE 127**
Like the eyes of an animal, this specimen features one eye on either side of its "head." Approx. 1.5" x 1.5" (3.8 cm x 3.8 cm)

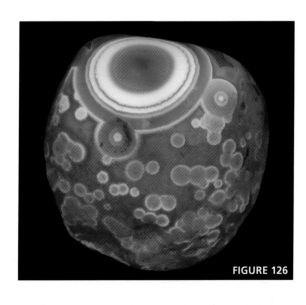

FIGURE 126

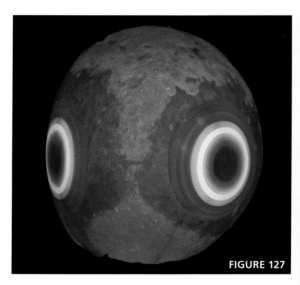

FIGURE 127

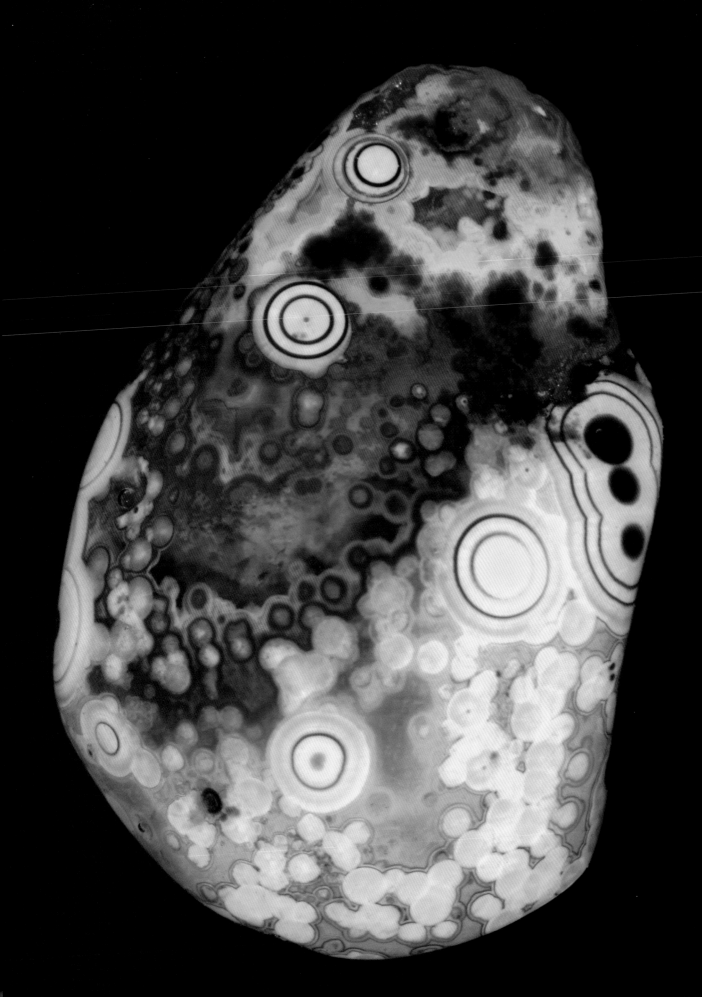

FIGURE 125

**FIGURE 128**
Eyes on the surface of whole, unbroken nodules are common. Approx. 1.5" x 1.5" (3.8 cm x 3.8 cm)

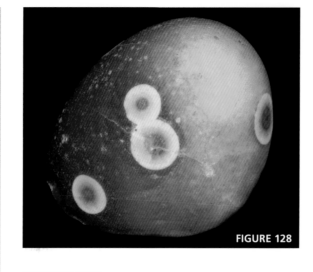

FIGURE 128

**FIGURE 129**
A ghostly, unbanded eye on red carnelian. 2x magnification

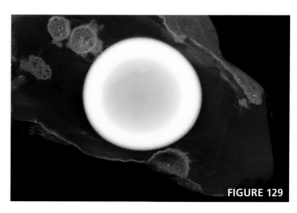

FIGURE 129

this theory on observations that the chemical reaction creates patterns remarkably similar to eye agates, but this idea has several problems. Primarily, it does not explain why eyes typically only form within the outermost layer of chalcedony. In 2009, Eckart Walger introduced the most probable theory, when he suggested a simple yet viable mechanism to explain why these spherulites significantly increased in size. He noted that

eyes are primarily present only on small agates generally no larger than a golf ball, and he proposed that the size of the vesicle was a primary factor in the formation of agates with eyes. If the thick outermost layer of an agate was attempting to form in a very small vesicle, its spherulites would fill most of the available space and leave little or no room for internal banding, resulting in a mass of gel. When this thick mass of chalcedony spherulites was still in a soft gel state, silica solutions remaining in the surrounding rock could not help this mass grow thicker (as it normally would) because there was no room left for it to grow. Instead, the additional silica would interact with the still-soft spherulites, enriching certain spherulites with more silica resulting in their expansion and formation of an eye. Banded eyes would result from repetition of this process.

## FORMATION

As we well know, the very first chalcedony layer of an agate, often known as the husk, forms very differently than the interior bands. Instead of forming as a layer of parallel chalcedony fibers, the outermost layer develops when silica molecules begin to nucleate, or accumulate, at various points along the inner walls of the vesicle. This initiates the growth of chalcedony spherulites, which are tiny spheres composed of chalcedony fibers. As the spherulites continue to increase in size, they eventually contact each other and continue to do

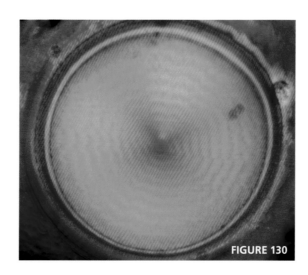

FIGURE 130

**FIGURE 130**
The fibers of the chalcedony spherulite that formed this eye are clearly visible in this large eye. Contrast increased 15% 5x magnification Specimen courtesy of Christopher Cordes.

so until a solid layer of chalcedony is formed. This is relevant to eye agates, because eyes are actually chalcedony spherulites that are exceptionally large and complex.

Throughout the years, many possible mechanisms for the formation of agate eyes have been proposed, some of which are rather far-fetched. According to Pabian and Zarins' theory from 1994, agate eyes form due to the occurrence of the Belousov-Zhabotinskii reaction. They based

**FIGURE 131**
A common agate eye. 4x magnification

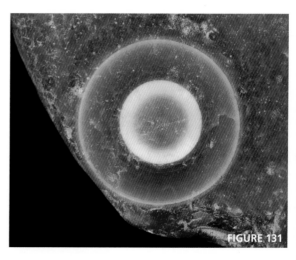

FIGURE 131

As previously mentioned, eyes can sometimes be found deeper within an agate, though they typically remain very small, as in Figure 133. These specimens are troublesome, but not completely in opposition to Walger's ideas. Spherulites can often be observed all throughout

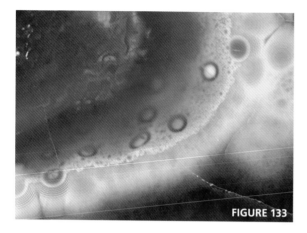

FIGURE 133

an agate, and a similar enriching process could have affected interior spherulites, resulting in additional eyes.

While a spherulite is a sphere by definition, agate eyes grow on the outermost layer of an agate; this only allows them to expand inward, resulting in the formation of a hemisphere, or half-sphere. This explains why agate eyes shrink in size when they are polished; the polishing process actually removes material from the agate, and a lower

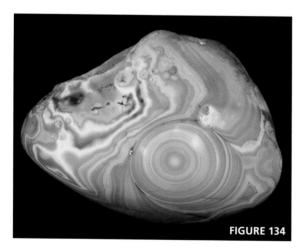

FIGURE 134

(and therefore smaller) portion of the eye is being revealed. Agate eyes can actually disappear altogether if polished too aggressively.

## COLLECTIBILITY

Eye agates always have been—and always will be—one of the most popular varieties of agate. Both novices and experienced collectors alike

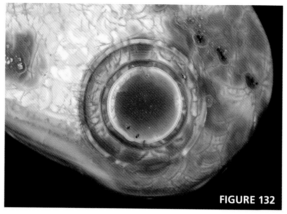

FIGURE 132

find the little eyes endearing, and everyone has a prized eye agate specimen. While agate eyes are not rare, even very small stones will command relatively high prices, so long as they contain a large, well-formed eye, or many smaller eyes that are equally as beautiful. Traditionally, the most desirable agate eyes are those that are coin-sized or larger and have highly contrasting bands. Alternating red and white bands are particularly sought after, and are sometimes referred to as "bull's-eye agates," after the pattern they resemble. Specimens in which two eyes meet at their edges, forming a figure-eight, are also popular. But because eyes typically are only found on small agates and are not particularly rare, the values of eye agates do not reach the lofty heights of adhesional banded agates or floaters.

## NOTABLE VARIATIONS

Some inexperienced collectors speak of "half eyes," which in reality are no different from any other agate eyes. Half eyes are simply agate eyes that have been broken or cut perpendicular to their structure so that a curving, semicircular cross section is observed instead of the entire eye. While not a unique form of an agate eye, they are fantastic illustrations that eyes are hemispheres that only extend partway into the agate.

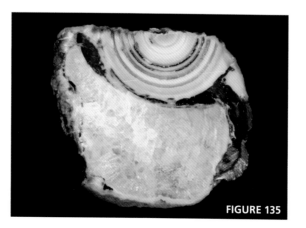

FIGURE 135

FIGURE 132
A large eye with a peculiar "crackly" appearance.
2x magnification

FIGURE 133
A close-up look at spherulites grown on the surface of an interior layer, some of which have developed banding.
6x magnification

FIGURE 134
An agate eye with the unusual habit of asymmetrical banding.
Approx. 2.5" x 1" (6.4 cm x 2.5 cm)

FIGURE 135
This "half eye" is just a regular eye cut perpendicularly to its banding. This particular specimen contains copper.
Approx. 1" x 1" (2.5 cm x 2.5 cm)

# *Floater* AGATE

*Agates containing bands of chalcedony "floating" within colorless macrocrystalline quartz*

**CHARACTERISTICS:** There are two common appearances exhibited by floater agates; many contain a core of banded agate surrounded by a thick shell of macrocrystalline quartz while others consist of alternating layers of banded agate and macrocrystalline quartz

**SYNONYMS:** Suspended center agate, floater

**DISTRIBUTION:** Floater agates can be found virtually anywhere in the usual range of Lake Superior agates

**RARITY:** Floaters are fairly common, though they are generally not quite as abundant as adhesional banded agates

.........................................................

## DESCRIPTION

The term "floater agate" is purely a collectors' name, but it is commonly used because few other well-known labels exist for this variety of agate. A favorite among Lake Superior agate collectors, floaters contain areas of chalcedony banding that are surrounded by macrocrystalline quartz, appearing as if "floating" on the quartz. Floaters can be observed in two distinct types, both of which can produce beautiful specimens. The more common of the two types of floaters consists of a thin outer layer of chalcedony surrounding a thick band of macrocrystalline quartz just beneath the surface of the nodule. At the center of the macrocrystalline quartz layer is an adhesional agate pattern that continues to fill the agate, which is illustrated in Figure 137. In this chapter, this type will be referred to as "type one." The second type, or "type two," is slightly less common, but more desirable to collectors, and consists of alternating layers of macrocrystalline quartz and banded chalcedony. This creates the appearance of multiple "floating" banded areas, as pictured in Figure 136.

With the exception of the prominent regions of macrocrystalline quartz, floater agates are essentially adhesional banded agates, and as such they can take on many appearances and colors. Perhaps the most noticeable difference in floater agates' banding is the boundary at which the macrocrystalline quartz and chalcedony layers meet. The pointed tips of the well-formed quartz crystals provided an uneven base from which the subsequent chalcedony layers grew, resulting

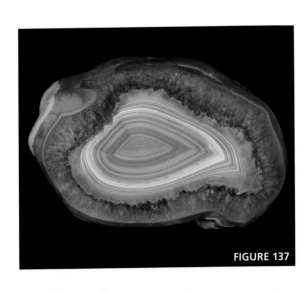

FIGURE 137

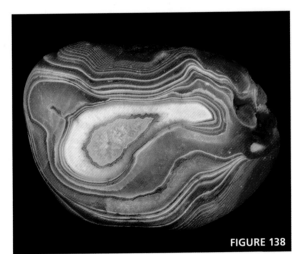

FIGURE 138

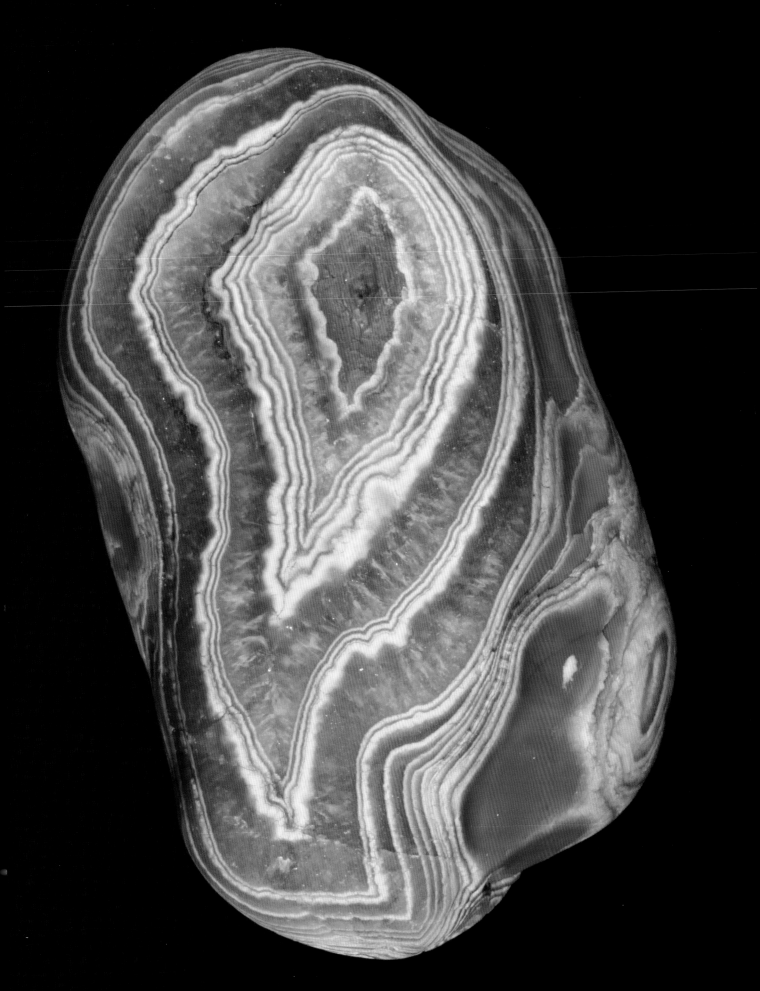

FIGURE 136

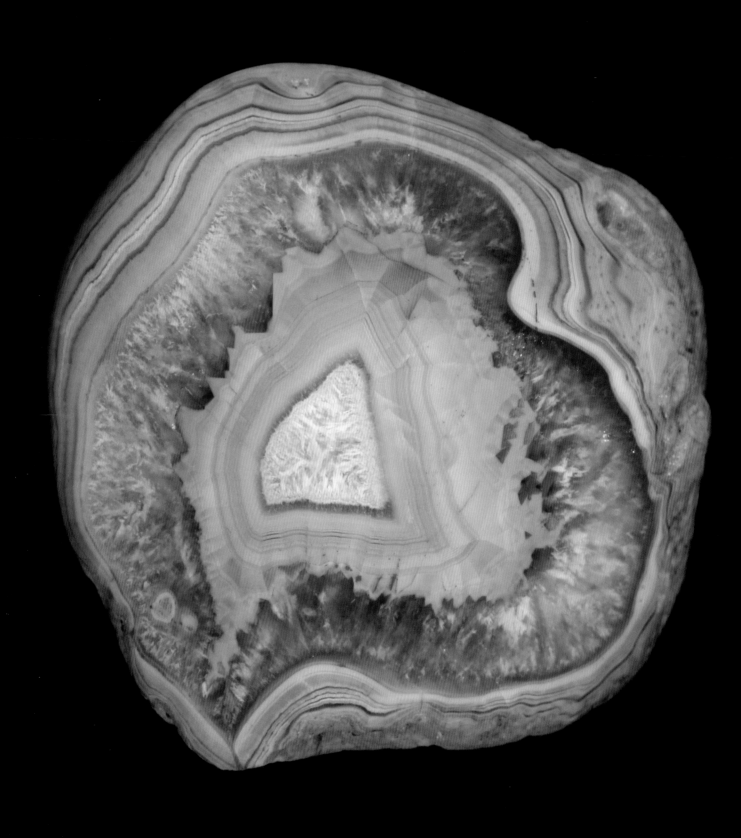

FIGURE 140

in irregular, jagged banding, which is clearly illustrated in Figures 137 and 140. As with the patterns in adhesional banded agates, the chalcedony layers initially closely follow the contours of the serrated macrocrystalline quartz growths, but the layers eventually become smoother as they progress toward the center of the agate.

## FORMATION

Many aspects of the formation of floater agates are easily understood. Unlike adhesional banded agates, which formed through an uninterrupted banding process, floaters clearly formed due to alternating periods of silica abundance and silica deficiency; this resulted in fibrous chalcedony bands and macrocrystalline quartz layers, respectively. In the case of "type two" floaters, such as the one pictured in Figure 136, the amount of silica available varied several times before the agate was complete, but "type one" floaters (see Figures 139 and 141) were subjected to only one change in silica availability. As with banded quartz agates, floaters are a variety of Lake Superior agate that is more easily explained by accumulation theories rather than differentiation theories. Differentiation theories assume that macrocrystalline quartz is created from the remaining silica-poor solution left over at the

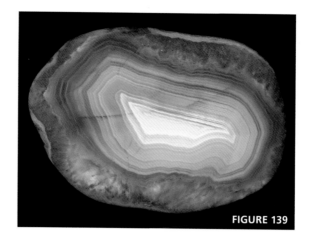

**FIGURE 139**
A perfect floater with odd pink coloration. Approx. 2.5" x 1.5" (5 cm x 3.8 cm)

agates have a core of banded chalcedony surrounded by a thick layer of macrocrystalline quartz. This indicates there was only one change in the amount of available silica, but why was there only one temporary decrease? This is such an abundant occurrence that we must wonder if the development of so many "type one" floaters is merely a coincidence or if there were dramatic volcanic or climatic events that affected many, but not all, Lake Superior agates. If agates are indeed a result of primarily an accumulation process, such drastic regional changes outside of the vesicle could easily uniformly affect the banding in many agates.

## COLLECTIBILITY

Often visually interesting and colorful, floaters are very collectible and are one of the most popular agates with collectors. As with any variety of Lake Superior agate, many collectors dislike floaters that contain excessive amounts of macrocrystalline quartz. Nevertheless, with the right balance of chalcedony banding, quartz thickness and vivid coloration, floaters can be extremely valuable and beautiful additions to any agate collection.

**FIGURE 140**
A beautifully formed floater exhibiting rather unusual coloration. Approx. 2.5" x 2.5" (6.4 cm x 6.4 cm)

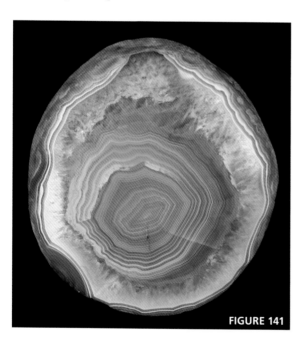

**FIGURE 141**

**FIGURE 141**
The very definition of a floater agate. 2" x 2" (5 cm x 5 cm)

center of the agate, but they do not sufficiently account for macrocrystalline quartz found in other parts of an agate.

One of the puzzling aspects of floaters is found in the more abundant "type one" agates. These

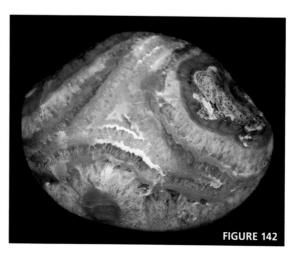

**FIGURE 142**

**FIGURE 142**
In this specimen, only certain bands are "floating," but this, too, is considered a floater agate. Approx. 2.5" x 2" (6.4 cm x 5 cm)

# AGATE *Geode*

*Agates containing a cavity at their core that is often lined with drusy quartz*

**CHARACTERISTICS:** Agates containing a hollow center, often lined with many tiny crystals

**SYNONYMS:** Geode

**DISTRIBUTION:** Can be found anywhere in the usual range of Lake Superior agates, but are more common on Minnesota's northern shores

**RARITY:** Agate geodes are quite uncommon because of their fragile nature; they survive best when still embedded in host rock (or when very recently removed)

............................................................

## DESCRIPTION

A geode is a rounded mass of material that contains a hollow space at its center. The void typically contains small crystals of various minerals, but particularly quartz. There are many different kinds of geodes worldwide, each composed of different rocks or minerals, but agate geodes are generally the most popular and well-known type. Agate geodes consist of common concentric agate banding surrounding an empty cavity. More often than not, the hollow space is lined with thousands of tiny macrocrystalline quartz crystals, a formation called quartz druse or drusy quartz.

With the exception of the central cavity, agate geodes most resemble adhesional banded agates. The amount of chalcedony banding in agate geodes can vary greatly from agate to agate; the chalcedony banding can sometimes be very thick and almost fill the geode entirely (as in Figure 143), or the banding can be very thin (as in Figure 144). But because thin-walled geodes with large interior cavities were brittle and easily crushed, they were no match for the immense weight of the glaciers. For this reason, most Lake Superior agate geodes found in areas of glacial till have thick regions of chalcedony banding surrounding relatively small cavities; this helped them survive weathering. Such was the case with the large specimen in Figure 143. More fragile agate geodes do exist in the Lake Superior region, but they are typically still embedded within their host rock, where they were protected from the glaciers.

All geodes can provide a cavity in which crystals of other minerals can form. Agate geodes are no exception and sometimes other minerals formed

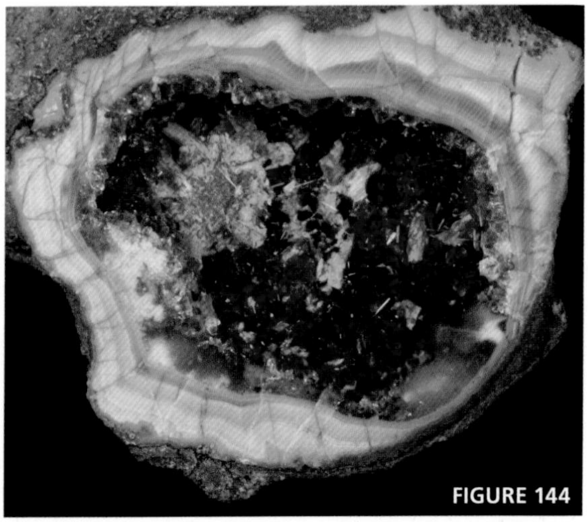

**FIGURE 143**
While thoroughly stained with limonite, this large agate is "incomplete," exhibiting a very small geode center. Approx. 3.5" x 4" (8.9 cm x 10.2 cm)

**FIGURE 144**
This geode is lined with a druse of dark reddish, iron-stained macrocrystalline quartz and crude orange crystals of laumontite. Approx. 1.5" x 1.5" (3.8 cm x 3.8 cm) Courtesy of Christopher Cordes.

**FIGURE 145**
Uncommon yellow banding encircles a geode center lined with a macrocrystalline quartz druse. Approx. 2.5" x 2" (6.4 cm x 5 cm)

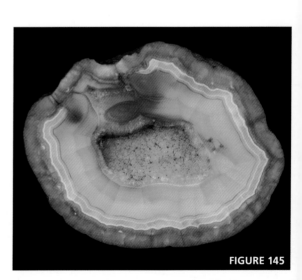

FIGURE 144

FIGURE 145

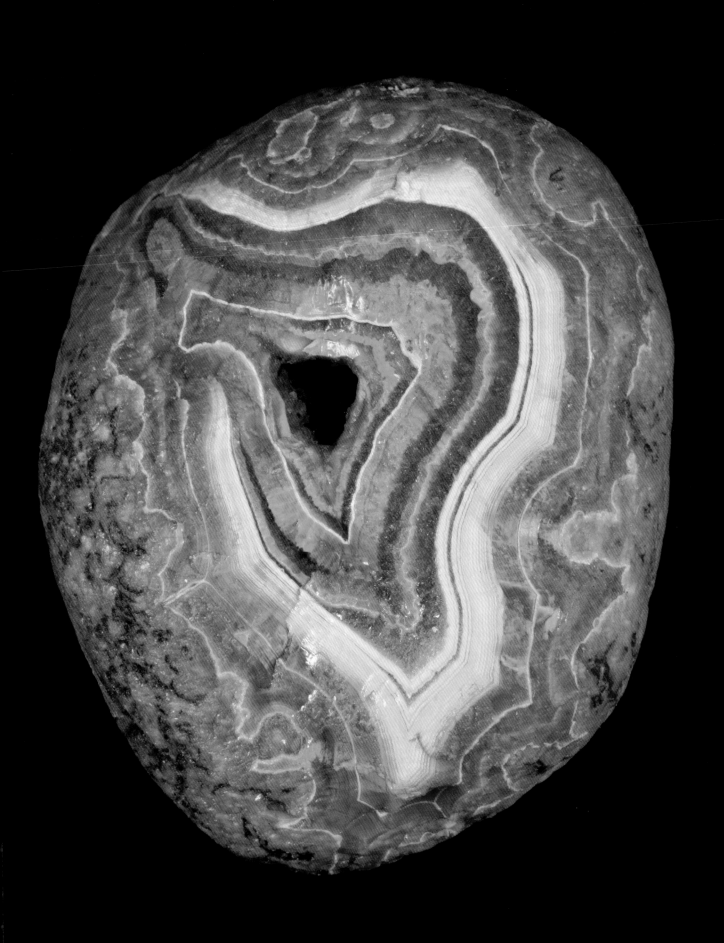

FIGURE 143

FIGURE 147

FIGURE 146
This thin-walled agate
geode still embedded
in rhyolite contains
the usual quartz
druse, but the large,
double-terminated
calcite crystal and
small, orange
laumontite crystals
are very unexpected—
and very rare—in
Lake Superior agates.
Geode approximately
2" long (5 cm).
Specimen courtesy of
Christopher Cordes.

in the cavity after the agate itself hardened (as in Figure 144). In fact, it is the additional mineral growths that make geodes as popular and collectible as they are. In Lake Superior agate geodes, the crystals of calcite or zeolites within the geode cavity often garner more attention than the agate itself.

## FORMATION

Agate geodes are fairly well understood. In essence, they are incomplete agates that weren't supplied with enough silica to develop into a whole agate. Historically, differentiation theories have not been able to account for hollow spaces within an agate, as their presence almost certainly means that the vesicle was not filled with a single mass of silica gel. The traditional accumulation

theories, however, can easily explain agate geodes. If the external source of silica was interrupted and never restored, silicic acid would not return to the vesicle and the agate would remain incomplete and partially empty. The quartz druse would have then formed from what little silica solutions remained in the vesicle after the last chalcedony layer developed.

After the formation of the chalcedony banding and drusy quartz layer, the porosity of the hardened agate could allow other mineral-bearing solutions to percolate through the agate and enter the void at its center. In this situation, crystals of other minerals would then grow within the geode. The minerals that can form within a Lake Superior agate geode primarily include calcite and various zeolite minerals, all of which are softer and more easily weathered than the agate itself. While these additional, secondary mineral growths are common in geodes from elsewhere in the world, Lake Superior agate geodes, such as that in Figure 148, generally lack them, possibly because they weathered away after the agates were broken open by the glaciers or because they simply never formed in the first place.

Nevertheless, not all Lake Superior agates geodes are devoid of secondary growths in their cavities. Whole, unbroken agate geode nodules still embedded in their host rock have often been sufficiently protected from weathering, and careful breaking or sawing can reveal beautifully formed crystals of secondary minerals contained within. The agate in Figure 147, for example, is

FIGURE 147
These are some of
the most perfectly
formed crystals of
Lake Superior stilbite
the authors have ever
seen, which in itself
is exciting. But
considering that these
are within a Lake
Superior agate geode
makes this a jaw-
dropping specimen.
10x magnification.
Specimen courtesy of
Christopher Cordes.

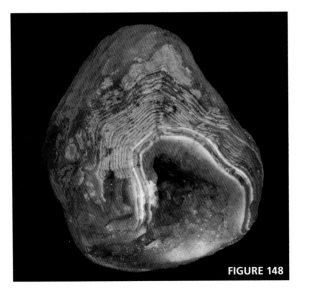

FIGURE 148
A common agate
geode, typical of those
found in Minnesota
gravel pits.
Approx. 3" x 2"
(7.6 cm x 5 cm)

an extraordinarily rare, one-of-a-kind specimen
containing perfectly developed crystals of stilbite,
a zeolite mineral. Specimens like this may be
more common from other parts of the world, but
they are nearly unheard of from Lake Superior.
Geodes filled with crude, irregular masses of
calcite (see Figures 149 and 150) are more
abundant in the Lake Superior region.

## COLLECTIBILITY

Hobbyists who frequent rock and mineral shops
will no doubt have encountered hundreds of
inexpensive agate geodes exported in bulk from
Brazil. While many are dyed gaudy colors, the

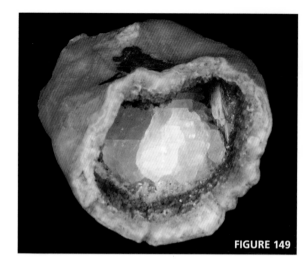

FIGURE 149

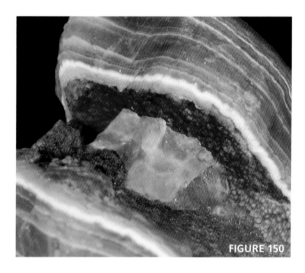

FIGURE 150

sheer volume of Brazilian geodes sold is a testament to the popularity and collectibility of all
agate geodes. Lake Superior agate geodes are far
less common that Brazil's, making them not only
more collectible, but more valuable as well.
While the interplay of the agate banding with the

geode cavity can be visually interesting, the
additional crystals that form within them are the
real draw. And due to the fact that secondary
mineral growths within the geode cavity are rare
in the Lake Superior area, the presence of any
additional mineral instantly makes specimens
more desirable and adds value.

Lake Superior agate geodes have traditionally
held few surprises in their cavities, predictably
containing only masses of calcite, a common
zeolite mineral such as laumontite, or nothing but
the quartz druse. However, recent discoveries on
Minnesota's North Shore have stunned collectors;
geodes have been discovered that contain mineral
growths never seen before in Lake Superior
agates. Broken directly out of rhyolite, Figure 147
shows a geode containing perfectly developed
crystals of stilbite. The geode in Figure 146
contains not an irregular mass of calcite, but a
very well-formed calcite crystal with termina-
tions, or points, at each end. Figure 151 features a

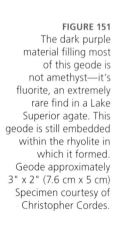

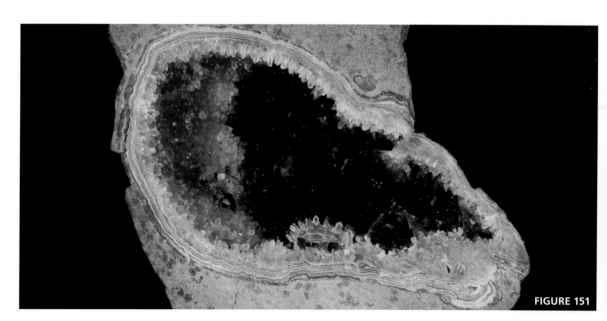

FIGURE 151

thin-walled agate geode nearly completely filled with purple fluorite. This is one of the most striking examples of a discovery that is entirely new to Lake Superior agate collectors. Fluorite itself is rare on Minnesota's shores, but finding it in an agate geode is truly exciting.

But even without additional crystals, geodes are still very collectible. If freshly exposed, the thousands of crystal points of the quartz druse found in nearly every agate geode can appear to sparkle as they each reflect light in a different direction. Indeed, unless significantly damaged or otherwise marred by weathering, agate geodes continue to be one of the most endearing varieties of agates.

FIGURE 153

## NOTABLE VARIATIONS

Thunder eggs are a common variety of geode around the world. Thunder eggs consist of a core of agate surrounded by rough, fine-grained rock. Thunder eggs form within bodies of volcanic ash or tuff. As hot gases violently expanded in the rock as it formed, irregularly shaped cracks and voids appeared. When the silica-rich ash later weathered, silica solutions filled in the hollow spaces and generated agate banding.

Thunder eggs can be found in northern Minnesota, near Lake Superior's shore in the area around Grand Marais. Though no volcanic ash or tuff exists in northern Minnesota today due to the past glacial activity, the thunder eggs found there, called "five-mile geodes" by collectors because of their geographic location five miles from Grand Marais, MN, are evidence that violent, ash-producing volcanic eruptions did indeed take place. Many specimens are hollow, as a geode is expected to be, while others are solid

FIGURE 152

and completely filled with agate banding or macrocrystalline quartz. Though non-hollow thunder eggs aren't technically geodes, collectors still consider them to be geodes as well.

Five-mile geodes can be difficult to identify when whole, as they simply appear as more or less spherical rocks with rough, nonuniform surfaces. When cut or broken open, however, they exhibit easily recognizable traits, including jagged, pointed cavities lined with bright red or orange chalcedony banding. Figure 153 shows a whole thunder egg from Minnesota that was found in a riverbank. Figure 152 shows a five-mile geode of similar size and shape sawn in half to reveal the characteristic thunder egg appearance. Note that the interior of the geode is lined with a white material—this is a thin coating of clay minerals, also derived from the weathering volcanic ash. Finally, Figure 154 shows that a single geode formation can actually contain several pockets of banded chalcedony.

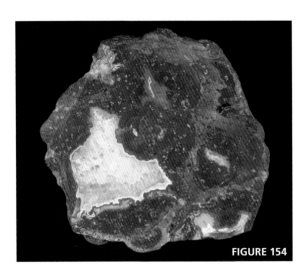

FIGURE 154

FIGURE 152
The characteristic interior of a thunder egg from Minnesota. Approx. 2" x 2" (5 cm x 5 cm)

FIGURE 153
A typical whole, unbroken thunder egg from Minnesota. Approx. 2.5" x 2.5" (6.4 cm x 6.4 cm)

FIGURE 154
A large five-mile geode with several areas of chalcedony. Approx. 4" x 4" (10.2 cm x 10.2 cm) Specimen courtesy of Dave Woerheide.

# *Gravitationally Banded* AGATE

*Parallel, horizontal layers at the bottom of a specimen are the primary characteristic of these agates*

**CHARACTERISTICS:** Agates containing a portion of horizontal, parallel bands at the bottom of the specimen

**SYNONYMS:** Horizontally banded agate, water-level agate, onyx, Uruguay-type agate

**DISTRIBUTION:** Gravitationally banded agates can be found anywhere in the usual range of Lake Superior agates, though they appear to be more abundant in Minnesota

**RARITY:** Gravitationally banded agates are not uncommon, but are less abundant than adhesional banded agates

## DESCRIPTION

Many theorists state that if impurities, inclusions and other "foreign" substances and structures are ignored, we are left with only two types of agates: adhesional banded agates and gravitationally banded agates. Whereas adhesional banded agates contain concentric chalcedony bands lining the inner walls of the vesicle, gravitationally banded agates exhibit flat, level, parallel bands that obviously developed by a very different process.

Like adhesional banded agates, gravitationally banded agates are known by many names. In the community of Lake Superior agate collectors, they are referred to as "water-level agates," while many researchers know them as "Uruguay-type agates," named for the fact that agate-bearing regions of Uruguay produce only gravitationally banded agates. But it is the term "onyx" that has been used since antiquity to refer to this specific type of agate. Originating from the Greek word *onychion*, onyx has been used as a decorative carving material for millennia, and today we know it to be another form of agate.

Gravitationally banded agates are immediately identifiable and cannot easily be confused with any other kind of agate. They consist of parallel layers at the bottom of the agate, sometimes with common adhesional banding or macrocrystalline quartz above, as in Figure 156, while at other times the gravitational bands fill the agate completely, as in Figure 157. Often the parallel bands will turn into common adhesional banding near the edges of the specimen; a trait visible in Figure 155. The parallel bands themselves are usually flat and straight, but most are not evenly

**FIGURE 155**
A typical gravitationally banded agate from Lake Superior. Note that macrocrystalline quartz formed above the banding. Also note the odd inclusion of rock at the top of the specimen. Approx. 3.5" x 3" (8.9 cm x 7.6 cm)

**FIGURE 156**
A rough, unpolished "water-level agate." Approx. 3.5" x 3" (8.9 cm x 7.6 cm)

**FIGURE 157**
A "leaning" vesicle filled entirely with gravitational bands. Approx. 3" x 1" (7.6 cm x 2.5 cm)

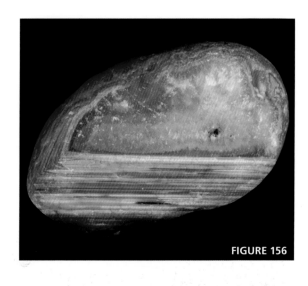

FIGURE 156

FIGURE 157

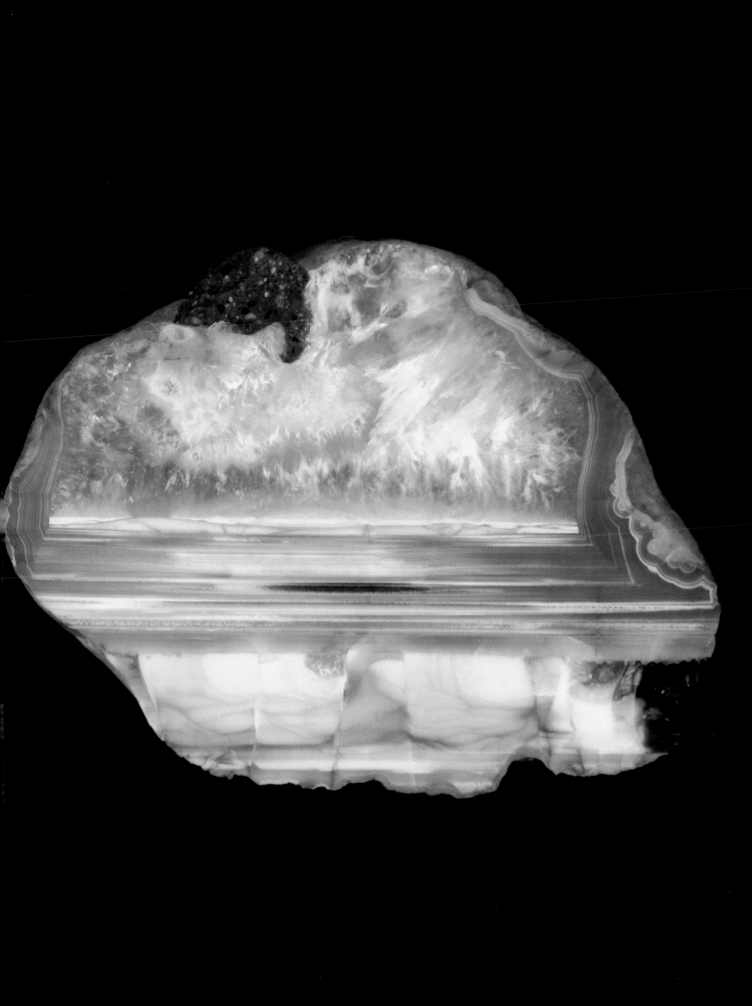

FIGURE 155

FIGURE 158
Intense red bands
surround bright yellow
gravitational bands.
Approx. 2" x 1.5"
(5 cm x 3.8 cm)

colored and contain odd blotches of differently colored material, often in shades of gray or black that appear out of place. In addition, the boundaries between layers are often indistinct and sometimes hard to see. Finally, the horizontal, parallel bands tend to be thicker and contain more material than common adhesional bands.

## FORMATION

The formation of gravitationally banded agates has long been studied due to the drastic differences between them and all other types of agates. We may not fully understand all of the conditions in the vesicle at the time of agate formation, but we do know with certainty that gravity played a major role in agate formation. Adhesional banded agates were able to overcome gravity's downward pull and form uniform bands on all sides of the vesicle, but for unknown reasons, in gravitationally banded agates the silica particles sank and collected in flat layers, not unlike sediment settling at the bottom of a pond. As the process repeated, the flat, parallel layers accumulated to provide the characteristic appearance and descriptive name of gravitationally banded agates.

Many researchers have noted that the parallel bands in gravitationally banded agates consist of microgranular quartz, not fibrous chalcedony. This is an important distinction, as it is another indication of how different their formation was from that of adhesional banded agates. In addition, it is universally accepted that only gravity could have organized the parallel bands. As a result, there are a number of formation theories for such agates, all centered around the reasons why gravity was able to so strongly impact these agates.

By nature, gravitationally banded agates are more easily explained by the accumulation theory. In

FIGURE 159
A small, but unique,
gravitationally banded
agate with a unique
mixture of color.
Approx. 1.5" x 1.5"
(3.8 cm x 3.8 cm)

FIGURE 160
A small gravitationally
banded agate.
Approx. 2.5" x 1.5"
(6.4 cm x 3.8 cm)

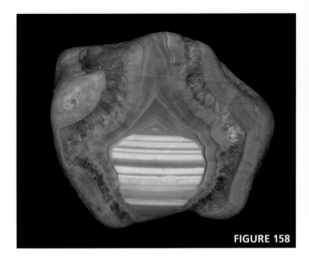

FIGURE 158

his 2009 article, Walger suggests that repeated inflows of silica solutions containing too much water and too little silica were unable to form a gel layer, and instead the particles of silica within the thin solution sank to the bottom of the vesicle. This idea is supported by the fact that gravitationally banded agates are found to contain

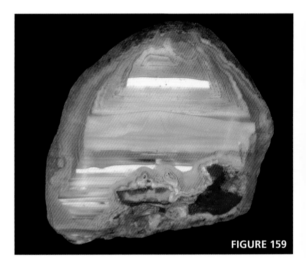

FIGURE 159

an unusually high amount of water. But while this idea may account for part of their formation, other authors have proposed more complex solutions to the problem.

Sunagawa and Ohta's theory of silica polymers, first published in 1976, may provide a more complete explanation of gravitational band formations. They suggested that the silica enters the vesicle as a very thin, watery solution containing polymerized silica, or linked silica molecules. After the vesicle is filled with silica-rich water, the polymers would begin to coagulate, or clump up and thicken, to form tiny particles of silica gel. They argued that if the vesicle were undisturbed, the coagulated silica particles suspended in the fluid would accumulate on the walls of

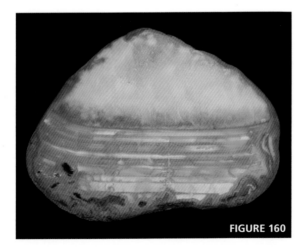

FIGURE 160

the agate and contribute to the formation of fibrous chalcedony. However, they proposed that if an event caused the silica clumps to become agitated, particularly by the movement of water, they would sink and build up to form a horizontal band. Because the silica would settle as tiny coagulated chunks, the microgranular texture of the bands would develop. While there are issues with Sunagawa and Ohta's ideas, they provide both a mechanism for parallel band development and an explanation of why the horizontal bands consist of granular quartz.

In 2004, Petránek developed a more complex model for the development of gravitationally banded agates by suggesting that their formation is possibly more dependent on conditions outside the vesicle than within. Petránek's research shows that gravitationally banded agates are considerably more abundant in rocks that formed during periods of a tropical climate and virtually absent from those that formed during very arid conditions. In addition, he notes that most gravitationally banded agates are formed in continental flood basalts, which are enormous formations of basalt that formed when lava "flooded" a large area. Some continental flood basalts can span more than one million square miles, and such a basalt formation exists in Brazil and Uruguay, which produces huge amounts of gravitationally banded agates. With any volcanic eruption, some gases are released into the atmosphere, but the eruptions that produced continental flood basalts pumped enormous amounts of carbon dioxide and other reactive gases into the air for long periods of time. These gases can be trapped within atmospheric moisture and return to earth in rain.

Petránek's article explains that the tons of carbon dioxide produced by large eruptions in wet, tropical climates would develop highly corrosive acid

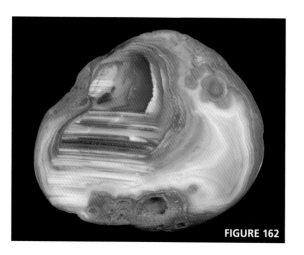

FIGURE 162

rain. As the caustic water attacked the basalt, the elements in the rock were dissolved and carried downward into the vesicles. Positively charged molecules of elements such as magnesium and calcium interacted with the silica solution already

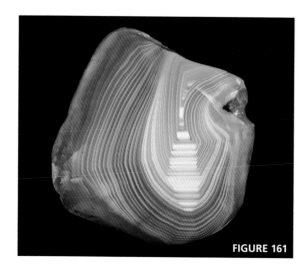

FIGURE 161

in the vesicle and caused the negatively charged silica molecules to bond and coagulate. As tiny particles of coagulated silica are heavy, they sank to the bottom of the liquid-filled vesicle, forming a horizontal band. Because some gravitationally banded agates contain adhesional banding, such as the one in Figure 155, we know that sometimes a small amount of silica is able to form a gel. Petránek's model for the development of gravitationally banded agates is unique because it focuses exclusively on this type of agate while virtually ignoring adhesional banded agates.

It is largely agreed upon that gravitationally banded agates formed when an abundance of water was present during agate formation, because nothing else could have formed such flat, parallel banding. Petránek's theory takes this idea one step further by assuming that a completely different process of agate formation developed horizontal banding.

Such drastically different types of banding could possibly be the result of two different silica sources. Perhaps a hydrothermal silica source rose and filled vesicles from below, allowing a gel to form, producing adhesional banded agates in a calm, still environment. Gravitationally banded agates may have formed in very wet climates where atmospheric water inundated the rock, providing the vesicle with considerable amounts of impurity-rich water that was moving enough to disturb the silica and cause it to sink. In addition, infiltration channels are almost never seen in

FIGURE 161
Resembling a stairway, this odd agate slice exhibits adhesional banding except for a small region of stepped horizontal bands. Approx. 1.5" x 2" (3.8 cm x 5 cm)

FIGURE 162
This specimen shows the typical way in which horizontal bands will shorten as they approach the center of the agate. Approx. 2.5" x 2" (6.4 cm x 5 cm)

gravitationally banded agates, further distancing themselves from adhesional banded agates.

There is one primary problem with Petránek's theory, however. His article focuses on relatively young agate-producing continental flood basalts, such as those in Brazil and Uruguay. The Mid-continent Rift rocks in the Lake Superior region, however, are neither young nor a continental flood basalt formation, yet gravitationally banded agates were still produced in the region. In addition, while Uruguay's agate-bearing basalt exclusively produces gravitationally banded agates, Lake Superior's basalts are home to many types of agates, including those with adhesional bands.

## COLLECTIBILITY

Throughout the world, gravitationally banded agates are highly collectible, and Lake Superior's are no exception. As with any agate, the most desirable specimens are those with colorful banding and attractive features, such as agate eyes or adhesional banding around the edges of the nodule. One of the most interesting aspects of gravitationally banded agates, however, is that we know exactly how the agate was oriented when it was forming. In certain specimens, this may help us determine how (or in what order) certain structures formed, while in others it may just prove visually interesting, such as the "leaning" agate nodule in Figure 157. But perhaps one of the most intriguing specimens in the authors' collection is pictured in Figures 164 and 165. These images portray two sides of the same agate nodule. When looking at this specimen, it's hard not to wonder why gravitational banding and macrocrystalline quartz formed in one half of the nodule while a classic concentric, adhesional pattern formed in the other half.

Because of their significance, no Lake Superior agate collection is complete without several

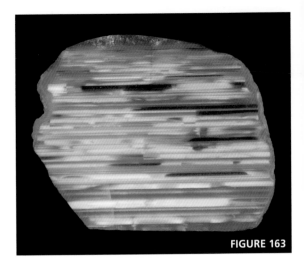

FIGURE 163

specimens of gravitationally banded agates. Particularly fine specimens can command high prices, though they typically are less sought after than adhesional banded agates.

## NOTABLE VARIATIONS

There are two variations of gravitationally banded agates that can be found in the Lake Superior region; collectors refer to them as "mosaic agates" and "cloud-bank agates." Both are strange, beautiful and highly collectible variants of gravitationally banded agates.

Figures 163 and 166 show agates completely filled with gravitational banding; however, the bands are not uniform along their entire length. There are peculiar changes in coloration, sometimes separated by sharp edges and containing different textures. These agates have been polished perpendicular to the band direction, as gravitationally banded agates generally are. However, the agate in Figure 166 was also polished along its top side, parallel to the horizontal bands. The result is the mosaic seen in Figure 167. Obviously named for their mosaic-like appearance, mosaic agates contain odd, geometric shapes composed of the

FIGURE 164
The front of this specimen exhibits two distinct regions of horizontal bands. Approx. 2.5" x 1.5" (6.4 cm x 3.8 cm)

FIGURE 165
The back side of the same specimen as in Figure 164 contains not horizontal bands, but adhesional bands. Approx. 2.5" x 1.5" (6.4 cm x 3.8 cm)

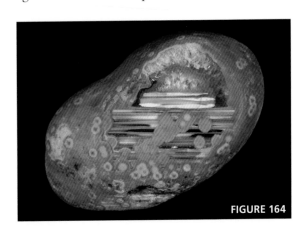

FIGURE 164

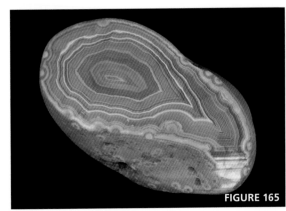

FIGURE 165

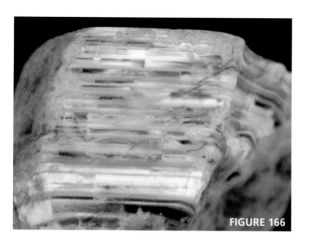

FIGURE 166

FIGURE 167

FIGURE 166
The blocky appearance of these horizontal bands is a telltale sign that a mosaic will appear when the stone is cut parallel to the bands.
2x magnification

FIGURE 167
The mosaic seen on the top of the specimen in Figure 166.
2x magnification

changes in quartz color and texture along the horizontal bands, as seen in Figure 167. Another mosaic is pictured in Figure 168, which has not been polished. Natural weathering has eroded only certain areas of the mosaic, leaving spaces behind. But why do mosaics occur? They show us that the parallel layers of gravitationally banded agates are seldom consistent and contain variations in structure and impurities, but it's not clear why this occurs. Mosaic agates are indeed one of the many remaining mysteries of agate formation.

Cloud-bank agates are another common variation of gravitationally banded agates, and they are named for their resemblance to low clouds. The bands in these agates are only somewhat parallel, containing rounded curves, bumps and slanting

While research articles hardly mention cloud-bank agates, the authors believe that the coagulated silica may have been particularly thick in these bands, causing them to shrink and pull to one side of the agate as they dried and solidified. If this process happened in stages, the slanted, lumpy, overlapping shapes could have formed.

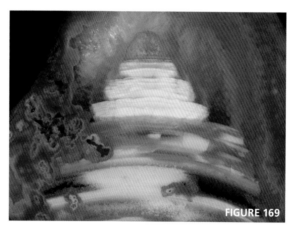

FIGURE 169

FIGURE 168
This rough mosaic has the same odd, geometric shapes as in Figure 167, but some are missing due to weathering.
Approx. 2.5" x 2" (6.4 cm x 5 cm)

FIGURE 169
The typical cloud-bank formation in a separate section of banding above the regular horizontal bands.
1.5x magnification

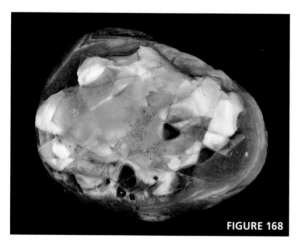

FIGURE 168

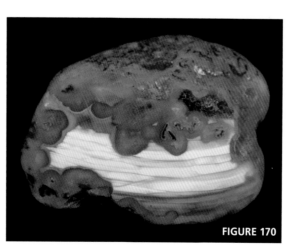

FIGURE 170

sections that seem to overlap with each other. In addition, the bands are virtually always an odd mixture of opaque yellow, pink and tan color-ations. Cloud-bank bands are also nearly always found as a secondary filling in a gravitationally banded agate; they typically grow within a pocket at the center of a macrocrystalline quartz formation that resides atop common gravitational banding, as seen in Figures 169 and 170.

FIGURE 170
This small agate consists entirely of cloud-bank banding surrounded by a gray husk.
Approx. 1.5" x 1" (3.8cm x 2.5 cm)

# *Skip-an-Atom* AGATE

*A peculiar variety of agate displaying opaque, bluish gray or white macrocrystalline quartz*

**CHARACTERISTICS:** Opaque, bluish gray or white macrocrystalline quartz with a "crackly" appearance and typically very little chalcedony banding

**SYNONYMS:** "Opalized quartz" agate

**DISTRIBUTION:** Skip-an-atom agates are inconsistent in their distribution and very few "hunting grounds" exist, though they are more common on Minnesota's Lake Superior shoreline than other areas

**RARITY:** Skip-an-atom agates are rare and few areas will consistently yield specimens

## DESCRIPTION

Of all the strange and unique variations in agate structure that can be found within Lake Superior's agates, none are more compelling and puzzling than the skip-an-atom agates found along the lake's shores. Everything about them, including their name, is perplexing. They predominantly contain opaque, bluish gray or white macrocrystalline quartz divided into growth layers (not unlike the layers in banded quartz

agates), and they occasionally exhibit chalcedony banding that is typically brown or yellowish in color. To the authors' knowledge, no studies or research has been published that take a direct look at these strange agates, leaving many collectors to come up with their own ideas for formation. Sometimes these ideas are far-fetched, such as the claims that these agates "skipped an atom" during their formation. (Perhaps the originators of the "skip-an-atom" name suggested this theory in jest because it makes little scientific sense.) Others refer to these agates as containing "opalized quartz," stating that the macrocrystalline quartz has somehow turned into opal or actually contains opal within its structure. This idea may be closer to the truth, but without in-depth research, we cannot know for certain.

It wouldn't be easy to confuse a skip-an-atom agate with another agate variety, as their appearance is very distinctive. The macrocrystalline quartz within these agates is opaque and light colored with a crackled or fragmented look. Typically, specimens contain little or no banded chalcedony, and resemble the specimens in Figures 171 and 173, respectively. However, rarer examples, such as the agate pictured in Figure 172, can exhibit beautiful, colorful concentric banding. These three specimens illustrate the wide range of variations that can be found in

**FIGURE 171**
The characteristic appearance of a skip-an-atom agate is exemplified in this fantastic specimen. Approx. 1.5" x 2.5" (3.8 cm x 6.4 cm)

**FIGURE 172**
Skip-an-atom agates typically don't have much banding, especially colored banding, making this a rare specimen. Approx. 3" x 2" (7.6 cm x 5 cm)

**FIGURE 173**
The most typical appearance of a skip-an-atom agate has no chalcedony banding. Approx. 2" x 1.5" (5 cm x 3.8 cm)

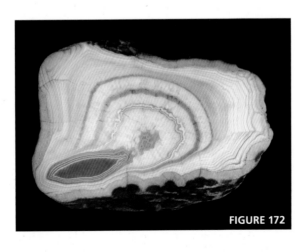

FIGURE 172

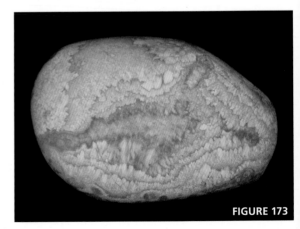

FIGURE 173

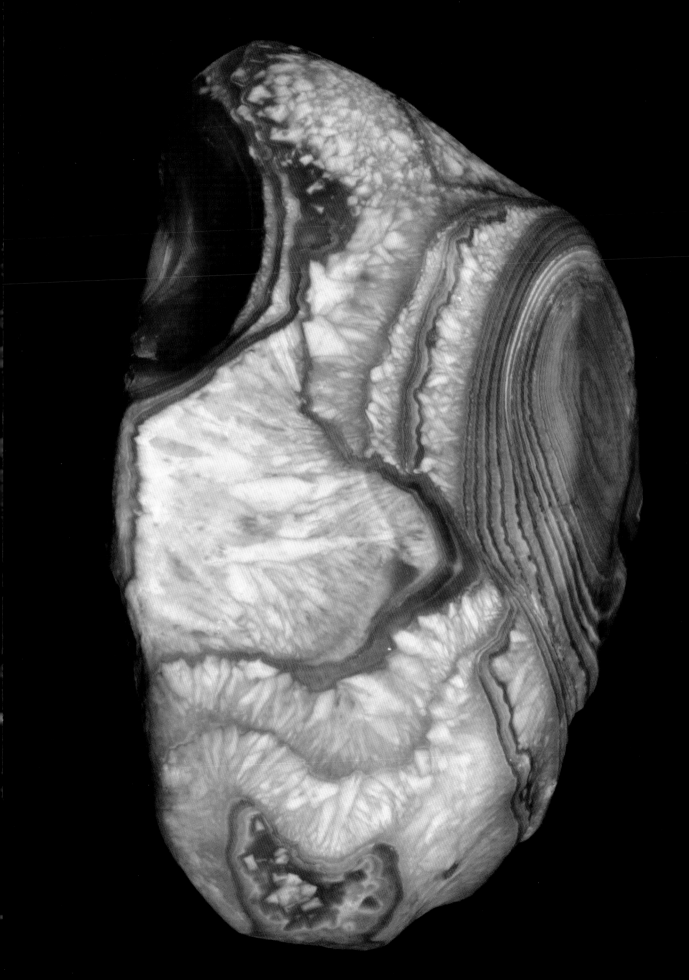

FIGURE 171

FIGURE 174
A rare specimen with ample chalcedony banding and only small layers of skip-an-atom quartz. Approx. 2" x 1.5" (5 cm x 3.8 cm)

FIGURE 175
A bright red shell of chalcedony surrounds this skip-an-atom agate. Approx. 2" x 1" (5 cm x 2.5 cm)

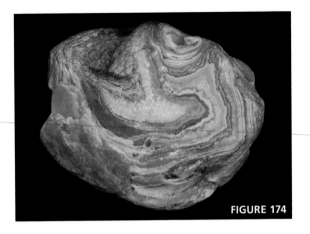

FIGURE 174

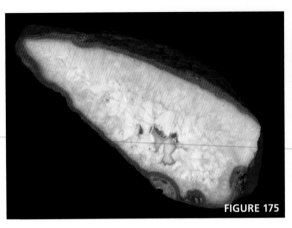

FIGURE 175

skip-an-atom agates and that there may be many different ways in which each forms.

## FORMATION

Skip-an-atom agates are absent from scientific literature and popular theories behind their formation are hardly credible, to say the least. While skip-an-atom agates may not actually be "opalized," there is certainly some value to the idea that the opaque, crackled macrocrystalline quartz may have undergone some kind of change. Several researchers throughout the past century have shown that various forms of silica will

FIGURE 176
A shell of chalcedony surrounds skip-an-atom quartz. Approx. 3" x 2" (7.6 cm x 5 cm)

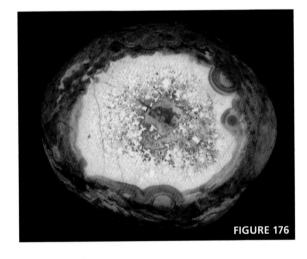

FIGURE 176

FIGURE 177
A characteristic skip-an-atom agate. Approx. 2" x 1.5" (5 cm x 3.8 cm)

transform into others when heated. For example, when heated, opal transforms into cristobalite, which in turn changes to granular quartz as the temperature is increased. In addition, Moxon's many studies on the size of the chalcedony fibers and microgranules in agates have shown that it is possible that some agates have undergone heating after they formed. Based on these findings and some of their own observations, the authors suggest that skip-an-atom agates are examples of agates that have been sufficiently heated after

their formation in order to cause significant changes to their structure and appearance.

When significantly heated by volcanic activity, the fibers in chalcedony merge and recrystallize into tiny quartz grains, or granular quartz. Similarly, macrocrystalline quartz turns into tridymite, a variety of silica that only forms under high temperatures. With further heating, tridymite then changes into a high-temperature form of cristobalite. After the heat dissipates, the tridymite or cristobalite then revert back to macrocrystalline quartz. It is this transformation process that may have permanently changed the silica in these agates, causing the macrocrystalline quartz to appear opaque and crackled. The authors present the specimen in Figure 178 as the strongest evidence for this idea. Note how the agate retains a vaguely banded structure, yet the darker bands appear to be formed of granular quartz, not fibrous chalcedony. In between the darker bands are the characteristic gray, opaque crystals of altered macrocrystalline quartz.

Admittedly, there are flaws with this theory. Heating may have caused specimens such as in Figure 173 to form, as it only contains altered macrocrystalline quartz, but other samples, such

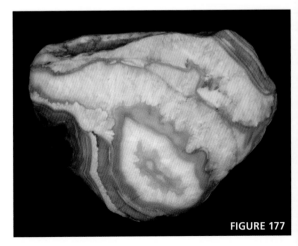

FIGURE 177

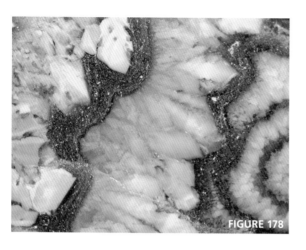

FIGURE 178

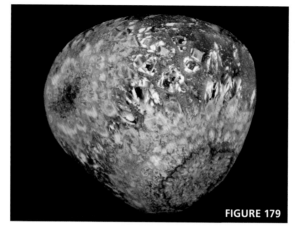

FIGURE 179

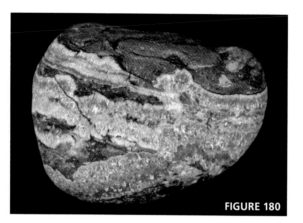

FIGURE 180

FIGURE 178
Skip-an-atom quartz divided by bands of dark granular quartz. 5x magnification

FIGURE 179
Very rare skip-an-atom amethyst from northern Michigan. Note the two large radial formations of quartz.
Approx. 3" x 3" (7.6 cm x 7.6 cm) Specimen courtesy of Terry and Bobbi House.

FIGURE 180
Another example of rare skip-an-atom amethyst from northern Michigan. Note that this specimen formed as veins within rock.
Approx. 4" x 3" (10.2 cm x 7.6 cm) Specimen courtesy of Terry and Bobbi House.

as that in Figure 174 or 177 still retain fibrous, unchanged chalcedony bands. Unless chalcedony requires significantly more heating than macro-crystalline quartz to transform, or is more resistant to changing forms, it would seem that this theory is not entirely viable. The thin chalcedony husks on the specimens in Figure 175 and 176 are also problematic, as they appear unchanged as well. Even so, the notion that volcanic heat may be responsible for altering and transforming macrocrystalline quartz may be the best explanation we currently have for the mysterious formation of skip-an-atom agates.

## COLLECTIBILITY

Skip-an-atoms are an "acquired taste" for some, but in general they have become very popular within the Lake Superior agate collecting community. The finest and most desirable specimens are those with macrocrystalline quartz with a rich bluish coloration combined with colorful chalcedony banding. To some collectors, skip-an-atoms are one of the most valuable types.

FIGURE 181

## NOTABLE VARIATIONS

Skip-an-atom agates were long only found in Minnesota, but recent discoveries on the eastern end of Michigan's Upper Peninsula have yielded rare skip-an-atom specimens that consist of amethyst. Amethyst is the purple, irradiated, iron-rich variety of quartz, and its presence in skip-an-atom agates makes their formation even more bewildering. Figure 179 shows one of these specimens, and it contains two large, radial "sprays" of gray quartz that extend upward into a body of amethyst. Figure 180 shows a similar formation of amethyst in a skip-an-atom agate that formed as veins within cracks in its host rock. Equally as strange is the specimen shown in Figure 181. This body of opaque, gray skip-an-atom quartz formed within a type of rock called basalt porphyry, which is similar to basalt but contains large crystals of feldspar minerals, which are visible here as the orange spots. Porphyry begins its formation deep underground, where high heat allowed its feldspar crystals to begin forming to a large, visible size. However, an eruption forced the lava to the surface, where it cooled quickly, freezing the feldspar crystals in place. Did the skip-an-atom quartz form before the lava erupted, or after?

FIGURE 181
Typical skip-an-atom quartz in a non-typical rock called porphyry.
Approx. 5.5" x 6" (14 cm x 15.2 cm) Specimen courtesy of Dean Montour.

# *Vein* AGATE

*Vein agates form in cracks instead of vesicles, giving them a thin, elongated appearance*

**CHARACTERISTICS:** Agates without a nodular, amygdaloidal structure, instead appearing as long, skinny patterns of banded chalcedony

**SYNONYMS:** Seam agate, fissure infill agate

**DISTRIBUTION:** Vein agates are not as widespread as other agates; though they can form in any type of rock, many are found in the iron-rich regions of Minnesota, Wisconsin and Michigan

**RARITY:** Seam agates are fairly uncommon

## DESCRIPTION

While nearly every Lake Superior agate formed as an amygdule in volcanic rock such as basalt or rhyolite, some agates did not. Though they are uncommon around Lake Superior, vein agates formed in small cracks—not vesicles—within rocks. The narrow nature of crevices and fissures give these agates a thin, elongated appearance that easily distinguishes them from their amygdaloidal

cousins. There are three types of vein agates found in the Lake Superior region, each of which is highly distinctive and easy to tell apart.

One variety of vein agate is still embedded in its matrix, which oddly is almost never basalt. Figures 183 and 184 show two vein agates encased in rhyolite that have been worn and rounded by Lake Superior. Of course, it is highly likely that vein agates formed within basalt as well, but perhaps the high silica content of the rhyolite helps the rough, irregularly shaped agates bond tightly to the rock, preventing them from easily separating. Other than the shape of the cavity they formed within, these vein agates differ little from regular agates, exhibiting similar colors, patterns and internal structures.

The second kind of vein agate is derived from iron-rich areas, namely in Minnesota and Michigan. These agates formed in cracks within bodies of iron ore, such as rocks rich with hematite and magnetite, and developed dark coloration as a result of a large amount of light-absorbing impurities. Vein agates of this variety resemble Figure 182; they have narrow arrangements of bright white opaque bands bordered by black a nd gray translucent chalcedony that rarely features anything other than poorly defined parallel layers.

**FIGURE 182**
A typical black and white vein agate from Minnesota. Approx. 2.5" x 4" (6.4 cm x 10.2 cm)

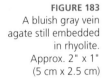

**FIGURE 183**
A bluish gray vein agate still embedded in rhyolite. Approx. 2" x 1" (5 cm x 2.5 cm)

**FIGURE 184**
An orange vein agate still in rhyolite. Approx. 2.5" x 2" (6.4 cm x 5 cm)

FIGURE 183

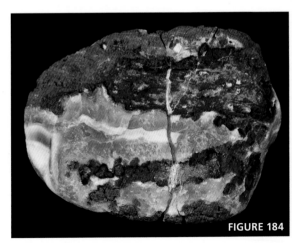

FIGURE 184

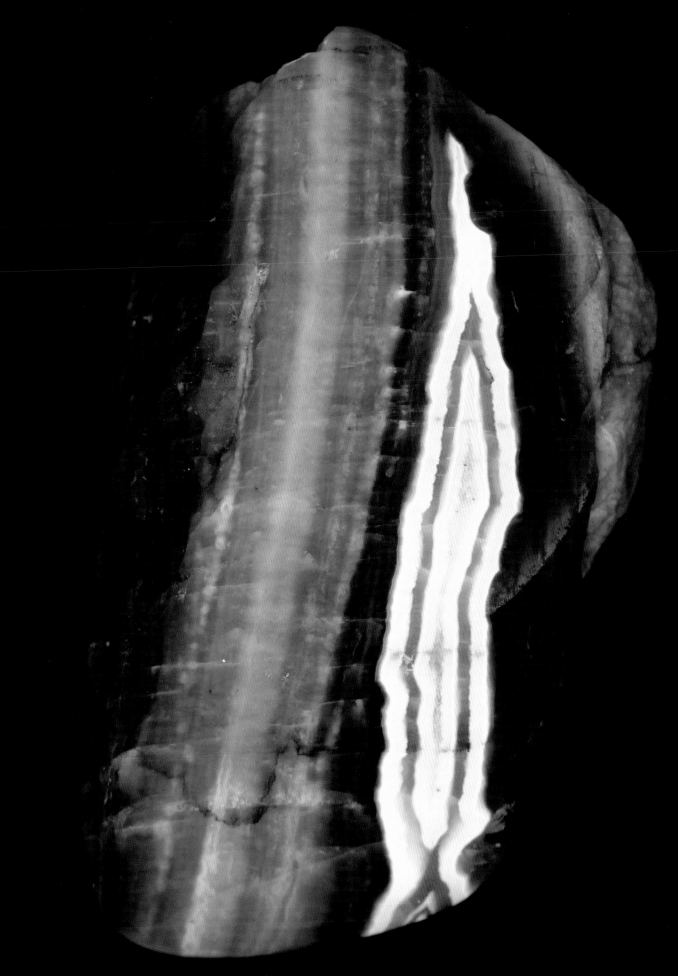

FIGURE 182

FIGURE 185
A black and white vein agate from iron-rich areas.
Approx. 3" x 2.5" (7.6 cm x 6.4 cm)

**FIGURE 186**
Vein agate in hematite.
Approx. 1" x 1.5" (2.5 cm x 3.8 cm)

The third variety of vein agate is rarer and formed within limestone, a soft sedimentary rock derived from ancient oceans. Due to the glacial activity in the region, limestone is uncommon around Lake Superior, and these agates are only found in one area near Thunder Bay, Ontario.

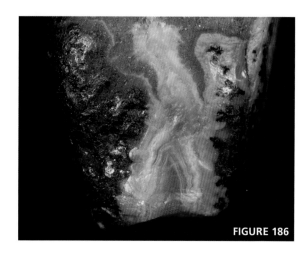

FIGURE 186

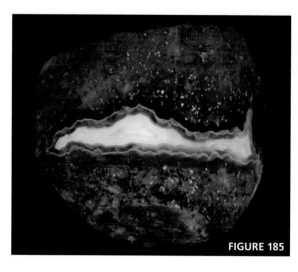

FIGURE 185

These agates exhibit intricate woven patterns that are light in color and rich with impurities and stalactitic structures.

## FORMATION

Vein agates formed fairly simply. Fissures in rock received influxes of mineral-rich waters (just as vesicles did) and eventually those minerals began to build up. If enough silicic acid found its way into the crack and remained there long enough, chalcedony began to form and the usual agate formation process would initiate. Observation of specimens tells us that vein agates do not, or cannot, form in very large cracks within volcanic rocks, presumably because not enough silicic acid could accumulate to fill such a large area.

Research into the varying amounts of certain oxygen isotopes in agates resulted in an interesting discovery in German vein agates. Götze and his colleagues found that while amygdaloidal agates from all over the world typically contain varying amounts of certain oxygen isotopes from band to band, the German vein agates tested did not. This signified that they likely formed more quickly and from the same source of silica. If the same were true for Lake Superior vein agates, then perhaps they formed quickly too and not from long-term repeated inflows of silicic acid.

The high concentration of vein agates in iron-rich areas is interesting and worthy of note. Agates like those in Figure 186, which is contained within

shiny, metallic hematite, are formed when a mass of iron ore ruptures and silica solutions flow into the cavity. The same is true for the polished agate in Figure 187, which formed within a mass of magnetite (a magnetic iron ore); the magnetite is visible on the bottom portion of the specimen. The mysterious black vein agates shown in Figures 182 and 185 are harder to understand, however. They are thought to originate from Minnesota's iron ranges, where taconite, a rocky mixture of chert and magnetite, is prevalent. The silica within these agates may have been derived from the weathering and decomposition of chert and taconite, but the exact process of their formation is unknown.

## COLLECTIBILITY

The desirability of Lake Superior vein agates is typically limited to those collectors looking for rare and unusual agates. Specimens in rhyolite

**FIGURE 187**
Known locally as "hematite lace agates," specimens of these vein agates were reportedly removed from deep within the Cliffs Iron Mine in Ishpeming, Michigan, decades ago. It is said that there is no access to more specimens and they have not been collected since. Oddly, the mass of iron ore at the bottom end of this specimen is magnetite, not hematite, and is magnetic.
Approx. 1" x 2" (2.5 cm x 5 cm)

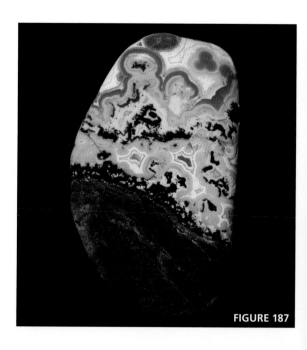

FIGURE 187

that exhibit bright coloration and fine banding can be as collectible as any other agates—sometimes more so, due to the added interest of the attached rock—but high-quality specimens are rare, and the average specimens aren't often considered valuable by collectors. Due to their dark coloration, high level of impurities and often underwhelming banding, most vein agates derived from iron-bearing rocks are generally ignored by collectors, despite being perhaps more unique than many other varieties of agate. Lake Superior vein agates might see more praise from collectors if they were more common, more colorful, and better known (as they are in places like Germany), but today few specimens garner any attention.

## NOTABLE VARIATIONS

The vein agates found within limestone near Thunder Bay, Ontario, known as "Thunder Bay agates," resulted from a completely different process of agate formation than those found elsewhere around Lake Superior. Formed as irregular, blocky masses in the sedimentary rock limestone, Thunder Bay agates contrast greatly with amygdaloidal Lake Superior agates, which formed within igneous rocks. While their formation is largely a mystery, they may actually prove to be a "side effect" of the Midcontinent Rift event, and may therefore be related to Lake Superior's more famous agates.

Because limestone consists almost entirely of calcite, it is highly susceptible to weathering. Acidic water can cause sections of the rock to dissolve and collapse, providing the spaces in which agates can form. Though the source of

**FIGURE 188**
A typical specimen of Thunder Bay agate. Approx. 2.5" x 1.5" (6.4 cm x 3.8 cm)

**FIGURE 188**

silica for the Thunder Bay agates is not entirely known, it is believed to stem from the Gunflint Formation, a nearly two billion-year-old mass of iron-rich chert that formed from sediment at the bottom of an ancient sea. Volcanic activity and rising hot water (possibly as a result of the nearby Midcontinent Rift event) may have carried silica from the chert up into the overlying limestone, eventually forming agates.

Thunder Bay agates can be enormous, as many formed in large cavities. All contain an abundance of soft calcite growths and macrocrystalline quartz amid the chalcedony, which gives the agates a segmented appearance. Agate stalactites, or icicle-shaped formations, are also prevalent within the limestone, caused by accumulations of silica around pendants of other minerals. Unfortunately for interested collectors, Thunder Bay agates come primarily from one particular location that is privately owned. A pay-to-dig service was once operated, but the mine has not been open for many years. Specimens rarely come up for sale, and are expensive when colorful.

**FIGURE 189**
Thunder Bay agate specimen with limestone still attached to its top side. Approx. 4.5" x 2" (11.4 cm x 5 cm)

**FIGURE 189**

# *Whorl* AGATE

*Agates with swirling patterns with "wispy" edges, often colored in shades of intense red*

**CHARACTERISTICS:** Swirling patterns of ill-defined bands, often in circular or curving patterns clearly different from other agates

**SYNONYMS:** Hurricane agate, veil agate, feathery plume agate, disrupted band agate, cloud agate

**DISTRIBUTION:** Whorl agates are generally only found in Minnesota

**RARITY:** Quite uncommon

## DESCRIPTION

Whorl agates exhibit some of the weirdest chalcedony banding of any agate variety, and they are known by many names, including "cloud agates" and "disrupted band agates." The most common name—whorl agate—stems from their wavy, circular-patterns. Whorl agates tend to exhibit a "fuzziness" to their banding, and the boundaries between bands are generally ill defined. Most of the bands consist of white chalcedony; under a microscope these bands exhibit a very jagged arrangement of fibers different from most other agates. In whorl agates, the chalcedony fibers are not as well organized as in other agates.

Coloration in whorl agates also differs from other agates. It is generally very spotty and uneven, appearing "smudged" across only some of the bands. When Lake Superior whorl agates are colored, however, they are very often intensely red, as in Figure 190, due to a high concentration of hematite particles.

## FORMATION

The formation of whorl agates is largely a mystery, and few hypotheses have been put forth. Perhaps one of the only easily visible clues in whorls is their vague resemblance to chalcedony "roses." Chalcedony roses are typically found in the southwestern United States, but they are not agates. Instead, they are formed as circular, bowl-shaped "blobs" of chalcedony with overlapping, rounded layers that resemble the petals of a flower. The banding in Figures 191 and 192 show very similar traits. It is therefore proposed that a chalcedony rose first formed in the vesicle, which was then later filled with chalcedony to result in an agate.

## COLLECTIBILITY

Whorl agates are interesting, but generally aren't sought after by serious collectors. Exceptions would be similar to the agate in Figure 190, with ample sweeping bands and vivid coloration.

**FIGURE 190**
The typical yet unusual intense red and white coloration of Lake Superior whorl agates is exemplified by this polished specimen. Approx. 2" x 2.5" (5 cm x 6.4 cm)

**FIGURE 191**
Typical whorl pattern and appearance, but without the bright red coloration. Approx. 2" x 2" (5 cm x 5 cm)

**FIGURE 192**
A large agate nodule with the common whorl pattern on one end. Approx. 5" x 3.5" (12.7 cm x 8.9 cm)

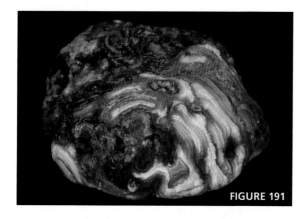

FIGURE 191

FIGURE 192

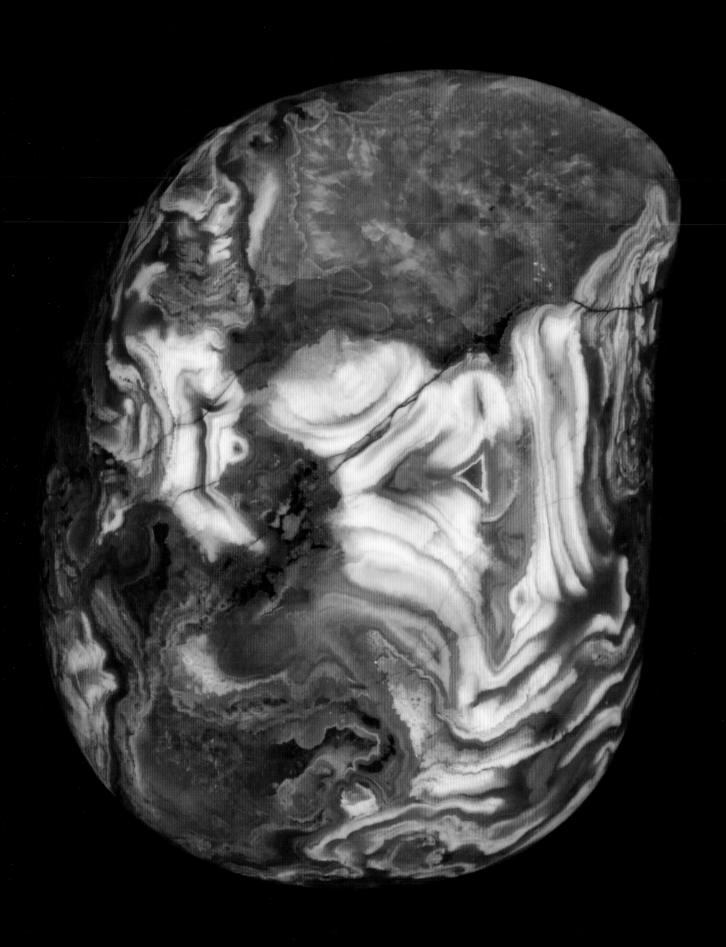

FIGURE 190

# Inclusions and Replacements

*Some agates contain structures formed by other minerals*

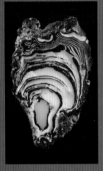 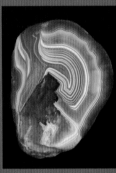 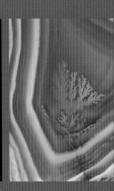 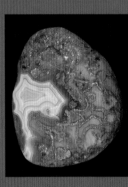 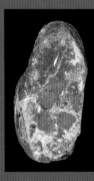 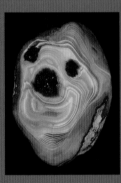

**COPPER REPLACEMENT AGATE**  **CRYSTAL IMPRESSIONS**  **DENDRITIC AGATE**  **FRAGMENTED MEMBRANE AGATE**  **JASP-AGATE**  **MINERAL INCLUSIONS**

**MOSS AGATE**          **PLUME AGATE**          **SAGENITIC AGATE**          **STALACTITIC AGATE**          **TUBE AGATE**

The rocks in which agates form are not inert. With the help of volcanic gases and groundwater, the minerals in basalt and rhyolite can break down and contribute their elements to the formation of new minerals. In essence, the rocks themselves contain the ingredients for vesicular minerals like zeolites, chlorite, celadonite and clay. When these minerals form before or during agate development, the resulting agate will contain evidence of them either as a soft mineral inclusion or a geometric cavity. These can appear in any of the previously discussed structural variations of agates.

## INTRODUCTION

Lake Superior agates didn't always form alone. Aside from the impurities of iron minerals and aluminum that color agate bands, nearly every agate contains some kind of additional mineral growths. These growths come in all shapes and sizes, from large masses of tangled tubes to tiny geometric shapes and fan-shaped arrangements of delicate needles, but all originate from other minerals growing in the vesicle before (or during) agate development. As the agate formed around these minerals, this caused the banding to warp and conform to their shape, creating some of the most interesting and complex banding patterns seen in Lake Superior agates.

These additional mineral growths are known by collectors as inclusions, and they can make for incredibly interesting specimens. But sometimes the soft mineral growths can be dissolved or weathered out of an agate, leaving a void. That cavity then provides a new space for more quartz or other minerals to form within, and the result is called a replacement. Inclusions and replacements can enhance the beauty of a specimen or degrade it, depending on how they affect the banding or aesthetics of an agate, but all are compelling and fascinating examples of the dramatic variability of agate formation.

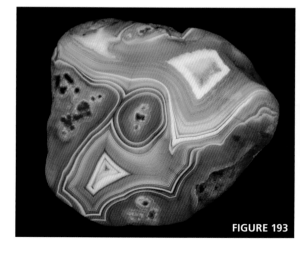

FIGURE 193

## PRIMARY VARIATIONS

Inclusions and replacements in Lake Superior agates are very common and come in many different varieties. Moss agates are one of the most common varieties, and they initially don't appear to be agates at all. Strange growths of tiny, branching tubes tangle and twist through translucent chalcedony to form moss agates, one of the oldest known agate varieties; they were first described in ancient Greece. Tube agates are closely related and contain long, hollow filaments that extend through an agate. They were formed when needle-like crystals of minerals were coated by the chalcedony of the developing agate. But

FIGURE 193
Dark inclusions caused this agate to form two distinctly patterned sections. Approx. 3" x 2.5" (7.6 cm x 6.4 cm)

FIGURE 194
Sagenitic agates, such as this, have radial arrangements of inclusions. Approx. 3" x 2" (7.6 cm x 5 cm)

FIGURE 195
An incredibly rare copper replacement agate still embedded in basalt. Agate approx. 1" x 0.5" (2.5 cm x 1.3 cm)

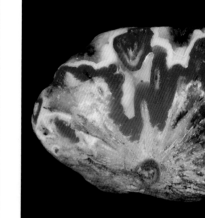
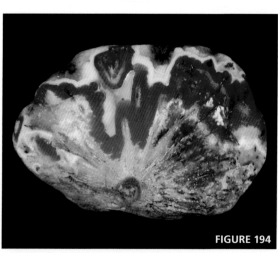
FIGURE 194

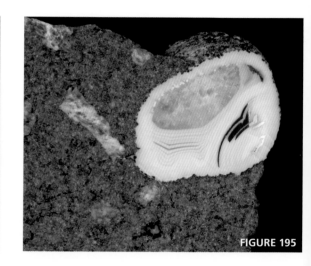
FIGURE 195

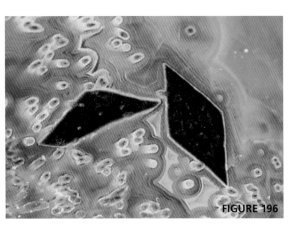

FIGURE 196

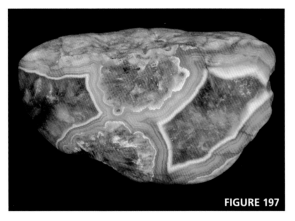

FIGURE 197

FIGURE 196
Two black
crystals of siderite
embedded within a
sagenitic agate.
8x magnification

FIGURE 197
This agate contains two
rounded aggregates of
barite crystals.
Approx. 2.5" x 1.5"
(6.4 cm x 3.8 cm)

FIGURE 198
A common moss agate.
Approx. 3" x 1.5"
(7.6 cm x 3.8 cm)

FIGURE 199
Tube formations
caused the banding to
bend around them in
this specimen.
3x magnification

FIGURE 200
"Floating" within a gray
chalcedony agate band,
these tiny, dark brown
cubic crystals of pyrite,
a common iron- and
sulfur-bearing mineral,
measure less than
0.25 mm across and are
encircled by yellow
discs of material formed
as a result of their
decomposition. Similar
to dendrites, the yellow
rings reside between
agate bands and are
microscopically thin.
100x magnification

some tubes elegantly curve and sweep through the agate banding, such as in Figure 199, which signifies that there are different methods of tube development.

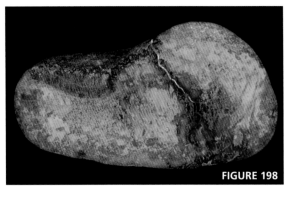

FIGURE 198

One of the most popular inclusions in Lake Superior agates is known as sagenite. Sagenite is not the name of a particular mineral, but rather is used to describe any mineral that forms radial, "fan-shaped" aggregates of needle-like crystals embedded within agates.

These are all large, highly visible inclusions that can easily be observed with no additional equipment. Put an agate under a microscope, however, and you will begin to realize how complex agates truly are. Figure 200, for example, shows two tiny cubic crystals of the mineral pyrite, often known as "fool's gold," that have weathered and formed a yellow stain in the chalcedony. However, each pyrite cube, including the yellow disc, is only 0.25 mm wide.

These are just a few examples of the many mineral growths you can find in Lake Superior agates. Inclusions and replacements represent one of the largest and most diverse groups of structural variations that can be observed within agates and are largely responsible for why so many varieties of agates exist. In this chapter, we will discuss these strangest of agates in detail.

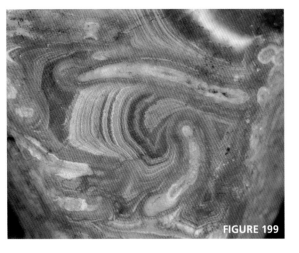

FIGURE 199

When crystallized mineral inclusions (such as the well-formed siderite crystals in Figure 196) are weathered and dissolved they leave a hollow geometric space called a crystal impression. A similar process is thought to have spurred the formation of the incredible copper replacement agates found in Michigan, which actually contain bands made of copper. Other specimens contain less graceful inclusions of chunky jasper, and are called jasp–agates.

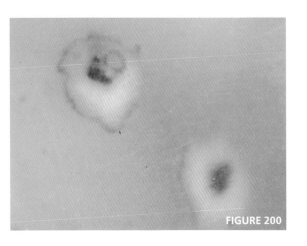

FIGURE 200

# *Copper Replacement* AGATE

*Native copper has completely replaced agate banding in these rare gems from Michigan*

**CHARACTERISTICS:** Small agates no larger than an inch or two containing bands consisting entirely of copper

**SYNONYMS:** Copper-banded agate, copper agate

**DISTRIBUTION:** Copper replacement agates are limited only to the northern end of Michigan's Keweenaw Peninsula, north of Houghton

**RARITY:** Copper replacement agates are one of the rarest varieties of Lake Superior agates and are extremely difficult to find

## DESCRIPTION

The first time the authors saw a copper replacement agate, they were stunned. The reaction from other collectors must have been the same, because these agates actually contain banding composed of solid native, copper alternating with chalcedony. Originally found on a single pile of waste rock from one of the many copper mines on Michigan's Keweenaw Peninsula, the location of these rare agates was a closely guarded secret until recent years. Now, several locations are known where these agates can be found, and the specimens have caused quite a stir among collectors.

The copper replacement agates, reportedly first discovered in 1951 by John and Frank Perona, got their name from one of the first theories of their formation, which stated that copper seeped into and replaced certain agate bands. (As mentioned earlier, they are found only on mine dumps, or piles of unwanted rock left over from Michigan's copper mining era.) The agates are tightly embedded in boulders of brownish-gray basalt that is heavily included with dark green chlorite formed during the weathering of the rock. The agate nodules, which must be broken out of the rock, are small, rarely larger than an inch or two and are coated with the same soft, dark chlorite found in the basalt. When cut or broken, they reveal white and nearly opaque tan-colored chalcedony banding, though not all agates from the known locations contain copper. Perhaps one in every twenty-five of these agate nodules will contain any copper banding, and only one in one hundred will contain very fine, well-developed copper bands. But that's if you've found agates at all. A large number of neighboring vesicles contain calcite, quartz or feldspars, but are all

**FIGURE 201**
As one of the finest specimens in the authors' collection, this copper replacement agate exemplifies the incredible formation of copper bands within agate. Approx. 0.5" x 0.75" (1.3 cm x 1.9 cm)

**FIGURE 202**
This specimen, still embedded in basalt, displays bands composed only partly of copper. Agate approx. 0.5" x 0.5" (1.3 cm x 1.3 cm)

**FIGURE 203**
This beautifully polished specimen exhibits many bands of copper as well as bands flecked with green chlorite inclusions. Approx. 0.75" x 0.5" (1.9 cm x 1.3 cm)

FIGURE 202

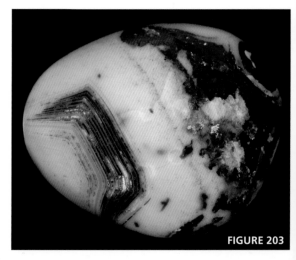

FIGURE 203

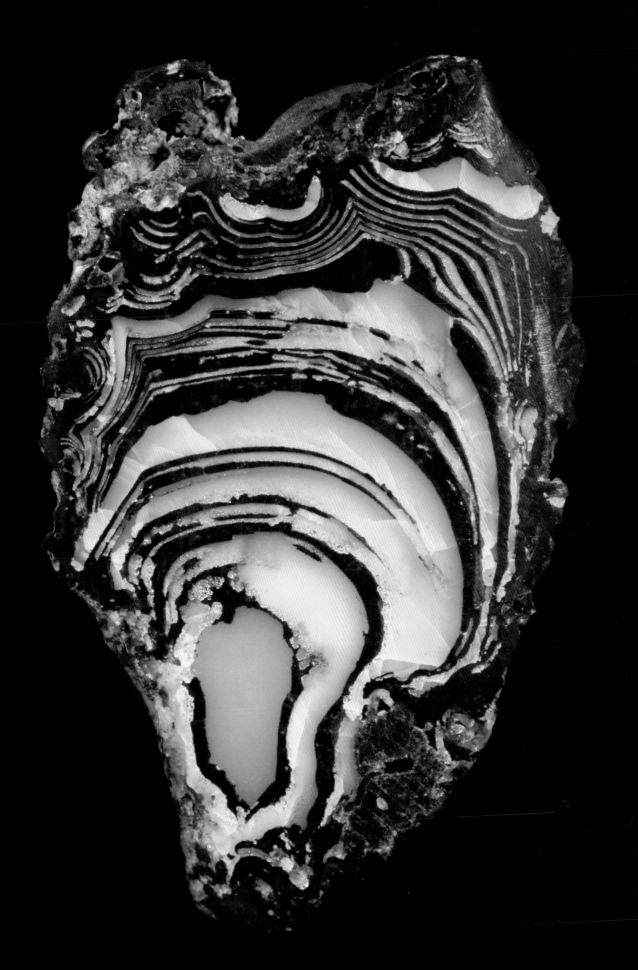

FIGURE 201

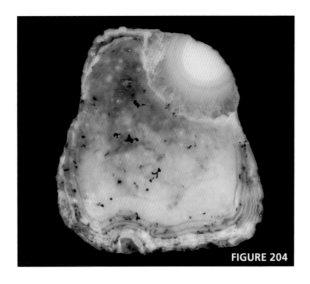

**FIGURE 204**

coated with the same chlorite as the agate nodules, making them impossible to distinguish until cut open. When copper banding is present, it is often in the form of tiny flecks or disjointed streaks that follow the length of some of the chalcedony bands, but the most desirable specimens contain thick, solid bands of copper alternating with tan chalcedony.

Copper isn't the only mineral inclusion found in these agates. Prehnite, a hard, apple-green mineral common around Lake Superior, is very abundant in many specimens, as are other green minerals, such as yellow-green epidote and the same dark green chlorite that coats the outside of the agates. Clearly, the copper replacement agates of Michigan have been subjected to a significantly larger amount of mineral-bearing waters than agates from other parts of Lake Superior, and their highly altered nature reflects this.

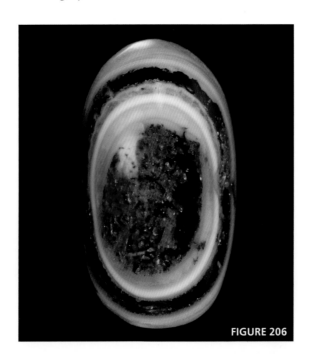

**FIGURE 206**

## FORMATION

With as much attention as copper replacements have gained recently, it is no wonder there are several theories of how they got their copper banding. While we don't know exactly how the copper got into the agates, there is little question where the copper came from—Michigan's Keweenaw Peninsula is the site of one of the world's largest copper deposits (and the most

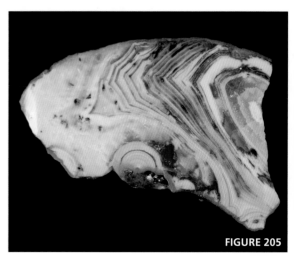

**FIGURE 205**

important) and formed when hydrothermal waters percolated through the basalt, depositing metals. The area saw significant mining for many decades as a result and unwanted rock from the digging of mine shafts was piled on the surface. Dozens of these enormous piles still exist today, and copper replacement agates are found in four or five. At least two piles at the site of the Wolverine Mine, near Kearsarge, Michigan, produce copper-banded agates, as well as two more at the Osceola Mine, near Calumet. The authors have also heard of a fifth "secret" mine where copper replacement agates are found, but its location is unknown. What the agates' presence in mine dumps indicates, however, is that they formed very deep within the basalt and were not exposed on the earth's surface.

Theorists attempted to explain how copper replacement agates formed; some suggested that the copper was present within the initial silica solution, or that agate bands somehow dried out and hardened prematurely, causing the banding to collapse, forming voids that were later filled by copper. However, none of the existing theories sufficiently explain everything observed in copper replacement agates. To complicate matters, there is the specimen shown in Figure 207, in which a knob of copper, perhaps formed

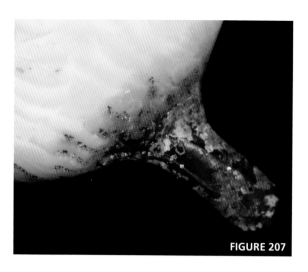

FIGURE 207

FIGURE 208

FIGURE 207
Could this unexplained knob of copper be the entry-point for the copper in these agate bands? It appears so, but this creates some issues with formation theories.
4x magnification

FIGURE 208
While it contains no copper, this agate contains pockets of calcite, possibly formed within the agate during its development. Approx. 0.5" x 0.5" (1.3 cm x 1.3 cm)

in a crack connected to the vesicle, appears to be feeding copper into the agate along certain bands as flecks; this cannot be accounted for by the foregoing theories. The authors' discovery of the agates shown in Figures 208 and 209, combined with their observations and application of recent research, have led them to their own theory which they believe is much more inclusive to all of the strange, copper-bearing agates of the Keweenaw Peninsula.

impurity band in front of the newest chalcedony band. If an accumulation theory of agate formation is employed, future inflows of silica- and calcite-rich water could begin this process again, resulting in alternating bands of chalcedony and calcite. As calcite is extremely susceptible to weathering and is easily dissolved by even weak acids, it is likely that later acidic solutions dissolved the calcite, but not the chalcedony bands, leaving voids filled in later by copper-bearing waters. Figures 208 and 209 corroborate this idea. The agate in Figure 209 was found embedded at the center of a basalt boulder as a whole nodule. The authors carefully sawed the agate in half in search of copper bands, but instead found band-shaped voids. Because this agate was not subjected to the effects of glaciers or other weathering on the earth's surface, these bands could have been dissolved, but the spaces left behind were not filled by other minerals or copper. The specimen in Figure 208, though highly weathered, shows a similar agate that still contains calcite. Note the disconnected chalcedony bands on the right side of the specimen that are filled in with calcite.

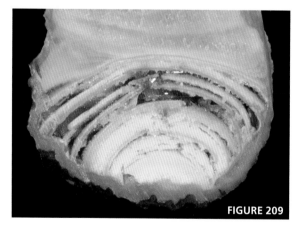

FIGURE 209

In 2010, Lakshtanov and Stipp published an article in which they showed that calcite will quickly precipitate when in the presence of a silica solution. This means that when dissolved calcite comes into contact with silica, the calcite rapidly crystallizes and solidifies. The authors believe that these findings could have significant implications for copper replacement agates because many agates in the Wolverine Mine dumps contain ample calcite. If solutions bearing calcite were present during the development of an agate, the calcite could precipitate as solid particles that would be pushed by the chalcedony crystallization front. As the calcite particles continued to build up, they would form an

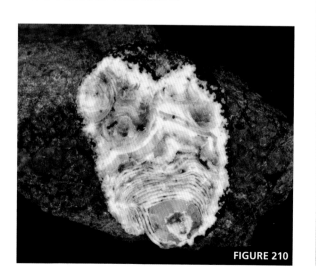

FIGURE 210

FIGURE 209
A possible clue about the formation of the copper replacement agates, this specimen contains no copper, but appears to be missing every other band. In the voids are tiny macrocrystalline quartz crystals.
6x magnification

FIGURE 210
Finds like this are much more common in the Wolverine Mine piles than well-developed copper replacement agates. This specimen, still in basalt, contains many calcite, prehnite, chlorite and feldspar inclusions in addition to many copper flecks and faint agate banding. Agate approx. 0.75" x 1" (1.9 cm x 2.5 cm)

FIGURE 212

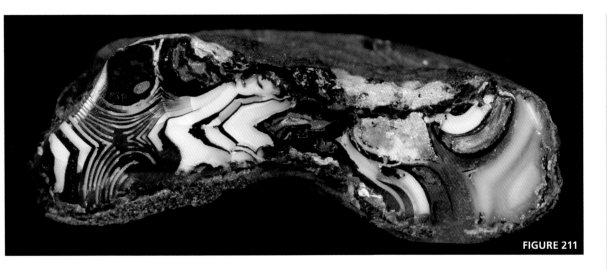

FIGURE 211
A tight, intricately banded example. Approx. 0.75" x 0.25" (1.9 cm x 0.64 cm)

This theory also explains why so many other agates from the copper mine dumps contain minerals like prehnite or chlorite in their banding. If calcite bands were dissolved, any mineral could grow in their place, not just copper. Specimens like those in Figures 210 and 213 are much more common than the copper-banded agates, and exhibit green prehnite intergrown among white chalcedony bands containing flecks of copper throughout.

mineral-bearing waters are the source of the silica needed for the formation of all agates. These waters would be a result of the volcanic activity that created the rocks, as suggested by Moxon.

## COLLECTIBILITY

Lake Superior's copper replacement agates are among the most collectible agates in the world; needless to say, they are very popular in the Lake Superior region. Because the original source of these agates is deep underground, there is only a finite supply of specimens available, making even very small specimens worth hundreds of dollars. But it should not be monetary gain that drives collectors to find or buy specimens; it should be the truly awe-inspiring beauty of the copper bands, their rarity and the scientific importance held by these small agates.

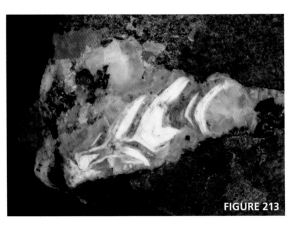

FIGURE 213

FIGURE 212
The first specimen found by the authors displays a unique coarseness to the copper bands, suggesting that macrocrystalline quartz growths grew in the voids before copper filled them. Approx. 0.5" x 1" (1.3 cm x 2.5 cm)

FIGURE 213
This specimen, still in basalt, is nearly completely replaced with green prehnite, dark green chlorite, and orange feldspar. Only the dense white chalcedony bands remain from the original agate. Agate approx. 1.5" x 0.5" (3.8 cm x 1.3 cm)

As for that strange copper knob in Figure 207, a 2001 article by Götze and his colleagues may explain it. They noted Lake Superior agates from Ontario that contain calcite that appears to be pseudomorphing, or replacing, chalcedony bands, starting from the edges of the agate. While it is unknown how the calcite is able to replace the chalcedony, we seem to have direct evidence that it can happen. If this took place in the agate in Figure 207, the calcite could have dissolved, leaving voids for copper to fill later.

Finally, because these agates originated deep in copper-rich rock, Michigan's copper replacement agates may be evidence that hydrothermal

FIGURE 214

FIGURE 214
A beautiful agate eye, completely replaced by copper. Approx. 0.5" x 0.75" (1.3 cm x 1.9 cm)

# Crystal Impressions

*Odd cavities in agate that have a definite shape are likely the impressions of dissolved crystals*

**CHARACTERISTICS:** Odd, specifically shaped holes or indentations within the surfaces of agates

**SYNONYMS:** Crystal imprints

**DISTRIBUTION:** Agates with impressions of other minerals can be found over the entire range of Lake Superior agates

**RARITY:** Impressions are common in Lake Superior agates

## DESCRIPTION

Occasionally, you may come across an agate with odd, specifically shaped holes. Unlike the common pitted surface typically displayed in an agate's husk, these holes are geometric, displaying very distinct edges, corners and angles. The nearby agate banding is affected by these cavities, bending and twisting around to accommodate them. Clearly there is something unique about these voids, but what are they?

The strange, geometric cavities found in some agates are known as crystal impressions, and are the result of minerals that once existed within the agate but are no longer present. Each particular shape, from the square impressions in Figure 217 to the ragged, pointed impressions in Figure 216, is derived from the crystal structure of different minerals. The primary culprits of impressions in Lake Superior agates are calcite and its various crystal forms, as well as barite, both of which are common, soft minerals found in agate-bearing rocks. Crystal impressions are most interesting when very well formed, as you can see the exact shape and structure of the missing crystals and how they interacted with the chalcedony bands.

## FORMATION

The term "crystal impression" is a bit of a misnomer, as that name implies that the crystals had impressed into the agate in order to form the geometric holes. In reality, the crystals of calcite, barite and other cavity-forming minerals were already present in an agate when it had finished developing.

There are two theories about how and when the crystals of other minerals formed in an agate. The traditional belief is that when the vesicle was still hollow and contained only the thin shell of chlorite or celadonite on its inner walls, mineral-

**FIGURE 215**
Calcite created the unique square-shaped impressions in this beautiful red and white adhesional banded agate. Approx. 2" x 2.5" (5 cm x 6.4 cm)

**FIGURE 216**
A mass of steep, sharply pointed crystals created the deep impressions in this agate. Approx. 3.5" x 2.5" (8.9 cm x 6.4 cm)

**FIGURE 217**
Small, rhombohedral crystals of calcite produced these impressions. Approx. 1.5" x 2" (3.8 cm x 5 cm)

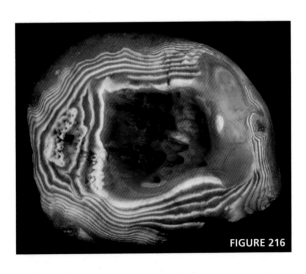

FIGURE 216

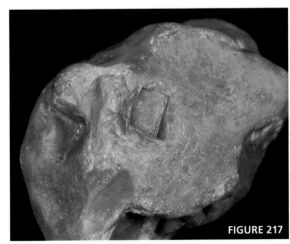

FIGURE 217

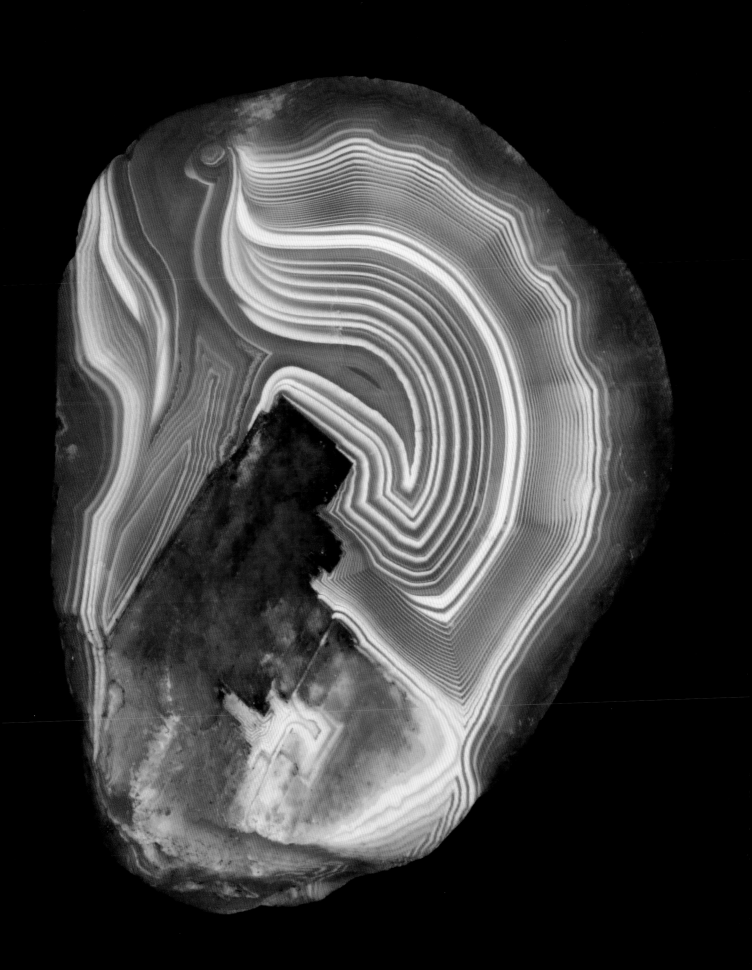

FIGURE 215

FIGURE 218
The deep, six-sided hole in this agate was produced by a large calcite crystal. Hole approx. 1" x 1" (2.5 cm x 2.5 cm)

FIGURE 219
A casting made from the hole in the agate in Figure 218 produces an exact replica of the calcite crystal that created the hole.

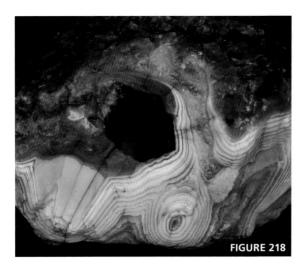

FIGURE 218

FIGURE 219

rich waters could easily flow through it. As certain molecules began to attach and nucleate to the walls of the vesicle, crystals of various minerals, such as calcite, began to grow. Later, when enough silicic acid had entered the vesicle for the agate formation process to begin, the crystals were then encased in chalcedony. While this two-step process is entirely viable, Pabian and Zarins suggested a second reason why different minerals crystallized within an agate. They proposed that molecules of other minerals (such as calcite) had entered the vesicle with the silicic acid. Since calcite contains calcium, an alkaline element that is chemically incompatible with silica, they suggested that the silica gel in the vesicle pushed the molecules of calcite into pockets which the agate then formed around. At the same time, the incompatible molecules in the "quarantined" impurity pockets crystallized as well, forming a calcite crystal. This process would be identical for other minerals as well, such as barite and siderite. Therefore, Pabian and Zarins proposed that the crystals of these additional minerals formed simultaneously with the

agate. Since these are both feasible ideas, one or both of these processes could have taken place to form the crystals.

In many specimens, this was the extent of the process and the crystals remained embedded within the agates; agates with embedded crystals are referred to as mineral inclusions. For a crystal impression to form, an additional step was required. At some point after the formation of the agate and the crystal inclusion, acidic water made contact with the vesicles. The acid could not affect the hard, resistant agate, but dissolved the soft minerals like calcite and barite, leaving the crystal-shaped voids that we call crystal impressions.

It is not always easy to determine what mineral left a particular impression, but a knowledge of the other minerals that can form within vesicles can offer some insight. Crystal impressions of calcite (a common calcium- and carbon-bearing mineral) are by far the most common impressions found in Lake Superior agates. It is important to note, however, that calcite crystals can grow in

FIGURE 220
This nearly square impression was formed by a rhombohedral calcite crystal. Hole approx. 0.25" x 0.25" (0.6 cm x 0.6 cm)

FIGURE 221
The casting made from the hole in the agate in Figure 220, on the left, is clearly of the same rhombohedral shape as the specimen of Lake Superior calcite, on the right.

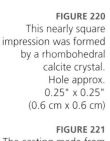

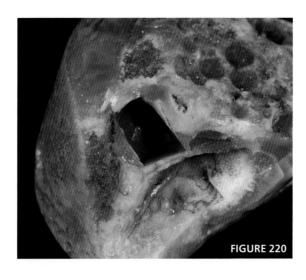

FIGURE 220

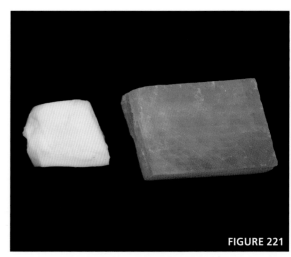

FIGURE 221

several distinct shapes, depending on the conditions in which they formed. For example, calcite can develop as six-sided prisms with steep points, or as rhombohedrons, which is a shape that resembles a leaning or tilted cube. The specimen in Figure 218 shows the characteristic hole left by a large, six-sided calcite crystal. The authors filled this cavity with silicone, which produced a perfect representation of the absent crystal, pictured in Figure 219. Similarly, the impression shown in Figure 220 appears to be cubic, but filling the cavity with silicone reveals that it was a calcite rhombohedron that formed this cavity. Figure 221 compares the silicone cast made from this specimen with an actual calcite rhombohedron found in a basalt cavity on Lake Superior's shore. Lastly, another very common crystal impression found in Lake Superior agates is pictured in Figure 222. This "coin slot," as collectors jokingly refer to them, was formed by a thin, bladelike crystal of barite. As a comparison, Figure 224 shows a barite crystal found near Duluth, Minnesota, in basalt on Lake Superior's shore. Note the sharp crystal edge on the right side of the photo and the way it resembles the shape of the impression in Figure 222.

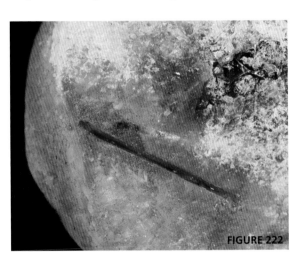

FIGURE 222

FIGURE 224

## COLLECTIBILITY

Crystal impressions see only limited collectibility, primarily from hobbyists interested in unique agate formations. Generally speaking, most Lake Superior agate collectors tend to disregard agates with large crystal impressions because their cavities are distracting or often obscure areas of banding. If the impressions are small, occur on the back side of an agate, or are non-intrusive to the banding pattern, they are generally ignored. Only when an impression adds to the visual interest and general aesthetics of a specimen does it garner more attention. Though rare, specimens like that in Figure 215 are examples of valuable and highly desirable crystal impressions.

## NOTABLE VARIATIONS

Finally, there is one particular type of agate rarely found in the Lake Superior region that appears to contain many tiny, hexagonal crystal impressions. But these were not caused by any mineral. The

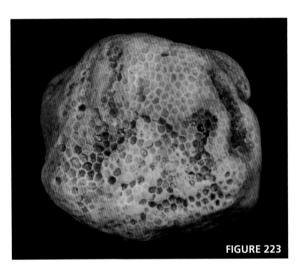

FIGURE 223

specimen shown in Figure 223 is an example of coral that has been turned to chalcedony and microgranular quartz; this is often referred to as "agatized coral." Found near Lake Superior, this fossil of ancient sea life is a reminder of the drastic changes the region has undergone. Because of the destructive glacial activity and the fact that most fossils are composed of soft, easily weathered materials, fossils are not common around Lake Superior. This specimen, however, consists of quartz, and like agates, it was able to survive countless millennia.

FIGURE 222
"Coin slots" are common in Lake Superior agates, and are caused by thin, bladelike crystals of barite.
Hole approx.
1" x 0.06"
(2.5 cm x 0.16 cm)

FIGURE 223
This specimen of agatized coral was found near Lake Superior.
Approx. 2" x 1.5"
(5 cm x 3.8 cm)

FIGURE 224
Barite crystals, a rare find along Lake Superior's shoreside basalt formations, are responsible for impressions such as the one in Figure 222.
Approx. 1" x 1.5"
(2.5 cm x 3.8 cm)

# Dendritic AGATE

*Tiny, two-dimensional arrangements of inclusions that appear "tree-like" are known as dendrites*

**CHARACTERISTICS:** Small, flat, tree-like growths on the surface of an agate band

**SYNONYMS:** Dendrite

**DISTRIBUTION:** Dendritic agates can be found throughout the Lake Superior agate's range, but are more common in Minnesota

**RARITY:** Dendrites in agates are common, but very well-formed and easily visible examples are fairly rare

## DESCRIPTION

Dendritic agates contain dendrites, which are some of the most interesting growths you can find hiding within an agate. Derived from the Greek word for "tree-like," dendrites do indeed resemble trees, ferns, or other organic, plant-like growths; however, they consist only of minuscule particles of various iron minerals, such as red hematite and yellow goethite. While a dendrite can measure up to an inch wide and long, they are microscopically thin, which essentially makes them two-dimensional objects. This allows them to form in the infinitesimally small spaces between chalcedony layers; they are primarily

revealed when freezing and thawing cause the bands to peel apart. Figures 226 and 227 show two different varieties of dendrites formed on the surfaces of peeled agate bands.

## FORMATION

As solid as agates seem, there are actually microscopic spaces between the bands. Dendrites form when iron-bearing water saturates part of an agate and finds its way into these spaces. As the iron particles move randomly within the solution, they eventually contact and adhere to each other. As more and more particles stick to each other, their accumulated surface area increases, which in turn allows additional particles to adhere to more points along the formation. As this process continues, the branching, tree-like growths result. In most specimens, the iron-rich water likely gets into an agate by seeping through its porous structure. The polished specimen in Figure 225, however, clearly derived its dendrite-producing waters from the crack at the bottom of the photo. Note how dendrites formed along every band on their way to the agate's center.

## COLLECTIBILITY

Well-formed dendrites are rare in Lake Superior agates, and breathtaking examples like that in Figure 225 are prized by collectors, especially those with an affinity for agate inclusions.

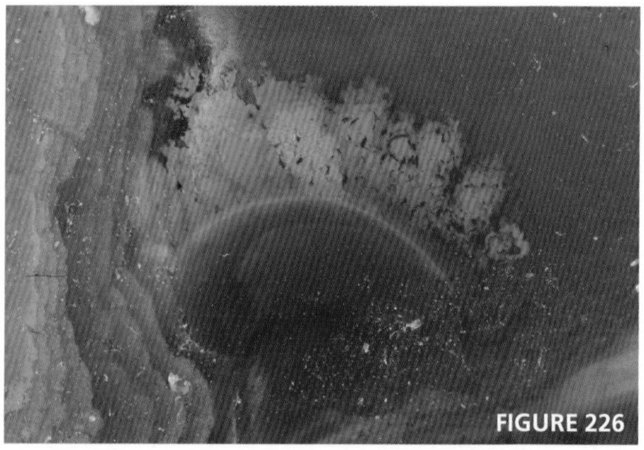

**FIGURE 225**
In this incredible specimen, a crack, visible at the bottom of the photo, fed iron-rich waters into the agate, which formed a dendrite between every band along the way. It is easy to note the dendrite's microscopically thin nature.
12x magnification

**FIGURE 226**
A "sunrise" dendrite, in which small dendrites rise from a larger iron stain.
5x magnification
Specimen courtesy of Mike Wendt.

**FIGURE 227**
A small, delicate dendrite on the surface of a peeled agate.
6x magnification

FIGURE 226
FIGURE 227

FIGURE 225

# *Fragmented Membrane* AGATE

*Small, slender, curving fragments of material create unique patterns in fragmented membrane agates*

**CHARACTERISTICS:** Agates with curving pieces of material embedded within the agate, particularly near the bottom portion of the specimen

**SYNONYMS:** Membrane agate

**DISTRIBUTION:** Fragmented membrane agates can be found anywhere in the usual range of Lake Superior agates

**RARITY:** Fragmented membrane agates are generally uncommon

.......................................................................................

## DESCRIPTION

Fragmented membrane agates are an odd but instantly recognizable variety of Lake Superior agate. These agates contain conspicuous inclusions that are thin, curving and ribbon-like, and softer than the rest of the agate. The ribbons, which appear to be broken into many segments, are actually fragments of the original vesicle-lining minerals present before the agate formed, namely chlorite, celadonite and various clay minerals.

These minerals typically remain on the walls of the vesicle, forming a membrane, or shell, for an agate to form within, but due to some destructive event, pieces of these minerals peeled away from the vesicle and fell into the center of the vesicle. Many specimens contain the fragments primarily in one half of the agate, signifying that gravity played a role in their dispersion.

The fragments in these agates frequently and dramatically affect the agate banding. In specimens such as the one pictured in Figure 228, the fragments, which were clearly present before the agate banding had begun to develop, prevented the crystallizing chalcedony bands from moving beyond their boundaries. Instead, the chalcedony between fragments often consists of patternless masses of color with a mossy texture. This can result in very unique patterns containing a lot of visual interest. Sometimes two distinctly different agate patterns can even be found in the same specimen, separated by a "wall" of membrane fragments.

The fragments themselves are typically thin, remain short and appear very jagged or rough on their edges. They rarely occur in any other colors

**FIGURE 228**
Large, curving fragments of the vesicle-lining membrane "float" within chalcedony, confining agate banding to small regions of the specimen. Approx. 2.5" x 3" (6.4 cm x 7.6 cm)

**FIGURE 229**
This paint agate contains multiple fragments of varying composition. Approx. 3" x 1" (7.6 cm x 2.5 cm)

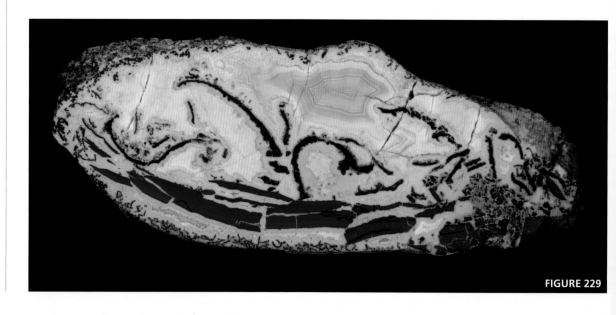

FIGURE 229

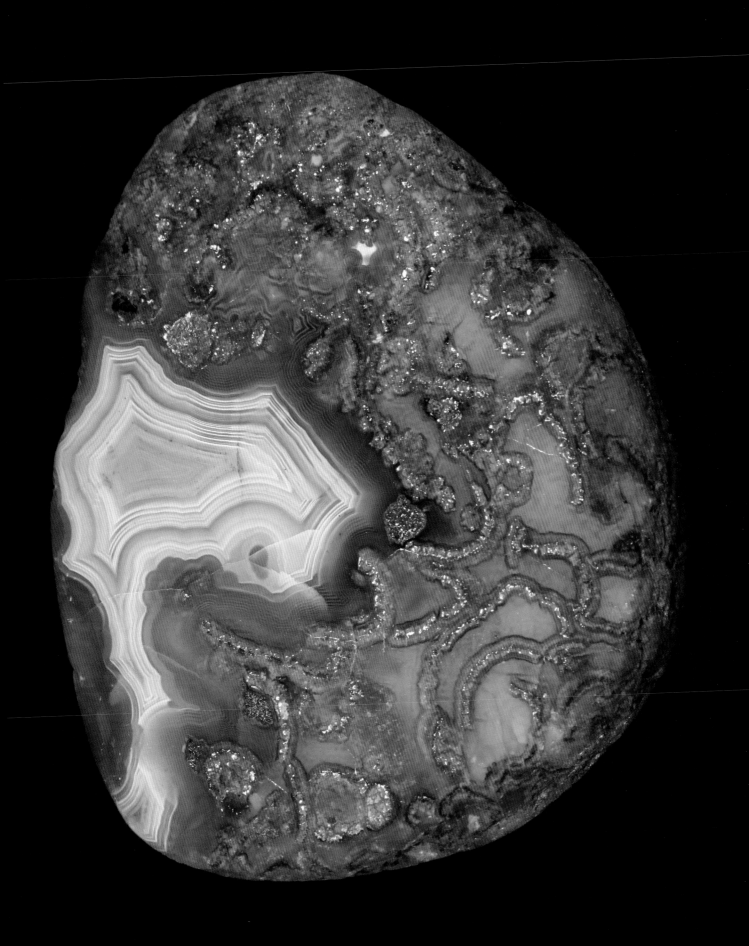

FIGURE 228

FIGURE 231

besides shades of brown, black or occasionally green. But because they are made of minerals much softer than quartz, they are easily weathered and form pits in the surface of the agate.

## FORMATION

Fragmented membrane agates form when the vesicle-lining minerals are disrupted and fall downward into the vesicle. However, it's not clear why the membrane of chlorite or celadonite would flake and break into many pieces. Perhaps a destructive geological event (such as an earthquake) occurred, or perhaps a chemical change within the vesicle occurred to dislodge the material. Whatever the cause, the fragments were then suspended in a fluid before the formation of the agate banding. Tension within the crystal structure of the individual fragments or pressure exerted upon the fragments caused them to curl and develop their characteristic appearance.

Fragmented membrane agates may provide an argument in favor of the differentiation theory of agate formation. Figure 229, for example, shows that the membrane fragments did not entirely sink, but were somewhat supported, possibly by a body of thick silica gel. Repeated inflows of silica solutions, such as in the accumulation theory, would likely disrupt the fragments and cause them to settle at the bottom of the vesicle. In addition, silica solutions, which are thinner than silica gel, could have easily filled in around the fragments to

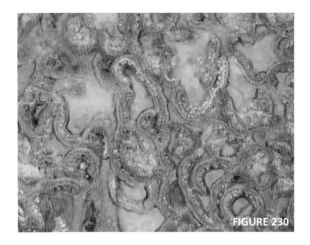

FIGURE 230

form banding, yet we only see banding in the large fragment-free areas of the agates.

## COLLECTIBILITY

Fragmented membrane agates can contain strange, unique patterns, making them desirable to some collectors. However, the large amount of inclusions and often "messy" appearance is off-putting to many veteran collectors, and specimens typically have low value. In addition, since the fragments consist of softer minerals, specimens often contain pits and holes affected by weathering. Polishing fragmented membrane agates has a similar effect, leaving the polished surfaces of a specimen pitted, uneven and littered with dull spots.

FIGURE 230
A close-up look at an agate that consists almost entirely of broken, curling fragments. 3x magnification

FIGURE 231
This large, disrupted fragment distinctly divides two different regions of adhesional banding, one more colored by iron than the other. Note how iron inclusions seem to funnel from the spaces in the fragment. 10x magnification

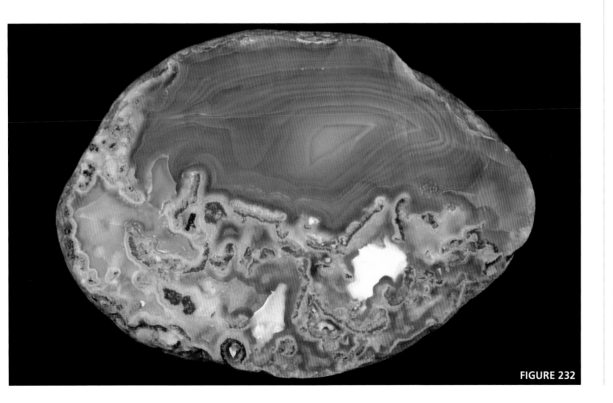

FIGURE 232

FIGURE 232
This specimen perfectly illustrates how the membrane fragments fall to the bottom of the vesicle. Approx. 2.5" x 2" (6.4 cm x 5 cm)

# Jasp-Agate

*Mixtures of banded agate and opaque jasper are generally classified as "jasp-agates"*

**CHARACTERISTICS:** Specimens contain various mixtures of opaque jasper and translucent banded chalcedony

**SYNONYMS:** Jasper agate, agate-jasper, jaspagate

**DISTRIBUTION:** Jasp-agates are found throughout the entire range of Lake Superior agates

**RARITY:** Jasp-agates are fairly common; much more common than most agate collectors would like

## DESCRIPTION

Jasp-agates are a loosely defined variety of agate that contain both jasper and agate banding. However, this vague description has led to confusion among collectors about what exactly a jasp-agate is, primarily because different parts of the world have different definitions. In the Lake Superior region, specimens containing large, irregular masses of opaque jasper intersected by banded chalcedony are referred to as jasp-agates. The jasper is often iron-rich and very red or brown in color, while the chalcedony can be any of the usual colors found in agate, particularly white or gray. In many specimens, it appears as if the agate formed in between the chunks of jasper, while in others it seems as though the jasper formed as inclusions within the agate.

## FORMATION

As both jasper and agate are forms of quartz, it is no wonder that they can sometimes grow together in the same specimen, and it appears that jasp-agates formed in at least two ways in the Lake Superior region. Some specimens, such as in Figure 234, appear to be amygdaloidal agates that formed within vesicles already containing growths of jasper, thereby causing the banding to fit around them. Other specimens, as in Figure 235, appear to have formed due to alternating depositions of granular opaque jasper and translucent fibrous chalcedony; these formed within a crack or space in rock, not in a vesicle.

## COLLECTIBILITY

Jasp-agates often fall into the category of "ugly" agates and are generally disregarded by serious collectors. While some specimens can certainly be very attractive, colorful and contain many interesting features, few ever make their way into hobbyists' permanent collections.

**FIGURE 233**
A classic Lake Superior jasp-agate, this specimen consists of agate banding formed between masses of jasper. Approx. 1.5" x 3" (3.8 cm x 7.5 cm)

**FIGURE 234**
A classic jasp-agate. Approx. 2.5" x 2" (6.4 cm x 5 cm)

**FIGURE 235**
This specimen appears to consist of alternating bands of jasper and chalcedony. Approx. 3.5" x 2" (8.9 cm x 5 cm)

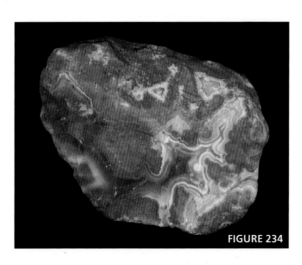

FIGURE 234

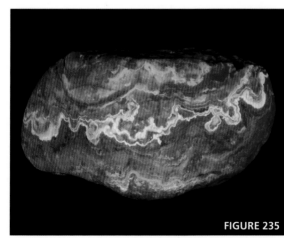

FIGURE 235

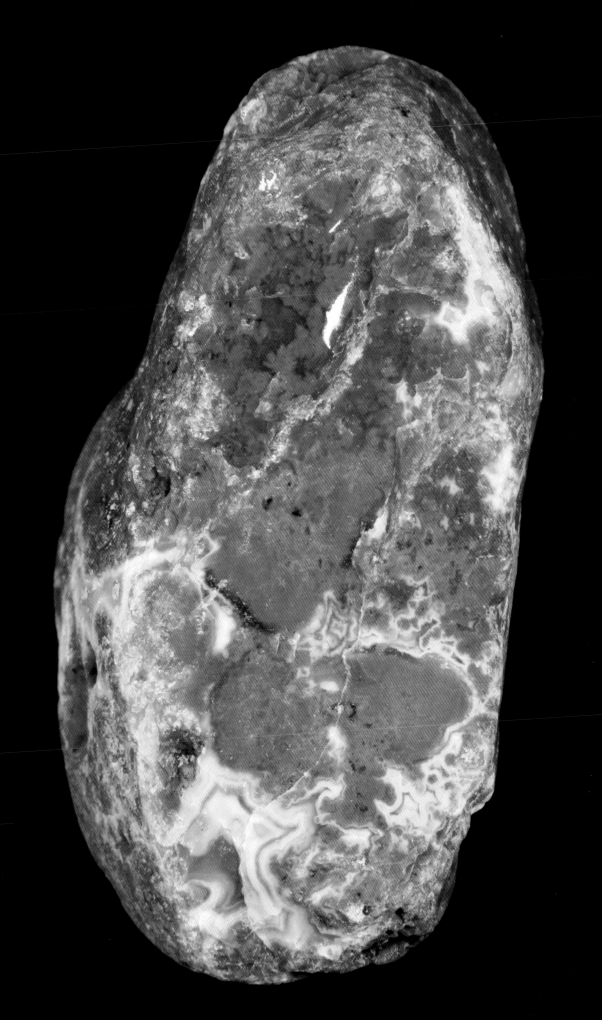

FIGURE 233

# Mineral Inclusions

*Formations of other minerals within an agate are called inclusions*

**CHARACTERISTICS:** Pockets, crystals, or tiny flecks of other minerals embedded within an agate

**SYNONYMS:** None

**DISTRIBUTION:** Inclusions can be found in agates from the entire range of Lake Superior agates

**RARITY:** Inclusions are very common

## DESCRIPTION

Agates certainly weren't the only mineral formations to grow within vesicles, nor were they always the first. There are dozens of minerals that can potentially crystallize within a basalt or rhyolite vesicle, all of which can be found encased within the chalcedony of an agate. When this happens, the mineral growth is known as an inclusion, and they are common in all agates from around the world, but particularly in Lake Superior agates. It's easy to spot an inclusion within an agate as they tend to appear obviously foreign to an agate's structure. In addition, many inclusions will exhibit a particular crystalline

shape and cause the agate banding to bend and conform to its figure. For example, the black inclusions of siderite, a common iron- and carbon-bearing mineral, embedded within the agate in Figure 236 clearly have crude crystal points that the developing agate had to accommodate. The same is true for the well-developed crystal in Figure 237. Interestingly, the inclusion in Figure 237 spawned the growth of agate eyes along its surfaces.

Not all inclusions are as conspicuous as these siderite crystals, however. Many were not present as large, well-formed crystals before or during an agate's formation, and instead were carried into the vesicle as tiny particles by the inflow of silicic acid. These inclusions tend to appear as tiny "blobs" or flecks of color hidden among the agate bands. For example, close inspection under a microscope reveals that the tiny orange flecks seen in the dark translucent chalcedony band in Figure 238 are actually copper.

## FORMATION

There are two ways that large mineral inclusions in agates could have formed, both of which likely took place in many specimens. The first process occurs when early flows of mineral-rich water,

**FIGURE 236**
It's hard not to smile when the agate smiles back at you. The "eyes" and "nose" on this agate face are growths of siderite that later became impregnated with quartz. Approx. 2.5" x 3.5" (6.4 cm x 8.9 cm)

**FIGURE 237**
A very well-formed crystal of siderite was encased by agate banding. Interestingly, the surface of the siderite crystal initiated the growth of many agate eyes. 3x magnification

**FIGURE 238**
A pink-orange smudge of color proves to be minute inclusions of copper flecks when viewed under magnification. 6x magnification

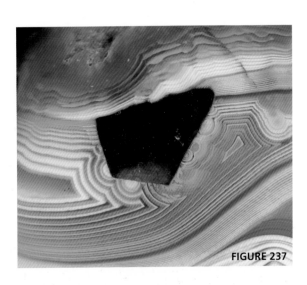

FIGURE 237

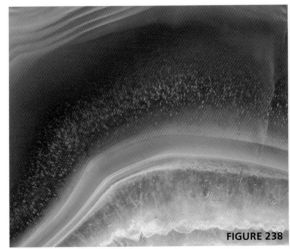

FIGURE 238

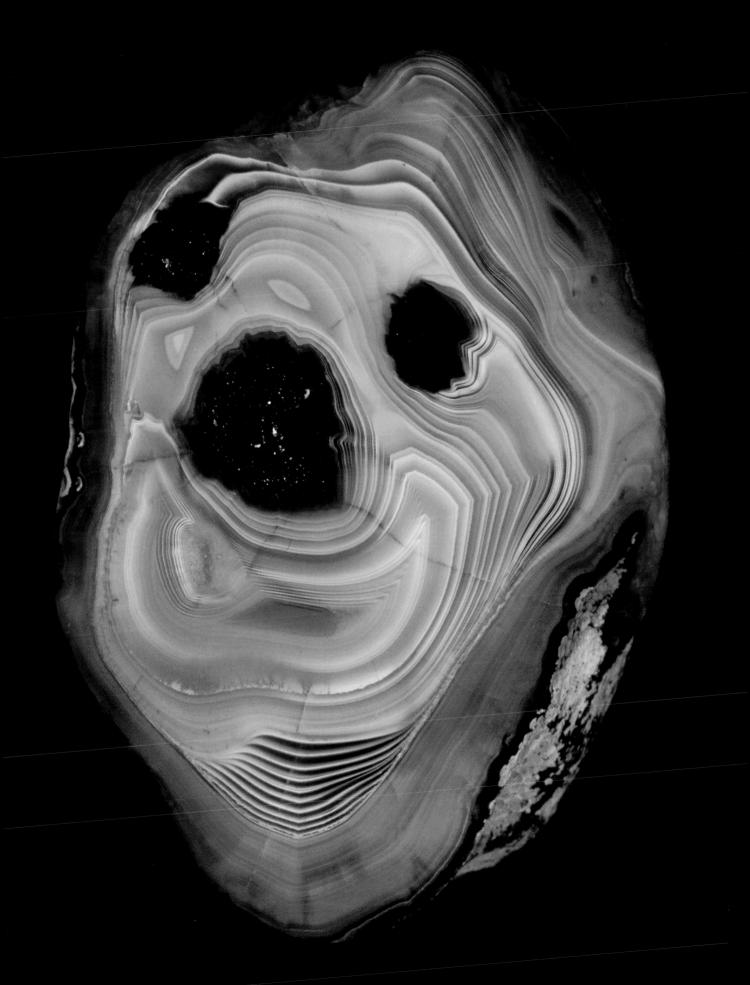

FIGURE 236

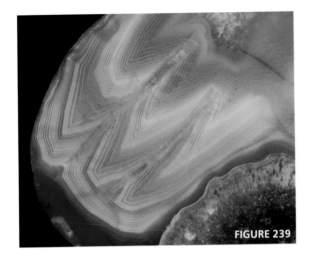

**FIGURE 239**
Two large barite crystals, still embedded within the agate, caused the agate banding to conform around them. 2x magnification

A common trait exhibited by crystal inclusions is an increased hardness. For example, if the siderite inclusions in Figure 236 were pure, they would exhibit a hardness of about 4 on the Mohs hardness scale. Instead, a hardness test finds them to be around 6, closer to quartz's hardness of 7. This is because they have been impregnated with silica during the formation of the agate, and the crystals now contain both siderite and quartz. Other crystal inclusions, however, remain unaltered by the agate. The long, narrow crystals of barite, a common barium-rich mineral, present within the agate in Figure 239, and the jagged calcite crystals interrupting the agate banding in Figure 240 both retain their proper hardnesses. The change in hardness, or lack thereof, could be an indication of which of the two processes formed the inclusions. More likely, however, the change in hardness could merely be the result of additional silica solutions interacting with the agate and seeping into the crystal structure of the inclusions.

likely derived from the volcanic activity that formed the host rock itself, fill the vesicles. As the molecules within the water begin to nucleate on the inner walls of the vesicles, the crystals begin to grow as they would in any cavity. Later, silicic acid concentrates in the vesicles and the process of agate development can begin. The crystallizing bands must then conform to the shape of the pre-existing crystals, encasing them within the agate as a result. The second way mineral inclusions could have formed was proposed by Pabian and Zarins in 1994. They stated that molecules of minerals like siderite and calcite entered the

Finally, crystallized mineral inclusions in agates may support the accumulation theory of agate formation. The beautiful agate in Figure 241A, for example, shows an infiltration channel completely filled with black siderite rather than quartz or chalcedony. Note also that the left edge of the innermost mass of siderite exhibits several sharp crystal points that affect the agate banding. If these channels were actually exit points for a build-up of internal pressure within a silica gel, as differentiation theorists claim, then the channel should unequivocally be filled with chalcedony or quartz. In addition, the way agate banding can distort around mineral inclusions, such as the barite crystals in Figure 239, is troublesome for the differentiation theory, as a single body of stationary gel would not likely wrap around the crystals in one particular direction. These

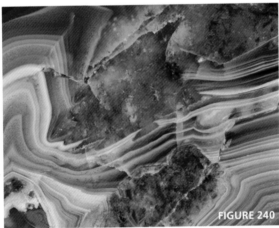
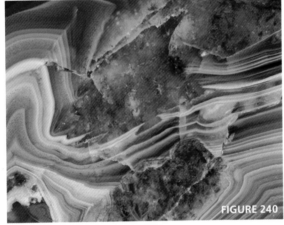

**FIGURE 240**
The beautiful pink, purple and white banding of this agate from Michipicoten Island is marred by large, brown calcite crystals. 3x magnification

vesicle at the same time as the silicic acid. Many of these molecules, particularly those containing alkaline elements such as calcium, are incompatible with silica, and would have been "pushed aside" by the growing chalcedony and quartz. By being forced into their own areas of the vesicle, the concentrated masses of molecules would begin to crystallize, theoretically at the same time as the agate. Either process is viable, and there is no reason why only one may have taken place in all agates. Therefore, both are likely equally responsible for large mineral inclusions in agates.

**FIGURE 241**
These strange, moss-like inclusions are composed of tiny particles of copper. 6x magnification

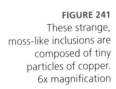

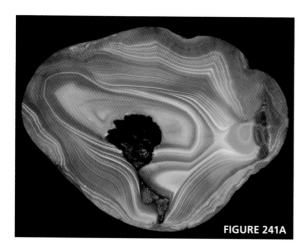

FIGURE 241A

conforming bands are better explained by an accumulation process where layers of chalcedony are deposited one at a time, thereby gradually enclosing the crystals.

## COLLECTIBILITY

From a collectors' standpoint, mineral inclusions can "make or break" an agate, depending on how well they are formed or how disruptive they are to the agate banding. For example, the specimens in Figures 236 and 237 are quite enhanced by the presence of mineral inclusions, and the inclusions have actually become the focal points of these agates. Rare inclusions, like the mass of copper flecks in Figure 241, can also add value to otherwise average agates. On the other hand, specimens such as that in Figure 240 are blemished and their beauty lessened by large, crude crystals. In the end, the desirability of inclusions is a matter of personal preference, but most collectors value and can appreciate well-formed, interesting mineral growths in agates.

## NOTABLE VARIATIONS

Few minerals that can form within a vesicle are as hard or resistant to weathering as quartz and agates. When soft minerals like barite, calcite and siderite are embedded within an agate that is still in its vesicle, acidic waters can dissolve these minerals and leave a crystal-shaped void, called a crystal impression. Later, solutions of silica can

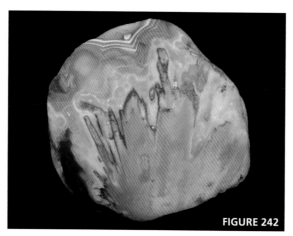

FIGURE 242

return to these voids and deposit quartz or chalcedony. The crystal impression acts as a mold for the silica, and the new quartz material fills the spaces and takes on the shape of the dissolved crystals. When one mineral retains the shape of another, it is called a pseudomorph, or replacement. The agate in Figure 242 contains orange chalcedony that pseudomorphed, or took the shape of, an unknown mineral (likely aragonite, a hard calcium-based mineral), while the intriguing shapes shown in Figure 243 are barite impressions later filled with granular quartz.

FIGURE 241A
A black, siderite- and goethite-filled infiltration channel dominates this specimen. Approx. 2.5" x 2" (6.4 cm x 5 cm)

FIGURE 242
Crystallized inclusions of sharply pointed crystals were later pseudomorphed by chalcedony. Approx. 1.5" x 1.5" (3.8 cm x 3.8 cm)

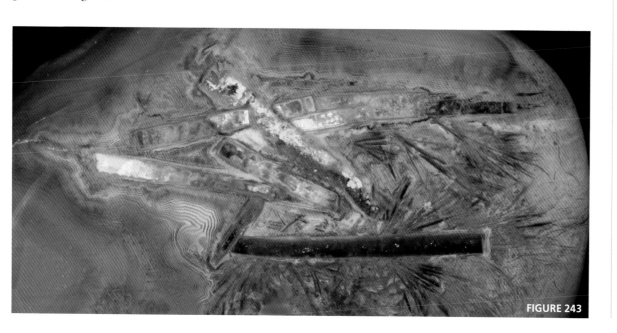

FIGURE 243

FIGURE 243
Interesting barite impressions, now filled with granular quartz. 3x magnification

# MOSS AGATE

*Moss agates exhibit seemingly organic, plant-like growths within masses of chalcedony*

**CHARACTERISTICS:** Tubular, moss-like growths embedded within chalcedony, occasionally also containing common agate banding

**SYNONYMS:** Tree agate

**DISTRIBUTION:** Moss agates can be found anywhere in the entire range of Lake Superior agates

**RARITY:** Moss agate specimens are extremely common, whether very large or very small

## DESCRIPTION

Moss agates are easily the best-known variety of agate that contains inclusions. In fact, moss agates are one of the earliest documented varieties of all agates, described in Greece by Pliny the Younger in 77 AD. These masses of chalcedony contain tangles of branching, filamentous growths that greatly resemble moss, hence their name. Believe it or not, for many centuries the seemingly organic appearance of moss agates led people to believe that moss agates were actually formed of fossilized moss. Finally, in 1776, Collini

discovered that many moss agates he had observed contained a magnetic material (iron) and therefore could not have originated from organic sources. He was then the first to suggest that moss agates were not formed of actual moss, but of an inorganic substance with the mere appearance of moss.

Today we know that the "moss" in moss agates is formed of various iron-rich compounds. They can be of any color, but as they are primarily derived from iron minerals, shades of brown, red and yellow are common, as are green and black. While they can take several different forms, moss growths are typically narrow and branching, forming knots and twists within the body of chalcedony. Generally there are so many moss-like growths within a specimen that the entire agate takes on a "messy" appearance, not unlike overgrown vines. Upon close inspection, however, the moss growths can be observed to be tube-like structures, sometimes remaining hollow like a straw, signifying that they are not random and formed through a very specific process.

Some moss agates contain regions of concentric agate banding, often confined to small areas between moss growths, as seen in several spots around the agates pictured in Figures 244 and 246. However, the vast majority of moss agates

**FIGURE 244**
A typical Lake Superior moss agate, complete with small areas of banded chalcedony. Approx. 3" x 4" (7.6 cm x 10.2 cm)

**FIGURE 245**
A moss agate containing varying coloration. Approx. 3" x 2" (7.6 cm x 5 cm)

**FIGURE 246**
A classic Lake Superior moss agate. Note the regions of higher iron content. Approx. 3" x 2" (7.6 cm x 5 cm)

FIGURE 245

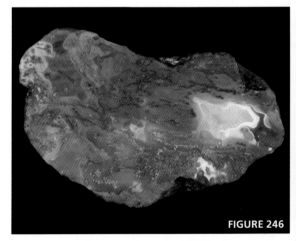

FIGURE 246

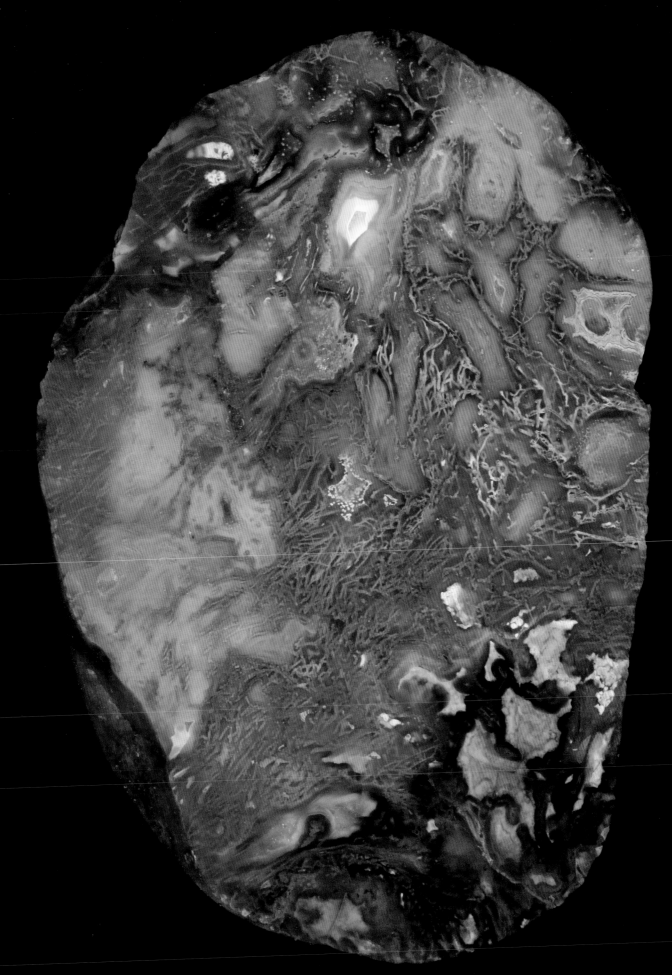

FIGURE 244

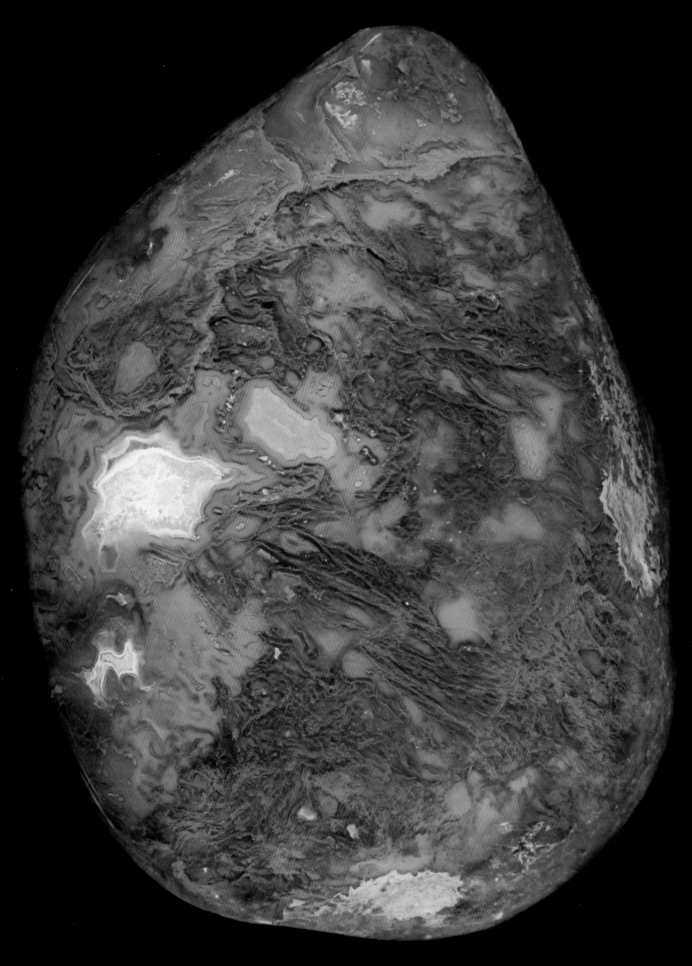

FIGURE 248

do not contain any banding, which means that moss agates technically are not agates, because agate consists of banded chalcedony. Yet moss agates with or without banding are considered agates, primarily because they are composed largely of chalcedony and because they have been considered agates for centuries.

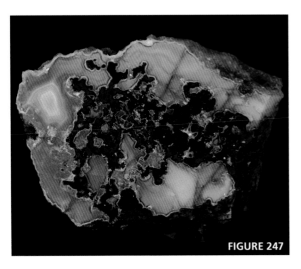

FIGURE 247

Finally, some agates appear to be moss agates but don't actually contain the well-formed, tubular filaments. Instead, they contain disordered masses of soft minerals that resemble the branching structure of many moss growths, but without the fine, delicate detail seen in true moss agates. One such specimen is pictured in Figure 247; it is marred with dark brown growths of chlorite and iron minerals. Despite not actually being a moss agate, specimens like this are generally labelled as such due to their similar appearance and collectors' tendency to not bother distinguishing them from true mosses.

## FORMATION

While the growths in moss agates may not be actual moss, as once believed, the real reason behind their formation may be equally as interesting. Because of moss agates' abundance and unique structure, researchers have theorized about their formation for decades, but no theorist has come closer to understanding how moss agates form than Raphael Liesegang.

While Liesegang's version of the differentiation theory of agate banding is largely disproved, his century-old hypothesis of moss agate growth still remains one of the best theories available today. During his many experiments with colloids (or gels) Liesegang noted a chemical reaction that

took place between ferrous sulfate, an iron- and sulfur-bearing compound, and sodium silicate, a thick gel containing molecules composed of sodium and silica suspended in water, also known as "water glass." When he placed grains of solid ferrous sulfate into the sodium silicate gel, the grains began to grow peculiar tubular growths, which Liesegang later realized greatly resembled the formations within moss agates. He determined that the reaction happening within the sodium silicate was causing the ferrous sulfate to change into a different iron compound.

While the chemical reaction itself is fairly complicated, the critical part of the process is easily understood. When the two substances meet, the iron in the ferrous sulfate combines with the silica in the sodium silicate to form an iron silicate, but only on the surface of the ferrous sulfate grain. The thin iron silicate shell surrounding the grain of ferrous sulfate causes high pressure to build in the grain, which releases by rupturing part of the iron silicate. The ferrous sulfate is then expelled through this rupture, where it once again contacts the sodium silicate, causing the iron and silica to once again combine and form a new shell of iron silicate around the grain. This process

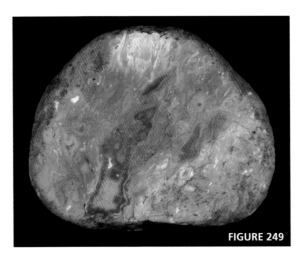

FIGURE 249

continues until the ferrous sulfate is depleted, at which point the reactions cease. During this reaction, the grain propels itself through the gel erratically, forming patterns similar to those seen in moss agates. In addition, the grain appears to "tunnel" through the gel as the hollow iron silicate shell is left trailing behind, which, if applied to moss agates, would account for the tubular structure of the moss growths.

Examples of this process are shown in Figures 250 and 252. In Figure 250 the grains were

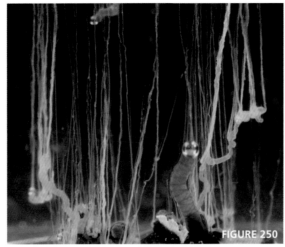

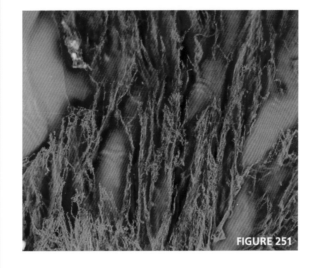

weaknesses inherent with the differentiation theory generally. Still, the uncannily similar structures seen in both Liesegang's experiments and moss agates are seemingly irrefutable evidence in favor of this process of formation.

## COLLECTIBILITY

Throughout the world, many varieties of moss agates are popular, especially with novices, but serious Lake Superior agate collectors have historically been more critical of the heavily included stones. Adhesional banded agates are the primary focus for collectors, and the sheer abundance and "messy" appearance of moss agates can be off-putting for discerning hobbyists. Moss agates can also be especially frustrating; on occasion, collectors discover what they think is a large, valuable banded agate only to realize that it is a moss agate upon closer inspection. Generally speaking, moss agates are largely valueless among Lake Superior agate collectors, even when very large.

But as with any variety of agate, there are exceptions. When polished, the true beauty of a moss

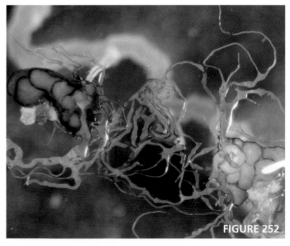

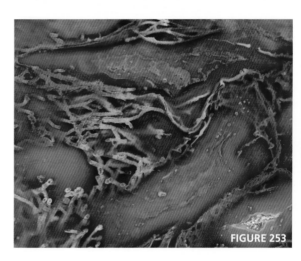

submerged in the sodium silicate, which caused them to rise and grow upwards as the reaction took place. Figure 251 shows strikingly similar structures within a Lake Superior moss agate. Likewise, the twisting, curved iron silicate growths in Figure 252 also greatly resemble moss arrangements seen in the agate in Figure 253.

Liesegang's theory of moss agate growth is supported both by lab tests and real-world observations in moss agates. We also know that iron-bearing compounds are abundant within the vesicle before, during and after agate formation, which makes this reaction a viable mechanism for moss agate development. In addition, it is clear that alkaline elements, such as sodium, are no doubt able to interact with the vesicle as they are contained within the surrounding rock and actually promote chalcedony growth. However, Liesegang's theory depends on the vesicle being initially filled with silica gel, and therefore supports the differentiation theory. This is not problematic until chalcedony banding within moss agates is considered, and it then suffers some of the same

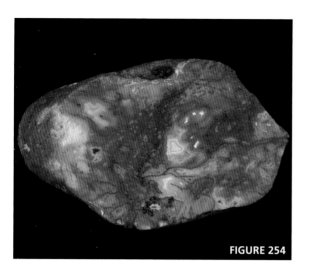

FIGURE 254

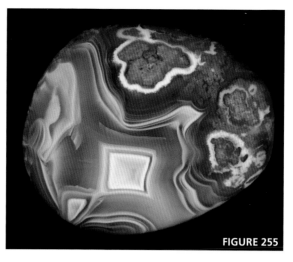

FIGURE 255

**FIGURE 254**
This moss agate contains greenish coloration that appears very similar to the color produced by the ferrous sulfate pictured in Figures 250 and 252. Approx. 3" x 2" (7.6 cm x 5 cm)

**FIGURE 255**
Pisolites are irregular, rounded formations of minerals that formed in the vesicle before the agate. Here, goethite pisolites are segregated by the agate banding. Approx. 2.5" x 2" (6.4 cm x 5 cm)

agate is allowed to show. Exceptional specimens like those in Figures 244 and 248 exhibit deep, rich coloration and well-formed moss structures. The translucency of the chalcedony within these moss agates gives them a sense of depth that beckons observers to gaze into the stone and pore over its details. If value and monetary gain are forgotten, it is easy to appreciate the wild patterns of moss agates, and no Lake Superior agate collection is truly complete without one.

Superior region is goethite, one of the world's primary ores of iron. As iron-bearing waters flow through the vesicle prior to agate growth, particles accumulate at certain points and begin to form the black, orange and brown goethite pisolites. Later, silicic acid enters the vesicle and the agate-formation process begins. Sometimes, only a small number of pisolites are formed, which allows plenty of room for chalcedony banding to form elsewhere in the vesicle, such as in Figure 255. However, large amounts of goethite pisolites can also result, leaving very little room for banded agate, as in the specimen in Figure 257. In either case, the pisolites are impregnated with silica during chalcedony formation, making them very hard.

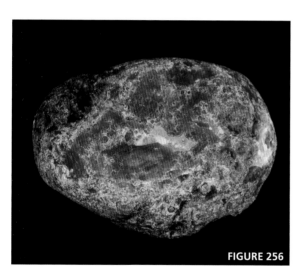

FIGURE 256

## NOTABLE VARIATIONS

As noted earlier, there are different growths of inclusions that can be present within an agate that are often classified as being "moss," despite not actually being formed of the typical moss structure. Pisolites are one such variety of inclusions.

Pisolites, which are somewhat common in Lake Superior agates, are more or less spherical formations of softer minerals that can grow within a vesicle before an agate does. A mineral that commonly exhibits this habit within the Lake

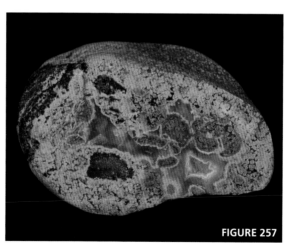

FIGURE 257

Though they are not moss structures, pisolites do share some superficial qualities of moss agates, such as their "messy" look and mottled, iron-derived coloration. Once you've learned the distinction, however, it should be easy to tell moss agates from pisolites.

**FIGURE 256**
This photo shows the back side of the agate pictured in Figure 244. Unpolished moss agates are both less attractive and more difficult for amateurs to identify. Approx. 4" x 3" (10.2 cm x 7.6 cm)

**FIGURE 257**
Bright orange goethite pisolites dominate this specimen. Approx. 3" x 2" (7.6 cm x 5 cm)

# Plume AGATE

*Plume agates contain rare, feathery, branching growths often found hiding among moss structures*

**CHARACTERISTICS:** Branching, three-dimensional growths that resemble feathers or brushes, often within colorless, translucent chalcedony

**SYNONYMS:** Paintbrush agate

**DISTRIBUTION:** Though rare, plume agates can be found in the typical agate-bearing regions of Minnesota

**RARITY:** Plumes are very rare in Lake Superior agates, though perhaps primarily because they are small and well disguised

## DESCRIPTION

Though common in agates from elsewhere in the country, plumes are one of the rarest growths in Lake Superior agates. Plumes are small branching growths of yellow or red iron minerals that resemble soft, fluffy feathers embedded within translucent chalcedony. Like dendrites, they look organic and tree-like, but differ in that they are three-dimensional and exhibit depth to their structures that dendrites do not. Lake Superior plumes are most often found within the tangled growths of a moss agate; this effectively camou-flages them, making them incredibly hard to see unless unusually large or the stone is polished and viewed under magnification.

## FORMATION

Despite their similarities with dendrites, plumes are considerably different. While dendrites form in the microscopic spaces between agate bands and are completely flat, plumes are not so restricted and grow freely within a vesicle filled with a silica solution, possibly in the form of a gel. They are composed of iron-bearing minerals derived from the weathering of the basalt. As the particles of iron minerals enter the vesicle, they begin to accumulate at a single point. Much like dendrites, the addition of more particles causes growth from that point to advance inward towards the center of the vesicle while simultane-ously branching out and increasing in width and complexity. Plumes are most often found in moss agates (see Figures 258 and 260) likely because plumes and moss structures are derived from similar iron compounds.

## COLLECTIBILITY

Plumes in Lake Superior agates are very rare and quite small, and some collectors prize even the poorest examples. They can be very valuable.

**FIGURE 258**
A rare mass of red hematite plumes found by looking at a moss agate through a microscope. 25x magnification

**FIGURE 259**
Rough hematite plumes grow in a region of translucent, band-free chalcedony that clearly formed during a separate period of growth than did the banded pattern at the center of this agate. 10x magnification

**FIGURE 260**
Typical limonite plumes found within masses of mossy growths. 6x magnification Specimen courtesy of Eric Powers.

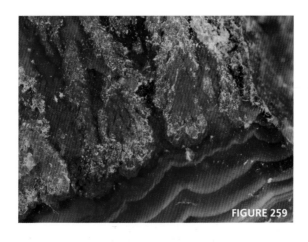

FIGURE 259

FIGURE 260

FIGURE 258

# *Sagenitic* AGATE

*Fibrous, radiating "eyes" formed of needle-like inclusions are the classic characteristics of sagenites*

**CHARACTERISTICS:** Radiating "sprays" of needle-like structures forming eye-like shapes within a mass of chalcedony or agate

**SYNONYMS:** Sagenite

**DISTRIBUTION:** Sagenitic agates can be found anywhere in usual range of Lake Superior agates, but most specimens are found in Minnesota

**RARITY:** Sagenites are uncommon, and very fine examples exhibiting well-formed radial formations and bright, varying colors are rare

......................................................................

## DESCRIPTION

Sagenitic agates, known more commonly as sagenites, contain some of the most peculiar inclusions that can be found in Lake Superior agates. Most often arranged into circular or radial "sprays," these inclusions are aggregates of fine, delicate, needle-like crystals of other minerals. The positioning of these inclusions creates eye-like shapes, though such inclusions shouldn't be confused with eye agates. Sometimes the needles in sagenitic agates are exceptionally fine, resulting in a "fuzzy" appearance, while others are large, coarse and sharp, signifying that the inclusions can be formed of different minerals. Typically, specimens are dominated by a single particularly large sagenitic growth that extends inward from the outer edges of the agate, but an agate can also contain many smaller growths around its perimeter. Sagenitic agates with inclusions that have no radial arrangement are also common; in such specimens, randomly oriented needles protrude through an agate. This, too, signifies the growth of a different mineral.

Sagenites don't always contain agate banding, but when they do, the bands generally wrap around the sagenite growth, separating it from the rest of the banded agate. Occasionally, agate banding can even develop in between the crystals. In addition, sagenitic agates can be found to exhibit any of the usual agate colorations, including the opaque colors normally only found in paint agates. Another unique trait is that the sagenite formations are often banded and contain differently colored zones. These are not agate bands, but merely layers of different amounts of color-causing impurities that were deposited along the length of the needle-like crystals. But in all

**FIGURE 261**
A perfectly formed sagenitic agate, showing all of the characteristic traits as well as unusually bright coloration. Approx. 2" x 2.5" (5 cm x 6.4 cm)

**FIGURE 262**
Coarse needles give this sagenite a unique look. Approx. 2" x 1.5" (5 cm x 3.8 cm)

**FIGURE 263**
A sagenitic agate with unique coloration. Approx. 3" x 2" (7.6 cm x 5 cm)

FIGURE 262

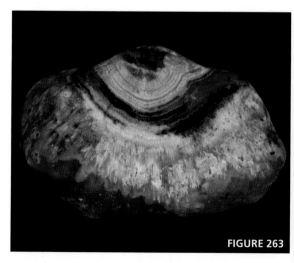

FIGURE 263

FIGURE 261

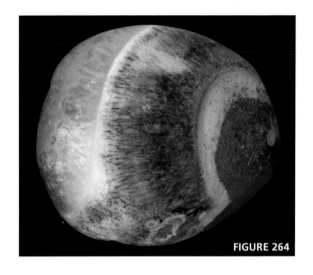

FIGURE 264

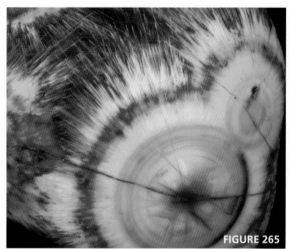

FIGURE 265

sagenitic agates, the inclusions are quite hard, signifying that they have been replaced by quartz and chalcedony.

## FORMATION

Though the name is now used to describe any needle-like mineral inclusions in agate, there is actually no such mineral as sagenite. The term "sagenite" was originally devised in 1796 to describe the mineral known today as rutile, an oxide of titanium with needle-like crystals that grow at perfect 60-degree angles to each other. Horace Bénédict de Saussure noted this unique trait and said it resembled a net, or *sagena* in Latin. In 1890, George Frederick Kunz adapted the sagenite name to refer to quartz crystals containing rutile or other crystals of thin, slender minerals. The definition of sagenite eventually expanded to include needle-like inclusions in agates. But thanks to this history, a popular misconception about sagenitic agates is that their inclusions are formed of rutile crystals. Lake Superior sagenitic agates generally do not contain rutile. Instead, inclusions usually consist of growths of zeolite minerals or goethite. (Rutile cannot be technically ruled out, however, since basalt contains small amounts of titanium-bearing minerals that could weather to form rutile.)

Zeolites form almost exclusively as alteration products of basalt, which means that they form from elements that are released from basalt as it weathers, particularly in the presence of alkaline groundwater. They are a large, closely related group of soft minerals consisting of silica, aluminum and water combined with alkaline elements, such as calcium, potassium or sodium. The majority of zeolites form as slender, delicate, needle-like crystals arranged into radiating

growths within vesicles. Thomsonite and mesolite are two zeolites that fit this description and are particularly common in the basalt formations along Lake Superior, especially in Minnesota, and are likely the two primary minerals that contributed to the sagenitic agates that originated from the Midcontinent Rift basalt flows.

It is very likely that zeolite formations in sagenites began to grow more or less simultaneously along with the agate in the vesicle. Studies and laboratory experiments have shown that silicic acid develops more readily in environments in which alkaline elements are present. Since silicic acid is believed to be the solution responsible for agate formation, and because alkaline elements raise the acidity of silica, which promotes silica polymerization and coagulation, we know that alkaline elements are certainly present in the vesicle during agate formation. As if that weren't enough evidence for the concept of contemporaneous growth of the zeolite and agate, we know that alkaline elements are incompatible with silica, and the crystallizing chalcedony would have pushed the calcium, potassium or sodium towards the boundaries of the vesicle, concentrating them

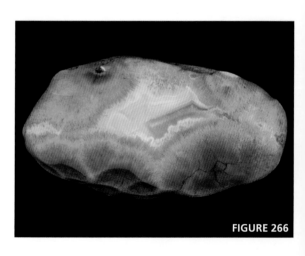

FIGURE 266

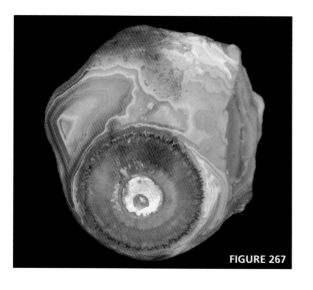

FIGURE 267

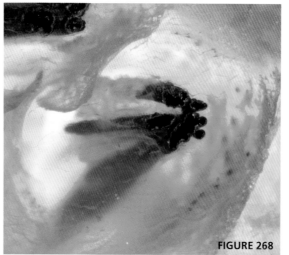

FIGURE 268

FIGURE 267
A fully formed sagenitic "eye" makes for an attractive specimen. Approx. 1.5" x 2" (3.8 cm x 5 cm)

FIGURE 268
Goethite needles, such as the ones pictured here extending into a backlit agate slice, have been coated by chalcedony in some specimens to produce sagenites like that in Figure 263.
15x magnification

as pockets of impurities. It is in these corners of the vesicle that the zeolites would subsequently form. But although the formation of the agate and zeolite mineral in a sagenitic agate may begin at the same time, the zeolite likely finishes forming long before the agate. This is evident in Figure 266, which shows that several zeolite growths formed on several sides of the vesicle and the agate remained in the space between. However, the agate does not extend past the boundaries of the zeolite "sprays," and the characteristic agate husk composed of chalcedony spherulites is not present on the outside of the zeolite growths. This suggests that the zeolites were already in place and formed before even the first layers of chalcedony could solidify.

Even though the chemistry and conditions in which both agates and zeolites form is evidence enough that zeolites led to the formation of the characteristic inclusions in sagenitic agates, there is no better confirmation than simply observing a zeolite specimen alongside a sagenite. The radially arranged needle-like crystals and banded appearance of the thomsonite specimen in Figure 265 are clearly evident in Figure 264, and especially in Figure 261.

Although Lake Superior agate collectors often consider radial zeolite inclusions to be the "true" sagenites, any agates with needle-like crystal inclusions are considered sagenitic agates. Goethite, the hydrous oxide of iron common tlined

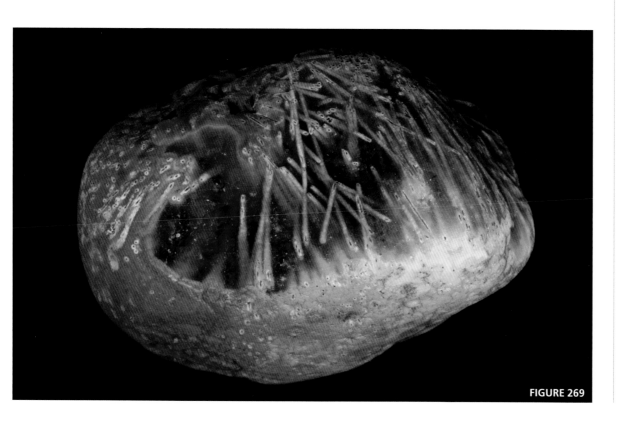

FIGURE 269

FIGURE 269
In a stunning example of a sagenitic agate not derived from radial zeolite inclusions, this agate likely began as a vesicle filled with goethite needles, such as those in Figure 262. Approx. 3" x 2" (7.6 cm x 5 cm) Specimen courtesy of Zack Jacobson.

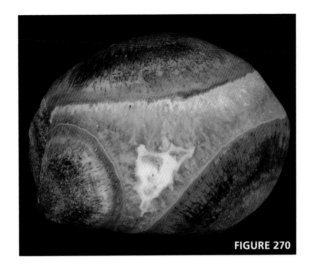

FIGURE 270

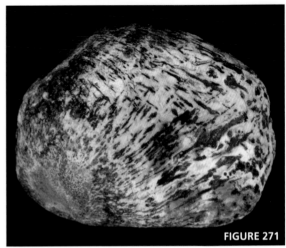

FIGURE 271

throughout the Lake Superior region, frequently crystallizes as coarse needles that can be found embedded in agates. Figure 268 shows a backlit agate slice in which a small arrangement of goethite crystals can be seen extending deeper into the stone. It was inclusions like these that were later coated with chalcedony to form the beautiful sagenitic agate shown in Figure 269.

Though many mineral growths within an agate are soft and weather easily, producing pits on the agate's surface (see the zeolite crystals in the agate in Figure 271), the needles of zeolites or goethite within Lake Superior agates are sometimes harder than they should be. Both types of minerals are normally much softer than quartz, but this is not always the case within sagenitic agates. This is because the inclusions have been impregnated or completely replaced with quartz. Over time, silica solutions can seep into the crystal lattices of other minerals and slowly turn them into quartz.

Alternatively, acidic waters can later flow through an agate, dissolving the softer minerals and leaving voids where more quartz or chalcedony eventually develop. In either case, the sagenite growths in Lake Superior agates are often colorful and well preserved, as they are rich with quartz and more weather resistant than they normally would be.

Finally, the small agate in Figure 273 tells us that sagenite growths can also form later in an agate's lifetime. In this specimen, the tiny zeolite growths formed deeper within the agate on the surface of a macrocrystalline quartz layer. This signifies that this specimen was likely a quartz-lined geode for quite some time, allowing zeolites to form within its cavity before more macrocrystalline quartz filled the rest of the agate.

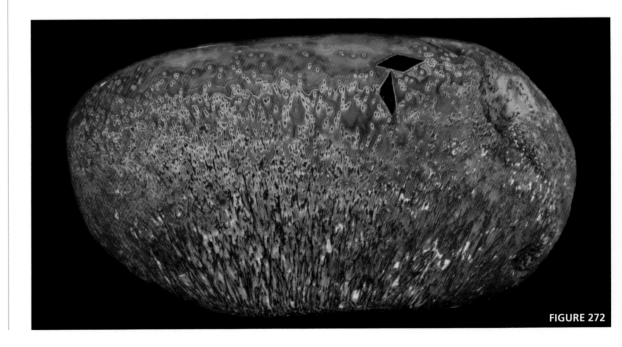

FIGURE 272

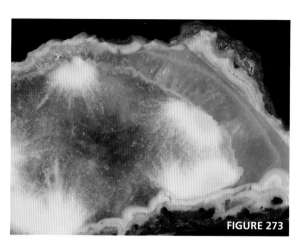

FIGURE 273

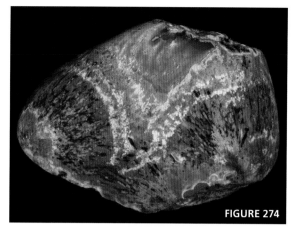

FIGURE 274

**FIGURE 273**
This specimen shows that the zeolite formations don't always form on the outer walls of the vesicle, but can also form at various stages of the agate's growth. 2.5x magnification Specimen courtesy of Chris Cordes.

**FIGURE 274**
An iron-rich sagenitic agate. Approx. 3" x 2" (7.6 cm x 5 cm)

## COLLECTIBILITY

Of all the Lake Superior agates containing inclusions, sagenites are without a doubt the most popular. While for some the large amount of inclusions can be off-putting, most collectors can appreciate the beauty of well-developed sagenitic inclusions embedded within agates. And because of the abundance of zeolites in the Lake Superior region, most collectors have more than a few sagenitic agates in their permanent collections. The finest specimens are, of course, those with bright coloration and unique formations, but the amount of regular agate banding can affect value as well. Most sagenites, however, contain little to no banding.

Whole agate nodules are notorious for their mysterious nature. Because many are undamaged and therefore give no hint what patterns, colors and structures (or lack thereof) may hide inside, many collectors tend to shy away from the gamble of buying and sawing a specimen, as some specimens contain only quartz or other less desirable minerals. But there are several external clues to help determine whether or not the nodule may contain a sagenite formation. Figure

276 shows a whole agate nodule that has telltale streaks of color along its sides and the appearance of many pinholes. These were formed by soft zeolite minerals, and cutting this specimen will likely reveal a large sagenite "spray." The specimens in Figures 275 and 277 are somewhat more obvious. Though polishing brings out a sagenite's true beauty, these specimens show what a sagenite formation looks like on the surface of a nodule when in its natural state.

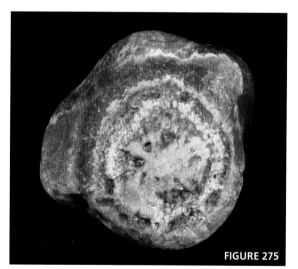

FIGURE 275

**FIGURE 275**
This rough, unpolished sagenite shows the rounded zeolite formation, but no fine details can be seen. Approx. 1.5" x 1.5" (3.8 cm x 3.8 cm). From the collection of Tom Bjugstad.

**FIGURE 276**
This large, rough agate nodule exhibits a surface that appears full of pinholes—a telltale sign of a sagenitic agate. Approx. 3.5" x 3" (8.9 cm x 7.6 cm)

**FIGURE 277**
This rough sagenitic agate exhibits three conspicuous zeolite formations. Approx. 2.5" x 2" (6.4 cm x 5 cm)

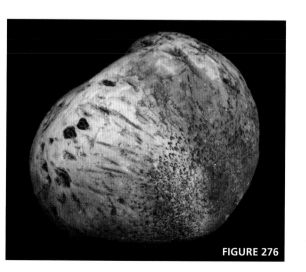

FIGURE 276

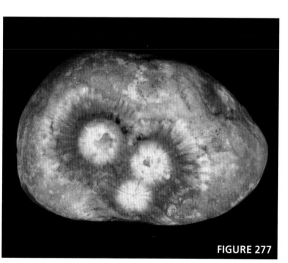

FIGURE 277

# *Stalactitic* AGATE

*Stalactitic agates exhibit long, slender, icicle-like formations extending from their top or bottom sides*

**CHARACTERISTICS:** Icicle- or carrot-shaped growths extending from one end of the agate into the center

**SYNONYMS:** Stalk agate

**DISTRIBUTION:** Stalactitic agates can be found primarily in Minnesota and Ontario

**RARITY:** Stalactitic agates are uncommon, and very fine examples are much more difficult to find

## DESCRIPTION

A stalactite is an icicle-like growth that hangs from the ceiling of a cavity. They are particularly well known in caverns, in which they are the rock formations extending downward from the roof of the cave. Therefore, a stalactitic agate contains the same kind of downward-growing formation. These growths apparently often formed before the rest of the agate banding, because the concentric banding bends and contorts around the tips of the stalactites, as seen in Figures 278 and 281.

In many specimens, a small, hollow opening may be seen where the top of a stalactite meets the surface of the agate. This is because stalactites in agates begin as slender, needle-like crystals of other softer minerals that later become coated with chalcedony. As the chalcedony continues to coat the inclusion, it grows longer and wider at its base, just like icicles do. Later, the original inclusion can dissolve or weather away to leave a small opening behind.

Stalactites are not very common, but can be found in several types of agates, from adhesional banded agates to moss and tube agates (page 166). In fact, stalactitic agates are very similar to tube agates and it can be very easy to mistake one for the other. Tube agates are essentially identical to stalactitic agates, but their chalcedony-coated mineral inclusions extend through the entire agate whereas the inclusions in stalactitic agates only extend partway. The real difficulty in telling the two apart occurs when a tube agate has been polished, cut or broken in such a way that the tube structures appear to end prematurely and resemble a stalactite. While there isn't a foolproof way of determining whether this has occurred in a particular agate, if a specimen has particularly translucent banding, it is easier to tell. For example, the specimen in Figure 278 has white stalactites visible deeper within the agate, and

**FIGURE 278**
This spectacular example of stalactites in an agate is made even more interesting by the translucent chalcedony allowing us to view stalactites deeper within the agate. Approx. 2.5" x 3" (6.4 cm x 7.6 cm)

**FIGURE 279**
Intensely colored stalactites. Approx. 2.5" x 2.5" (6.4 cm x 6.4 cm)

**FIGURE 280**
The irregular, curving structures indicate that these were likely stalks, not stalactites. Approx. 2.5" x 1.5" (6.4 cm x 3.8 cm)

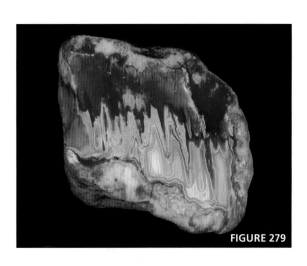

FIGURE 279

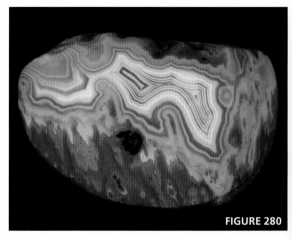

FIGURE 280

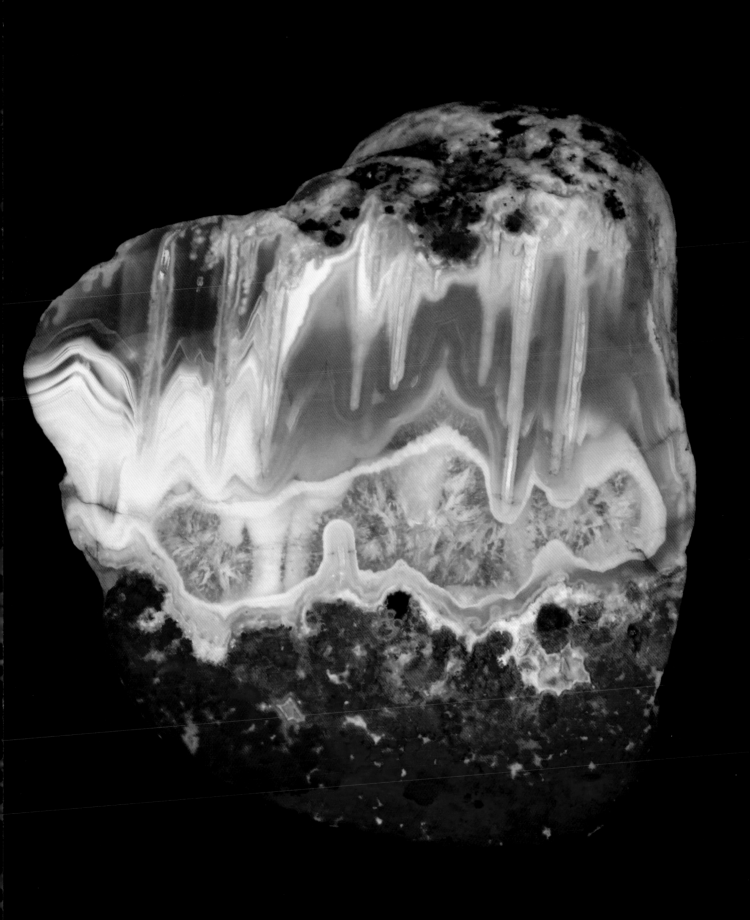

FIGURE 278

**FIGURE 281**
These stalactites are actually visible on the external surfaces of the specimen. Approx. 2" x 1.5" (5 cm x 3.8 cm)

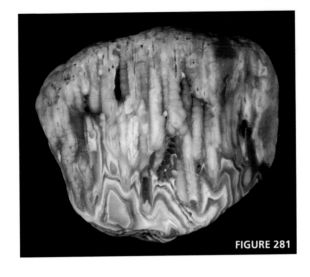

FIGURE 281

they occur behind the brownish gray bands near the upper-middle portion of the agate, proving that these are not long tubes.

When inspecting a specimen for stalactites, you may come across some that are very different, and are thinner and less regular in structure. These are known as stalks, and as Figures 280 and 283 show, they actually rise upwards through the agate. Known as stalk agates, these specimens contain fine, elongated growths that can sometimes appear to change direction. If there's no way to tell which portion of the agate was up or down during its formation, telling apart a stalactite from a stalk can be very difficult.

## FORMATION

Stalactites formed in much the same way as tubes: a long, slender, needle-like mineral inclusion provided the "seed" around which chalcedony began to accumulate. Unlike tubes, however, stalactites only protrude partway through the agate. As the mineral inclusions were likely present before the agate began to form, the banding twists

**FIGURE 282**
These stalks made a peculiar change in direction during their growth. Did the vesicle move? 10x magnification

**FIGURE 283**
Many stalks rise from various points within this agate. Approx. 3" x 2.5" (7.6 cm x 6.4 cm)

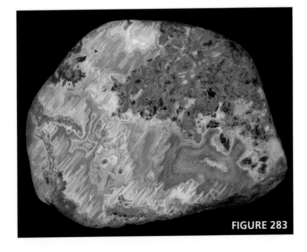

FIGURE 283

and contorts around them, creating interesting patterns such as that in Figure 281.

In terms of their formation, the stalks sometimes found rising from the bottom of an agate may be more compelling. These strange, gravity-defying growths tend to be more slender but less uniform than stalactites, often appearing lumpy or even changing direction. They also tend to remain much shorter than stalactites, but are more plentiful when they are present in an agate. So how do they form?

Stalks are simply the result of low-density particles rising through an agate, essentially floating upwards. This is why the stalks in some specimens (see Figure 280) appear to waver and make slight turns. Stalactites are very straight because they form along the length of a perfectly straight crystal, but rising stalks can be affected by motion or vibration within the surrounding rock or the thickness of the solution that the particles rose through.

FIGURE 282

One of the most interesting occurrences in stalk agates is shown in Figure 282. Clearly, the rising particles changed direction near their uppermost extent, but why? It is possible that the vesicle changed position, perhaps due to an earthquake, while these were forming, effectively altering which way was up. Or perhaps an unusually high amount of motion occurred within the solution in the vesicle. In any case, these hooked stalks are not actually rare, suggesting that whatever caused their unusual appearance may not have been as exotic as it initially seems. Finally, there is the question of what substance the stalks rose through. Was it a thick silica gel or a thin solution of silicic acid? There really is no way to tell, but specimens such as in Figures 282 and 284 show stalks within

FIGURE 284

a mass of macrocrystalline quartz containing very little or no chalcedony. Because macrocrystalline quartz requires relatively little silica to form, it may be safe to assume that these specimens resulted from a solution. However, specimens similar to that in Figure 280, which contains ample banding, may have begun with low-density particles rising through a gel.

## COLLECTIBILITY

Generally, any Lake Superior agate with a large amount of inclusions is only somewhat collectible; such agates are primarily only popular with collectors of "weird" agates. Stalactitic and stalk agates are no exception to this rule. Though most collectors can appreciate the unique growths in stalactitic agates, they always focus on adhesional banded and floater agates more than on agates with inclusions. Stalactitic agates with large, well-formed stalactites are the exception, as long as they add to the beauty and aesthetics of a specimen. Stalk agates, on the other hand, don't often see praise from serious collectors, no matter how colorful or interesting.

## NOTABLE VARIATIONS

A particular limestone formation near Thunder Bay, Ontario, produces a variety of vein agate called "Thunder Bay agate." Among the blocky limestone and seams of agate, true stalactites can be found hanging from the ceilings of cavities. These beautiful icicle-shaped agates grow freely and perfectly illustrate how a stalactite is formed, but are impure and many contain bands composed entirely of soft calcite derived from the

FIGURE 285

weathering of the limestone. Figure 285 shows an entire Thunder Bay agate stalactite while Figure 287 shows a fragment from the base of a stalactite where it was connected to the limestone. Note how there is a small, dark hole now at the center of each, signifying that another softer mineral initiated the accumulation of silica around it. Also note that each specimen has an exterior coating of rough, chalky calcite. Acquiring one of these uncommon stalactites for your collection is difficult, however, as they are found on privately owned land that is closed to collecting.

FIGURE 286

FIGURE 287

FIGURE 284
Countless stalks rise through this mass of macrocrystalline quartz.
Approx. 2.5" x 2" (6.4 cm x 5 cm)

FIGURE 285
Thunder Bay produces probably the only true agate stalactites in the entire Lake Superior region. Coatings of quartz, chalcedony and calcite accumulated layer-by-layer around a tiny mineral growth.
Approx. 3" x 1.5" (7.6 cm x 3.8 cm)]

FIGURE 286
Orange stalks rise through macrocrystalline quartz. Note the irregular, lumpy appearance.
8x magnification

FIGURE 287
The base of a broken Thunder bay stalactite shows the characteristic appearance.
Approx. 2.5" x 2" (6.4 cm x 5 cm)

# Tube AGATE

*Round, slender and often hollow structures extending through an agate are known as "tubes"*

**CHARACTERISTICS:** Tubular structures, hollow or otherwise, that penetrate an agate and appear as "eyes" when viewed on-end

**SYNONYMS:** None

**DISTRIBUTION:** Tube agates are found throughout the entire range of Lake Superior agates

**RARITY:** Tube agates are fairly common, but fine examples with very well-formed structures or completely hollow tubes are much more difficult to find

............................................................................

## DESCRIPTION

Impurities are common in Lake Superior agates and illustrate that agates did not form alone. In tube agates, long, straight and slender crystals of other minerals were encased in chalcedony, creating hollow filaments in the agate that extend through the specimen, resembling tubes. When a tube is viewed from the side, its length is evident, but when one is viewed from above, only the end is visible, and a circular, often banded formation can be seen. These are frequently mistaken for eye agates; according to many older definitions, tubes seen end-on were actually considered eye agates, though today tube agates and eye agates are considered distinct agate varieties. A small hollow that extends the entire length of the structure is at the center of many tubes, but this is not always the case in all tube agate specimens. As shown by the agate in Figure 288, many tubes are filled in with chalcedony that is often of a different color.

Though they are closely related to stalactitic agates, in which icicle-like tubular structures extend only partway into the agate, the tubes in tube agates are typically more banded, exhibiting growth rings not unlike those of a tree. In addition, the first chalcedony band surrounding the core of the tube is often thicker and of the same color as the agate's outermost chalcedony layer, or husk (if it is present), which signifies that the needle-like mineral inclusions that initiate tube growth were present in the vesicle before the agate began forming.

## FORMATION

The formation of a tube agate begins with a vesicle filled with long, slender crystals of miner-

**FIGURE 288**
This tube agate, beautifully worn by glaciers and water, exhibits all of the characteristic traits of a Lake Superior tube agate. Approx. 2" x 3" (5 cm x 7.6 cm) Specimen courtesy of Terry Roses.

**FIGURE 289**
Many tubes with hollow centers dot this iron-rich agate. Approx. 1.5" x 1" (3.8 cm x 2.5 cm)

**FIGURE 290**
This specimen contains so many tubes that they appear to merge into one large mass. Approx. 4" x 3" (10.2 cm x 7.6 cm)

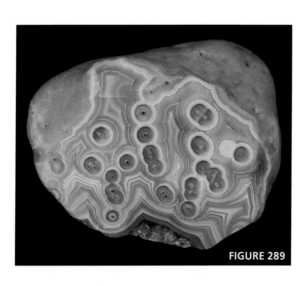

FIGURE 289

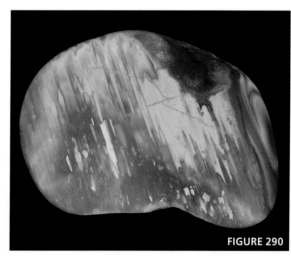

FIGURE 290

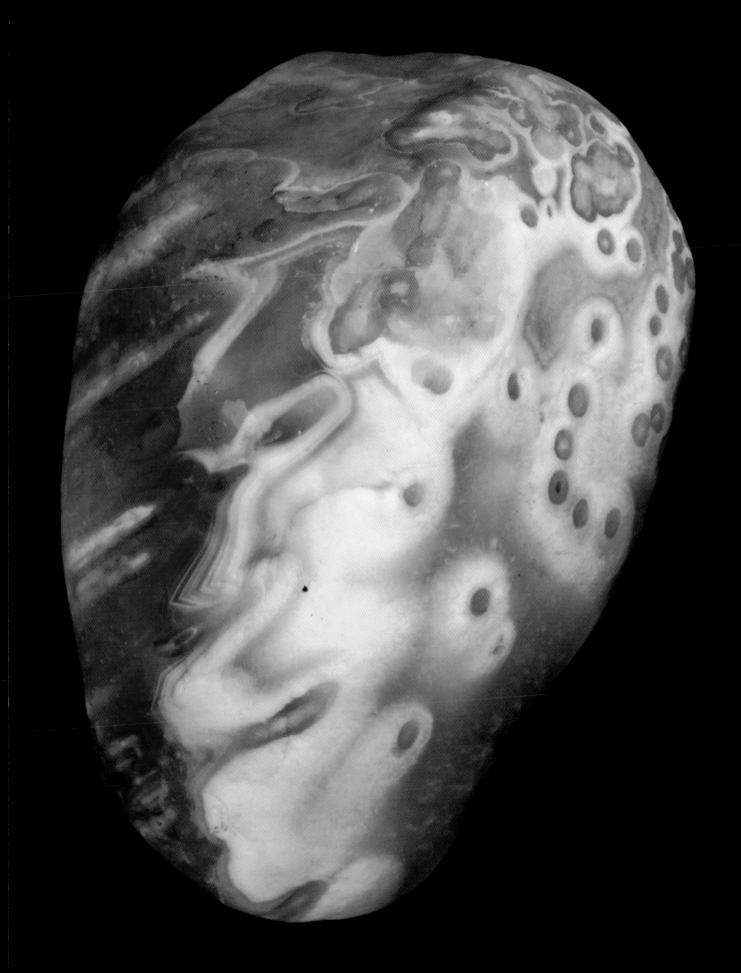

FIGURE 288

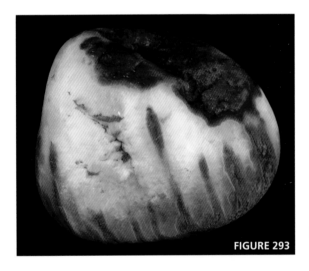

FIGURE 291

als like goethite extending across the entire interior of the cavity. As silicic acid later fills the vesicle, agate formation begins as usual, but the needle-like crystals are coated in chalcedony as well. As band development continues, the inclusions are coated again and again so that they are banded in a similar manner to the rest of the agate.

After banding formation completed and the entire agate solidified, acidic water may have flowed through the rock. It would have been unable to affect the chalcedony and quartz, but would easily have dissolved the mineral growth at the center of a tube. If this occurred, the characteristic hollow spaces would be left behind.

FIGURE 292
A quintessential Lake Superior tube agate.
Approx. 3" x 2.5"
(7.6 cm x 6.4 cm)

the tubes contain an unusually large hollow space, but they are lined with the same thick, gray chalcedony seen on parts of the husk in the top-left of the photo. This is also seen in Figure 289, though the husk is not present on most of that agate. These specimens are perhaps the best evidence that the mineral inclusions were present before the agate began to form, as the same chalcedony growths that formed the husk also encircle the tubes.

FIGURE 292

However, voids within agates generally don't stay hollow for long, as they create perfect openings for more silica to enter and form additional quartz or chalcedony. This was the case in the agates in Figures 288, 291 and 292, which all exhibit chalcedony-filled tubes.

Figure 294 exemplifies an interesting, but not always observed, trait of tube agates. Not only do

FIGURE 293
Red chalcedony tubes extend through white macrocrystalline quartz in this specimen from the far northern reaches of Lake Superior.
Approx. 2.5" x 2"
(6.4 cm x 5 cm)
Specimen courtesy of David Gredzens.

FIGURE 293

FIGURE 294

Occasionally, a tube will develop around a non-linear mineral growth. Figure 297 shows a well-developed tube structure that very evidently sweeps across the interior of the agate with a slight curve. Luckily, the tubes in this specimen are not hollow, and the polishing process slightly exposed the mineral contained within them. Visible as tiny black marks around the edges of the specimen, this tube agate resulted from soft, moss-like growths descending from the top of the vesicle. The horizontal bands at the bottom of the specimen also help to determine the direction in which the agate formed.

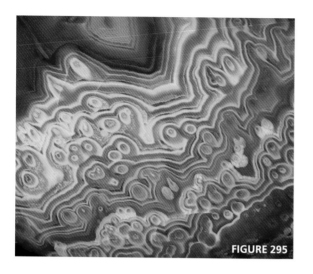

FIGURE 295

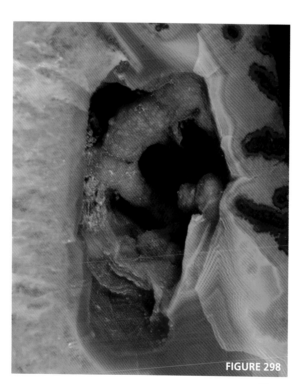

FIGURE 296

## COLLECTIBILITY

Though Lake Superior agates with a large amount of inclusions are generally not widely sought after, tubes do see some popularity among novice and experienced collectors alike. Unlike stalactitic agates, which generally contain simple, unbanded cone- or icicle-shaped streaks of color, tube agates are often more visually interesting. When a specimen contains banded tubes, such as in Figure 291, or wild patterns resulting from the agate banding forming around the tubes, as in Figure 295, the specimens can be very collectible, and even valuable, especially when vivid and contrasting color combinations are present.

## NOTABLE VARIATIONS

Not all tubes are deeply embedded within an agate. Sometimes they can be visible on a weathered surface (as in Figure 296), or inside a cavity,

Figure 296, for example, clearly began as a mass of perfectly parallel needle-like crystals that were later easily dissolved, as no trace of them still exists. What this mineral was, however, is unknown.

The agate in Figure 298 is equally confusing. The tube structures appeared to have grown freely within the cavity, but the cavity itself is a crystal impression. In addition, the tubes seem to be extensions of the dark mossy growths at

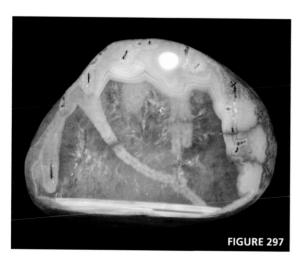

FIGURE 297

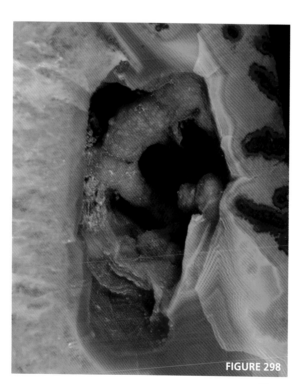

FIGURE 298

growing freely (as in Figure 298). Known simply as external tubes, these unique specimens offer rare insight into the formation of tubes in agates.

the right side of the photo. Did the tubes form after the crystal responsible for the impression had dissolved? Or did the tubes and the crystal form simultaneously? Specimens like this are as compelling as they are mysterious.

# Color Variations

*Some coloration in agates is so distinct that we classify it as a separate variety of agate*

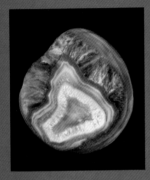

**COLORED MACROCRYSTALLINE QUARTZ**

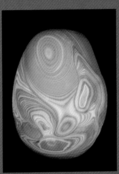

**PAINT AGATE**

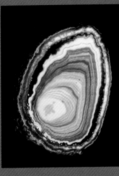

**RARE COLORATION**

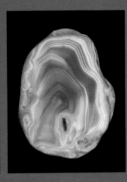

**SURFACE COLORATIONS**

Mineral impurities give Lake Superior agates their colors, but the striking differences in shade and intensity are a result of the amount of impurities coloring an agate, which minerals are doing the coloring and when
the coloration occurs. Some colorations are so common—or so uncommon—that collectors have classified them as a separate variety of agate.
The following unique color varieties can be found in many of the previously described structural variations of agates.

## INTRODUCTION

The beautiful banding and fascinating structures seen within agates would not be nearly as impressive if it weren't for the mineral impurities that stain them various colors. In fact, one of the most interesting qualities of agates is that they depend entirely upon other minerals to give them coloration. But agate coloration is not constant, and upon weathering, those colors can change drastically, sometimes over the course of just a few years on a collector's shelf.

Iron minerals are by far the most abundant colorant in agates. Hematite, goethite and limonite trapped within the twisted fibers of chalcedony are responsible for virtually every shade of red, brown, yellow and orange found in agates. Iron-stained agates are so common that certain shades of red or brown have several distinct names dating back to antiquity. Carnelian, for example, is the name given to rich red, translucent chalcedony. Containing a higher than usual amount of hematite impurities, carnelian is generally free of banding by definition, though the name is frequently applied to agates containing similar intense coloration. Another ancient name that still sees use today is sard, which is reserved for translucent brown or yellow-brown chalcedony with or without banding. Both of

these colorations are abundant in the Lake Superior region, and the area is home to dozens more that had not been named in the ancient Greek and Latin languages.

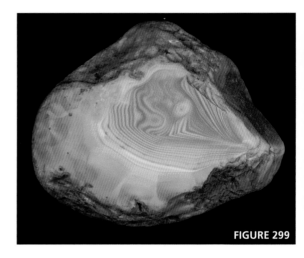

**FIGURE 299**

But not every agate exhibits the characteristic colors of iron. Aluminum, magnesium, manganese and even tiny water bubbles can result in shades of white, gray or black, as well as the bluish gray coloration caused by the Tyndall effect (see pages 19–20). Even copper, which is rare in the world's agates, is present and not uncommon in Lake Superior's agates, resulting in pink, orange or greenish coloration.

**FIGURE 299**
A very strange combination of colors makes this a unique agate. Approx. 2.5" x 2" (6.4 cm x 5 cm)

**FIGURE 300**
Sard, or brown chalcedony (top), and carnelian, or red chalcedony (bottom), are common finds on the beach. Both are colored by iron impurities. Largest specimen approx. 1" x 1" (2.5 cm x 2.5 cm)

**FIGURE 301**
Smoky quartz, or gray quartz, at the center of an agate. Approx. 2" x 1.5" (5 cm x 3.8 cm)

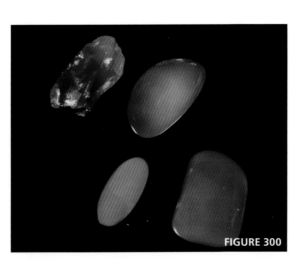

**FIGURE 300**

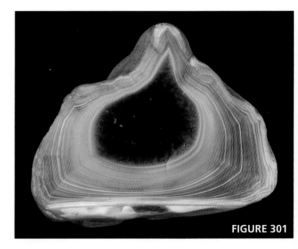

**FIGURE 301**

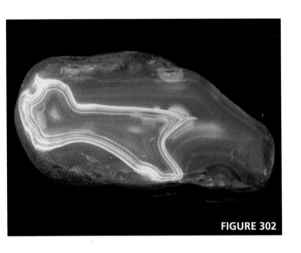

FIGURE 302

## PRIMARY VARIATIONS

In this chapter, we will discuss the causes of some of the most unique and compelling color variations found within Lake Superior agates. While we know the causes of the usual colors found in Lake Superior agates, others are more mysterious. For example, the macrocrystalline quartz sometimes found within agates can be tinted black, brown, purple and, rarely, yellow. Each of these colors is caused by atoms of certain elements actually incorporated within the crystal lattice of the quartz itself, not by impurities of certain minerals mixed among the crystals.

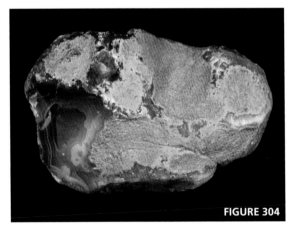

FIGURE 304

Every once in a while, you may come across a Lake Superior agate that exhibits unexpected colors in its chalcedony bands, such as vivid greens, lemon yellows and delicate purples and pinks. Some of these colors can be so odd that it's hard to determine what mineral impurity may have created them. Hues such as these may be common in other agates from around the world, but in Lake Superior's gems, they are very rare and valuable, as are certain combinations of colors. But one of the most popular variations in Lake Superior agate coloration is known as a

paint agate. The orange, brown and tan colors commonly exhibited in paint agates are distinctly opaque, offering little translucency except in thin sections of a specimen or when sliced. These colors are not caused by dense, compact concen-

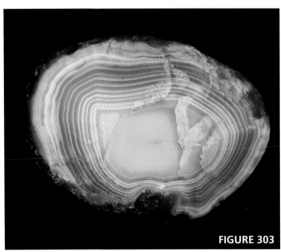

FIGURE 303

trations of iron mineral impurities, as popularly thought, but are instead the result of very fresh impurities that have not yet been sufficiently weathered to develop translucency. Finally, a large number of Lake Superior agates exhibit thin coatings of various minerals on their surfaces; these were deposited by iron-rich groundwater and are known as surface colorations. All of these colorations are variations of the usual, common hues and tints of Lake Superior agates and virtually all result from the same limited set of impurities. But because agates often formed under different circumstances, they developed different colorations.

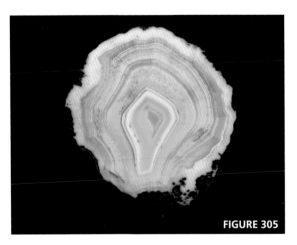

FIGURE 305

**FIGURE 302**
Greenish coloration is rare in Lake Superior agates. Approx. 4" x 2" (10.2 cm x 5 cm)

**FIGURE 303**
Bright yellow, such as that in the center of this agate, is uncommon, and caused by microscopic goethite impurities. Approx. 2" x 1.5" (5 cm x 3.8 cm)

**FIGURE 304**
Yellow coatings of limonite, as seen here, are very common on Lake Superior agates. Approx. 2.5" x 1.5" (6.4 cm x 3.8 cm)

**FIGURE 305**
Paint agates, exhibiting opaque coloration, are a fairly common and very popular variety of Lake Superior agate. Approx. 1" x 1" (2.5 cm x 2.5 cm) Specimen courtesy of Christopher Cordes.

# Colored Macrocrystalline Quartz

*Coarsely crystallized sections of gray, purple or yellow quartz within an agate are a rare occurrence*

**CHARACTERISTICS:** Agates containing macrocrystalline quartz that exhibits a unique color different from its usual translucent or white appearance

**SYNONYMS:** Amethyst; citrine; smoky quartz, morion quartz; Cairngorm quartz, root beer quartz

**DISTRIBUTION:** Agates with colored macrocrystalline quartz can be found anywhere in the usual agate-rich areas, but northern Minnesota is particularly known for these agates

**RARITY:** Gray and purple quartz within agate is fairly uncommon, whereas yellow, dark brown, or green quartz is very rare

## DESCRIPTION

Macrocrystalline quartz is not a rare occurrence in Lake Superior agates. It is a result of solutions containing low amounts of silica that were incapable of forming chalcedony, and signifies a dramatic change in the amount of silica available to the agate. Many specimens exhibit a core of large, coarsely developed quartz crystals that is generally white or colorless, or, at most, stained yellow or brown by particles of iron minerals. But there are those odd, compelling specimens that exhibit purple, black, gray or bright yellow macrocrystalline quartz that grew amid the agate banding. Upon close inspection, no tiny growths of impurities are present in or around the crystals, signifying that their coloration is the result of a very different process.

Smoky quartz, which is the name given to gray or black quartz, is one of the most common color varieties seen in agates, as is amethyst, the purple or violet form of quartz. In fact, amethyst is common in places along Lake Superior's shores, especially near Thunder Bay, Ontario, where enormous formations of amethyst are mined. Citrine is the name given to bright yellow quartz, and is one of the rarest types to see within an agate. It is easy to confuse citrine with quartz that has been stained yellow by limonite or other iron minerals, but close observation should reveal that citrine's color is derived from the crystals themselves and not iron particles. Finally, some rarer variations exist, including "root beer" quartz, which is intensely brown, and green quartz. All of these types of quartz are highly collectible in agates, but those from Lake Superior are especially desirable due to their rarity.

**FIGURE 306**
Greenish smoky quartz is an extremely rare and coveted find in Lake Superior agates. Approx. 3.5" x 4" (8.9 cm x 10.2 cm)

**FIGURE 307**
Most "citrine" in Lake Superior agates is actually deeply iron-stained quartz, but not in this rare specimen, which contains the coloration within the crystals themselves. Approx. 3" x 2.5" (7.6 cm x 6.4 cm)

**FIGURE 308**
Amethyst bands alternate with white chalcedony at the center of this agate. Approx. 2.5" x 1.5" (6.4 cm x 3.8 cm)

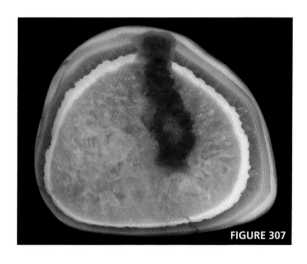

FIGURE 307

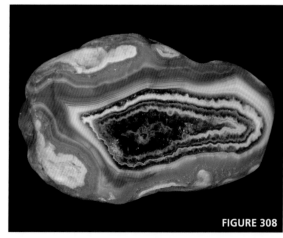

FIGURE 308

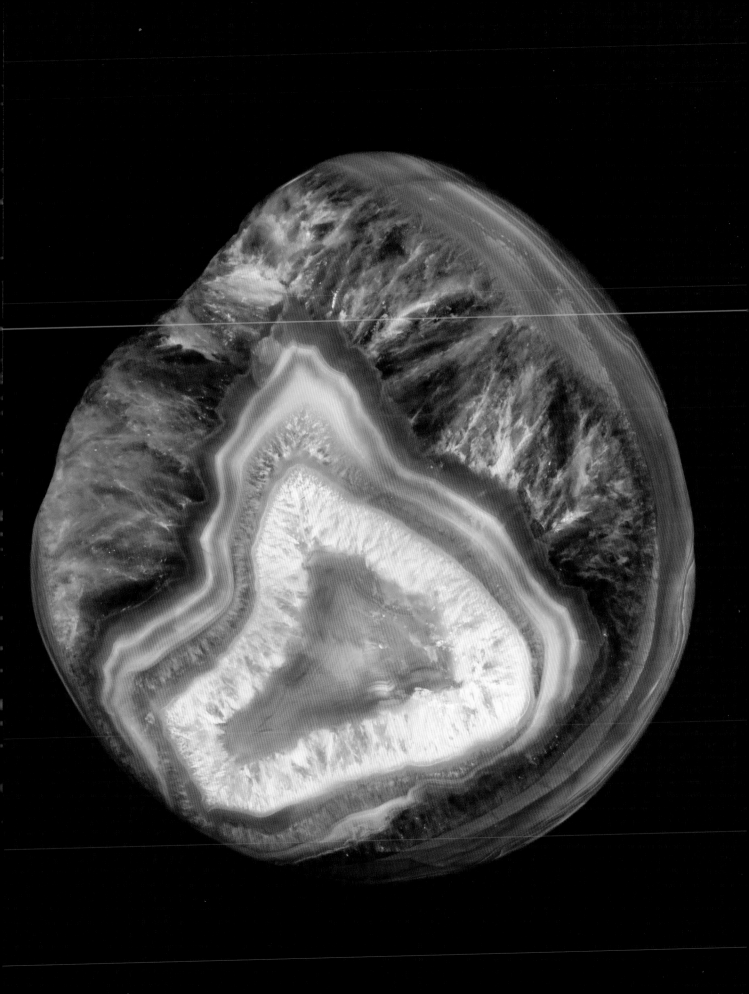

FIGURE 306

FIGURE 309
Not only do the chalcedony bands in this specimen have a strange assemblage of colors, but the smoky quartz center is unusually black. Approx. 2.5" x 1.5" (6.4 cm x 3.8 cm)

FIGURE 309

As the aluminum atoms rapidly move around the quartz, energized by the radiation, they are eventually caught in the microscopic spaces or holes between silicon atoms. Here, they continue to vibrate indefinitely, and this energetic movement of aluminum atoms causes gray or black coloration to appear in the quartz, otherwise known as smoky quartz. These trapped, vibrating atoms are called "color centers." The most interesting aspect of this phenomena is that heating a specimen of smoky quartz returns the missing electrons to the aluminum, causing its vibration to cease; this causes the smoky quartz to revert back to the white or colorless appearance of quartz.

## FORMATION

To determine why these colored varieties of quartz occasionally form within agates, we must first understand why the colorations occur at all. As discussed earlier in this book, certain elements can substitute for others in the crystal lattice of quartz. For example, a silicon atom can be exchanged for an aluminum atom if enough aluminum is present for it to be incorporated within a crystal at the time of quartz growth. In this case, the aluminum technically is an impurity, but not in the same way that hematite acts as an impurity in chalcedony because the aluminum is actually part of the crystal structure, rather than just an associated mineral growth.

FIGURE 310
This specimen illustrates how the coloration of the macrocrystalline quartz can be zoned into different varieties. Approx. 3.5" x 2.5" (8.9 cm x 6.4 cm)

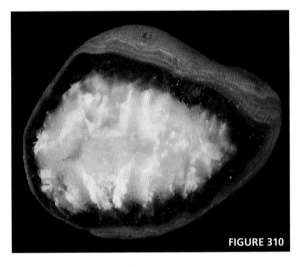

FIGURE 310

The exact same process is responsible for the coloration of amethyst, but it is an iron atom, not an aluminum one, that is vibrating. However, heating a specimen of amethyst doesn't result in color loss; instead, the purple quartz turns to a vivid yellow color called citrine. Citrine is rare in nature, and most store-bought specimens are actually artificially heated amethyst from Brazil.

FIGURE 311
Black smoky quartz, sometimes called "morion quartz," is particularly rich with irradiated aluminum to the point where it appears opaque. Approx. 2" x 2" (5 cm x 5 cm)

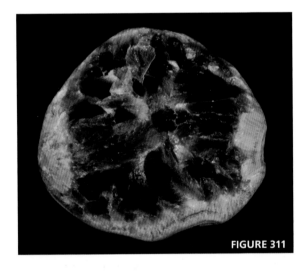

FIGURE 311

FIGURE 312
Wild banding, caused by barite inclusions, surrounds a center of pale amethyst. Approx. 2.5" x 2" (6.4 cm x 5 cm)

While aluminum-bearing quartz generally looks no different than quartz, or at most exhibits cloudy coloration, something peculiar happens when the quartz is subjected to radioactivity. The radiation can strip the aluminum atoms of essential electrons, or negatively charged particles, causing the aluminum atoms to vibrate and move from their positions in the quartz's crystal lattice.

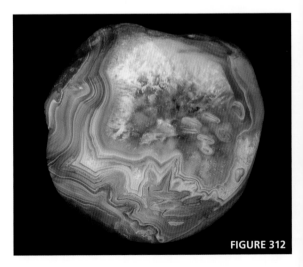

FIGURE 312

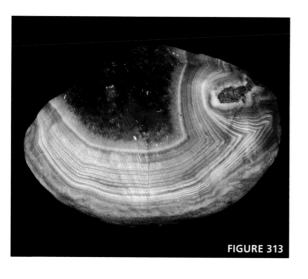

FIGURE 313

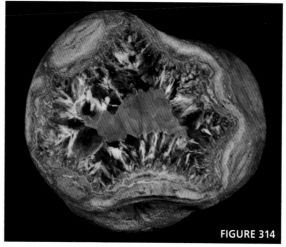

FIGURE 314

FIGURE 313
Intensely purple amethyst adds interest to this broken shard of a gray agate. Approx. 2" x 1" (5 cm x 2.5 cm)

FIGURE 314
Cairngorm quartz, the name given to very brown smoky quartz, is rare in Lake Superior agates. Approx. 2" x 1.5" (5 cm x 3.8 cm)

The presence of these colored forms of quartz in Lake Superior agates means that both natural radiation and heating must have occurred during an agate's lifetime. Luckily, there is evidence of both. The large formations of amethyst found near Thunder Bay, Ontario, are a direct confirmation that a major source of radiation once existed within the rocks of the Lake Superior region, and the dramatic volcanic events of the Midcontinent Rift event certainly could have heated agate specimens containing amethyst enough to form citrine. But in 2001, Götze and his colleagues published an article in which they tested agates for trace amounts of rare elements. They discovered that some agates contain tiny amounts of uranium, a radioactive element, and in higher concentrations than the rocks in which they formed. This would mean that the silicic acid flowing into the vesicle likely came from deeper within the earth, where uranium is more common. Given these results, Götze suggested that agates containing smoky quartz and amethyst may have irradiated themselves.

The irradiation of quartz in agates is particularly interesting in specimens such as in Figures 310,

313 and 315, which clearly display distinct zones of coloration. The quartz crystallization in Figure 310 began with amethyst, which later turned to standard white quartz. This could suggest that, if irradiated by the nearby rocks, the source of radiation eventually died out, as is common with unstable radioactive elements like uranium. But the agates in Figures 313 and 315 show a reversed growth of amethyst, which formed later than the standard quartz. It is unlikely that radioactive elements suddenly made their way into the surrounding rock, so were these growths the result of uranium-bearing waters entering the vesicle during the last stage of the agate's growth? This idea seems likely.

Finally, a rare variety of macrocrystalline quartz sometimes found in Lake Superior agates is called Cairngorm quartz, a variety of smoky quartz named for the Scottish Cairngorm Mountains where the material was first found. These specimens, such as in Figure 314, contain irradiated impurities of both aluminum and iron, which cause the quartz to appear chocolate-brown. Often called "root beer quartz" by collectors, these specimens are exceptionally rare.

## COLLECTIBILITY

Colored macrocrystalline quartz can make Lake Superior agates extremely collectible. Smoky quartz and amethyst are uncommon, but only very vividly colored examples (such as the specimen in Figure 313) are truly rare. Citrine, however, is very rare; beware when identifying or buying a specimen as it may actually be iron-stained quartz and not true citrine. Finally, brown Cairngorm quartz and green quartz are definitely the rarest colorations in Lake Superior agates and are most valuable.

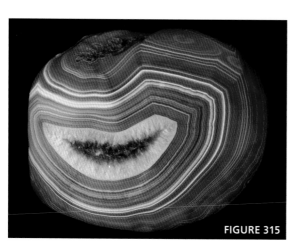

FIGURE 315

FIGURE 315
This gorgeous adhesional banded agate contains a center of zoned macrocrystalline quartz, with amethyst in the center. Approx. 3" x 2.5" (7.6 cm x 6.4 cm) From the collection of Jim Haase.

# *Paint* AGATE

*Paint agates exhibit opaque, non-translucent banding that appears as if "painted" on the stone*

**CHARACTERISTICS:** Opaque chalcedony bands, often in bright orange hues

**SYNONYMS:** Paint stone, painted agate, opaque agate

**DISTRIBUTION:** Paint agates can generally be found anywhere in the usual range of Lake Superior agates; however, high concentrations of paint agates are known from near Grand Marais on the far northern end of Minnesota's shores, and from the northern tip of Michigan's Keweenaw Peninsula

**RARITY:** Small paint agates aren't uncommon, though specimens larger than your fist are very rare

## DESCRIPTION

Paint agates get their name from their characteristic opaque bands, which appear to be painted onto the stone. In a standard Lake Superior agate, the bands are translucent except for the dense white chalcedony bands which only allow light to shine through them when the specimen is very thin. But paint agates (or "paint stones," as many collectors call them) differ in that every band is opaque, from the white chalcedony bands to the colored bands.

When looking at Lake Superior paint agates, one thing stands out more than anything else: aside from their white banding, they almost always exhibit shades of intense orange, yellow, pink, tan and brown, and rarely any other colors. As we know, these hues are caused by iron minerals, such as hematite and goethite, but clearly there is something unique about paint agates for these common colors to appear exclusively and in such an opaque manner. Perhaps surprisingly, any whole agate nodule recently removed from unweathered and intact host rock will reveal an agate with opaque bands when cut open.

## FORMATION

There is an old myth that says that agates are completely colorless until removed from the rock and allowed to contact air. The myth states that the iron impurities within the agate could only then oxidize, or combine with oxygen, and develop the recognizable browns and reds

**FIGURE 316**
In an incredibly stunning example of a paint agate, this specimen was polished not on a single side, but downward through its outermost chalcedony layers, revealing exotic swirls of color. Approx. 2.5" x 3.5" (6.4 cm x 8.9 cm) From the Dick Pyle collection; originally found by George Flaim.

**FIGURE 317**
This beautiful, unpolished paint agate is an example of how carefully documenting a specimen can increase its value. A tiny painted label on its back side tells us that it was found in 1969 by Joe Heininger in the Zumbro River, MN. Approx. 2" x 1.5" (5 cm x 3.8 cm)

**FIGURE 318**
This small, pink paint agate is one of the prizes in the authors' collection. An agate dealer once offered dozens of specimens for this one stone; needless to say, the authors didn't accept. Approx. 2" x 1" (5 cm x 2.5 cm)

FIGURE 317

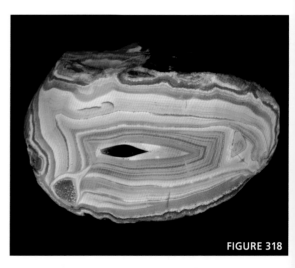
FIGURE 318

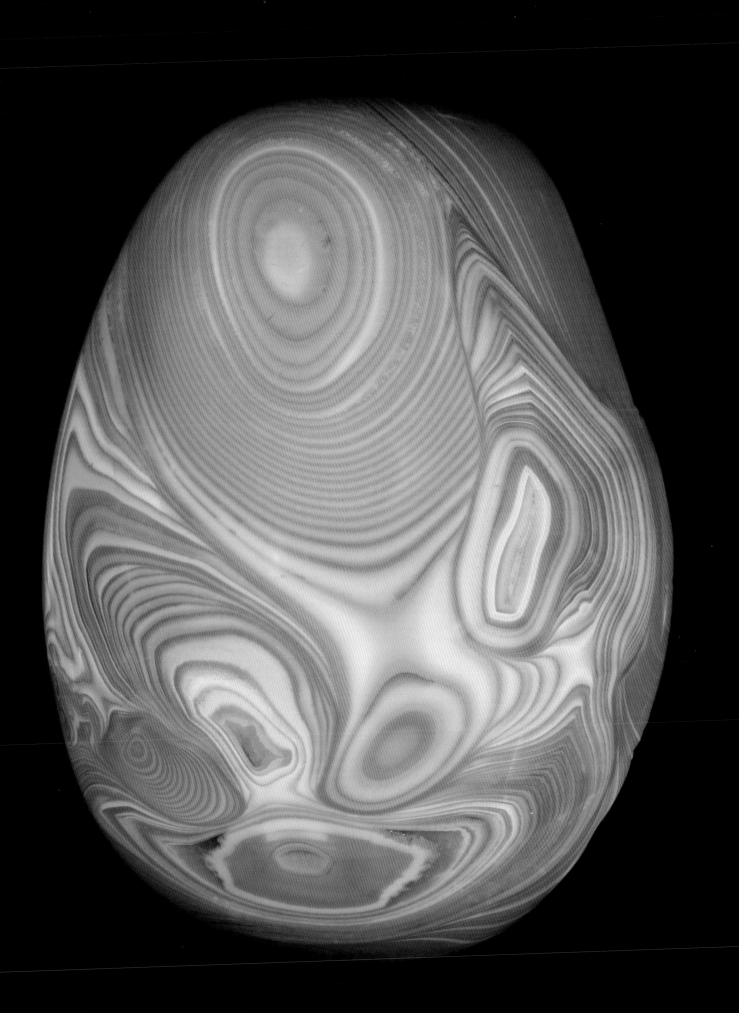

FIGURE 316

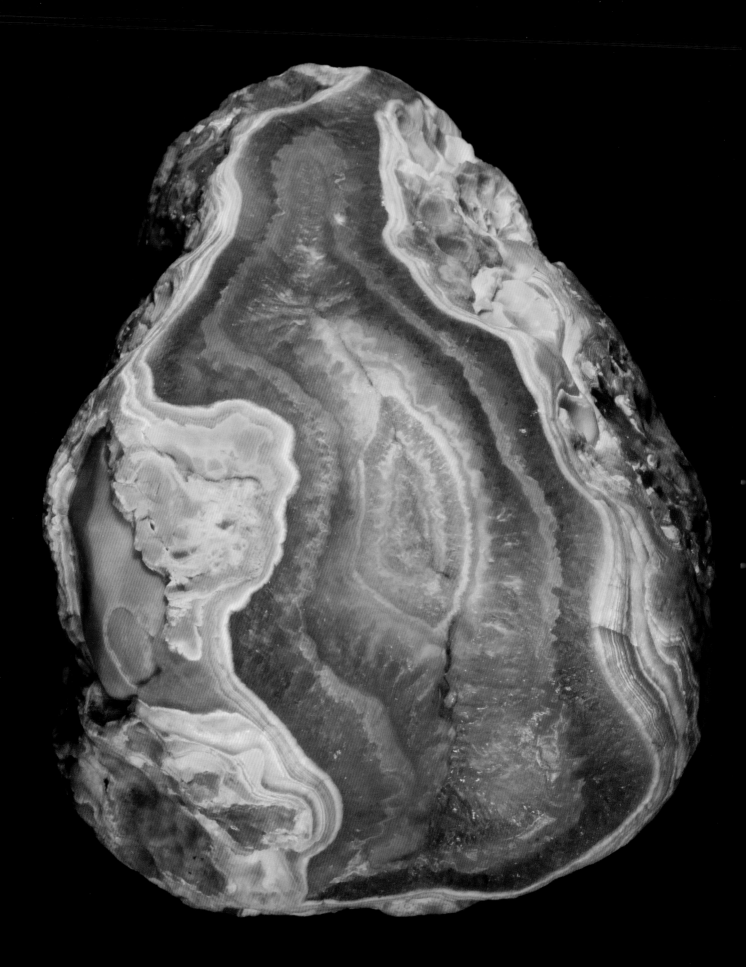

FIGURE 321

of hematite and goethite. Not only is this idea a complete misconception (after all, water deposited the iron, and the oxygen in the water would have already caused some oxidation), but countless direct observations of agates freshly broken from their host rock proves that they do indeed have color even when still embedded in rock. In fact, agates recently removed from their matrix

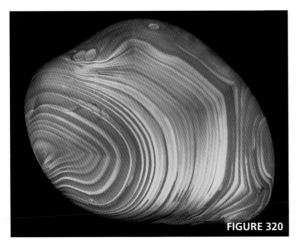

FIGURE 320

contain opaque banding and the characteristic coloration of paint agates. Many researchers have taken note of this fact as well and written about this phenomenon.

It is a common misinterpretation by collectors that paint agates are agates with extremely high concentrations of iron impurities. Most who believe this feel that the impurities must be so densely compact that it makes the banding appear opaque. While this idea seems entirely viable for paint agates found lying loose in glacial till, entirely separated from their matrix, the theory becomes problematic when agates still in their matrix are considered. Agates recently broken from the basalt in which they formed are always some kind of paint agate, provided that the basalt itself is not highly weathered or exposed. Though

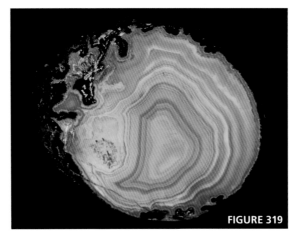

FIGURE 319

they may not always have the popular intense orange coloration, they will be opaque. If it were true that paint agates all had unusually high concentrations of impurities, why would nearly every agate recently removed from the basalt be a paint agate? It could be possible that some paint agates would be found, but certainly not the vast majority. This idea relies too much on coincidence.

There are two additional aspects of this misinformed theory that are problematic. First, this idea implies that paint agates have much higher amounts of mineral impurities scattered among their bands than do agates of regular coloration. Yet when we observe a vividly colored, translucent red band, for example, within a regular agate under a microscope, we can see countless mineral impurities. Clearly it is not a matter of the amount of impurities, but the properties of the impurities. Finally, if the impurity content of paint agates is supposedly so high, why do specimens like that in Figure 321 contain colorless macrocrystalline quartz? It is well known that macrocrystalline quartz typically retains fewer impurities than chalcedony does, but certainly if the agate contained a huge amount of iron, the quartz would also become stained.

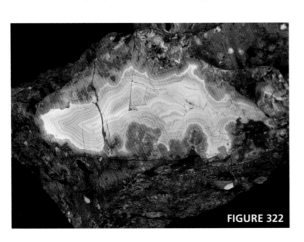

FIGURE 322

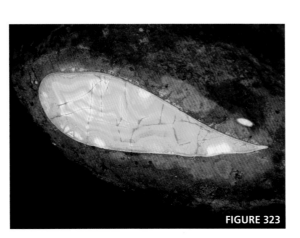

FIGURE 323

FIGURE 319
A small but intensely colored paint agate freshly removed from its host rock before being polished. Approx. 1" x 1" (2.5 cm x 2.5 cm) Specimen courtesy of Christopher Cordes.

FIGURE 320
Intense paint coloration. Approx. 2" x 1.5" (5 cm x 3.8 cm) From the collection of Dick Pyle.

FIGURE 321
This enormous, well-known agate consists of classic orange paint colors and macrocrystalline quartz. Approx. 5.5" x 7" (14 cm x 17.8 cm

FIGURE 322
A paint agate still embedded in basalt. Agate approx. 2.5" x 1" (6.4 cm x 2.5 cm) Specimen courtesy of Christopher Cordes.

FIGURE 323
The very definition of an amygdule, this paint agate is still tightly embedded in rhyolite. Agate approx. 2.5" x 1" (6.4 cm x 2.5 cm)

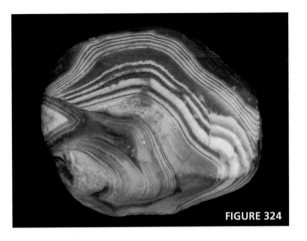

FIGURE 324

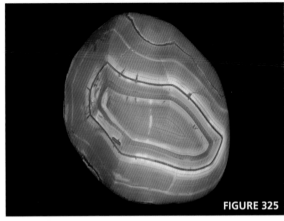

FIGURE 325

Several researchers have proposed a more likely explanation: paint agates are actually agates that have not yet been weathered. This theory implies that the longer a paint agate is exposed to air, water, ice, sunlight and possibly chemicals in the soil, the more translucent and varied in color it becomes due to changes occurring in the mineral impurities. This is why agates still embedded in their host rock exhibit the characteristics of paint agates—they have been protected from weathering. But since we cannot know exactly how long paint agates that were found loose in glacial till have been exposed, we must assume that they still have not been subjected to weathering long enough for their colors to change.

While color-changing chalcedony may seem unlikely at first, consider the specimen in Figure 324. This agate undoubtedly displays both regular agate coloration as well as characteristics of paint agates separated into two distinct zones. Because weathering would first affect the outer layers of an agate, it is proposed that this specimen is halfway through the weathering and color-changing process. This is why the center of the agate still contains paint agate attributes.

Paint agates also seemingly lack the colorless microgranular quartz bands seen in most regular agates. It has been noted by agate dyers for centuries that the clear granular quartz bands do not retain coloration for long, as they contain fewer impurity-catching pores than chalcedony bands. So it is conceivable that the microgranular bands are present in paint agates, but are impure and opaque. Upon weathering, they likely lose their impurities more readily, turning into the colorless microgranular bands we are more familiar with.

Finally, the authors can personally attest to the fact that Lake Superior agates can change color over time. This is particularly noticeable in newly polished specimens that are set on a sunny windowsill for a few years; the coloration of an agate can slowly brighten upon exposure to air and light, so it is not unbelievable that every red-and-white agate may have once been an orange-and-brown agate.

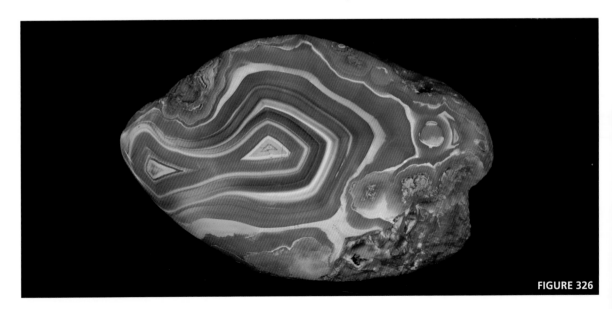

FIGURE 326

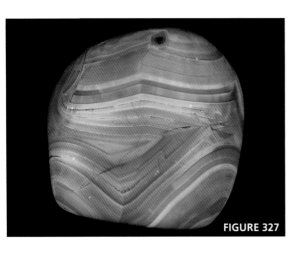

**FIGURE 327**

## COLLECTIBILITY

Other than adhesional banded agates, paint agates are undoubtedly the most collectible variety of Lake Superior agate. The most desirable specimens have vivid orange coloration and numerous white or gray bands that give the agates a high-contrast appearance. And as with any other variety of agate, the fewer fractures, the better the specimen.

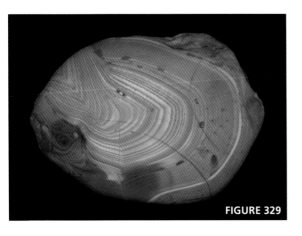

**FIGURE 329**

There is a unique praise given to paint agates from Paradise Beach, Minnesota. Said to produce the finest paint agates, Paradise Beach is now almost entirely private and off-limits to collectors, but specimens from the area, even those that are small and low-quality, are highly collectible and tend to sell for comparatively high prices. Collectors who can afford the finest examples spare no expense in obtaining agates from this historic Lake Superior agate collecting site.

## NOTABLE VARIATIONS

While the most common and popular paint agates exhibit the characteristic bright orange coloration, and are found in Minnesota gravel pits, there are two particular locations around

Lake Superior that consistently produce uniquely colored paint agates that are still embedded within basalt. The rocks around Grand Marais, Minnesota, have recently been known to contain strange paint agate nodules that contain dark, opaque green bands (like the specimen in Figure 331). Though these bands are beautiful and contrast vividly with the orange, iron-rich bands, the causes for their rare colors are unknown.

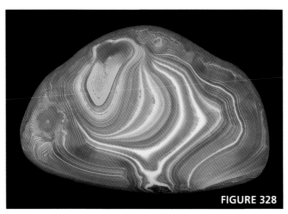

**FIGURE 328**

Certain beaches near Grand Marais have also produced paint agate nodules already freed from the basalt. These beach-worn nodules tend to have an opaque black coating on their surface. Also, Brockway Mountain at the far northern tip of Michigan's Keweenaw Peninsula has long been a well-known location for collecting whole agate nodules from the host rock. Brockway Mountain agates, as they are called, consist of grayish blue or pale orange chalcedony husks surrounding interiors of opaque pink, tan, orange and occasionally bluish gray. Of course these are not the only two places to find paint agate nodules embedded in basalt, but they are two of the best locations. But as always, beware of private property and dangerous lakeside cliffs.

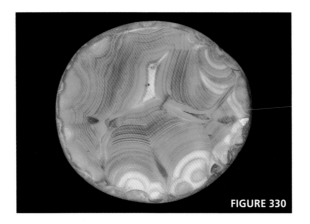

**FIGURE 330**

**FIGURE 327**
Polished Lake Superior paint agate.
Approx. 3.5" x 3.5" (8.9 cm x 8.9 cm)

**FIGURE 328**
Polished Lake Superior paint agate.
Approx. 3.5" x 2.5" (8.9 cm x 6.4 cm)

**FIGURE 329**
A quintessential Lake Superior paint agate, found by author Dan R. Lynch when he was 8 years old.
2" x 1.5" (5 cm x 3.8 cm)

**FIGURE 330**
A small and pale pink paint agate from Brockway Mountain, Michigan.
Approx. 0.5" x 0.5" (1.3 cm x 1.3 cm)

# *Rare Coloration*

*Shades of green, yellow and pink are examples of some of the rarest colors in Lake Superior agates*

**CHARACTERISTICS:** Agates exhibiting coloration vastly different from what is commonly seen in agates

**SYNONYMS:** None

**DISTRIBUTION:** Agates with unusual and rare colors can occasionally be found anywhere in the usual range of Lake Superior agates, though areas around Grand Marais, Minnesota, and various islands in Ontario consistently produce rare colors

**RARITY:** "Rare coloration" is, of course, rare

## DESCRIPTION

When it comes to color in Lake Superior agates, there generally aren't many surprises. Reds, browns, yellows, grays and white are the majority of what we find. But occasionally a specimen with a stunning coloration turns up at a mineral sale or in a gravel pit, and it makes our jaws drop. Deep greens, vivid yellows, delicate pinks and porcelain-like tans are among the rarest colorations in Lake Superior agates, and any combination of these colors is even rarer.

## FORMATION

Because we know that all agates derive their coloration from mineral impurities, the development of rare coloration in agate is not a question of why the colors are present or where they came from, but how they came to be so unique. All agates get their coloration from impurities that enter the vesicle alongside the silica, and later become intergrown with the chalcedony fibers. Observations of these impurities is easier with a microscope; some colors are a result of very dense concentrations of various impurities, while others are caused by a mixture of intergrown impurities, similar to mixing two differently colored paints together.

Of all the rare colors, bright, vibrant yellows are the most abundant and easiest to explain. The specimens in Figures 333 and 334 both contain such yellow coloration, which under a microscope is revealed to be a higher-than-usual concentration of goethite. Though even at nearly 100x magnification, the goethite growths still look like tiny specks of dust. Shades of pink and purple in chalcedony are caused by similar impurity growths. The specimen in Figure 332 is a slice of an agate from Michipicoten Island, the second-largest island in Lake Superior, and all rare agates from this protected location exhibit similar purple hues. Upon very close examination, the purple

**FIGURE 331**
Truly rare colors for a Lake Superior agate. Approx. 1" x 1.5" (2.5 cm x 3.8 cm) Specimen courtesy of Christopher Cordes.

**FIGURE 332**
A slice of an agate from Michipicoten Island, where all agates tend to have unique pink and purple hues. Approx. 4.5" x 3.5" (11.4 cm x 8.9 cm)

**FIGURE 333**
An incredibly strange lemon-yellow Lake Superior agate. Approx. 2.5" x 2.5" (6.4 cm x 6.4 cm)

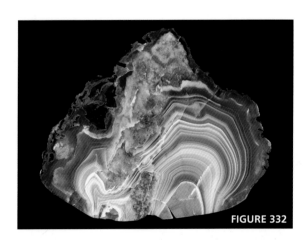

FIGURE 332

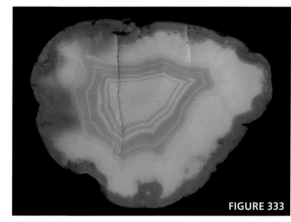

FIGURE 333

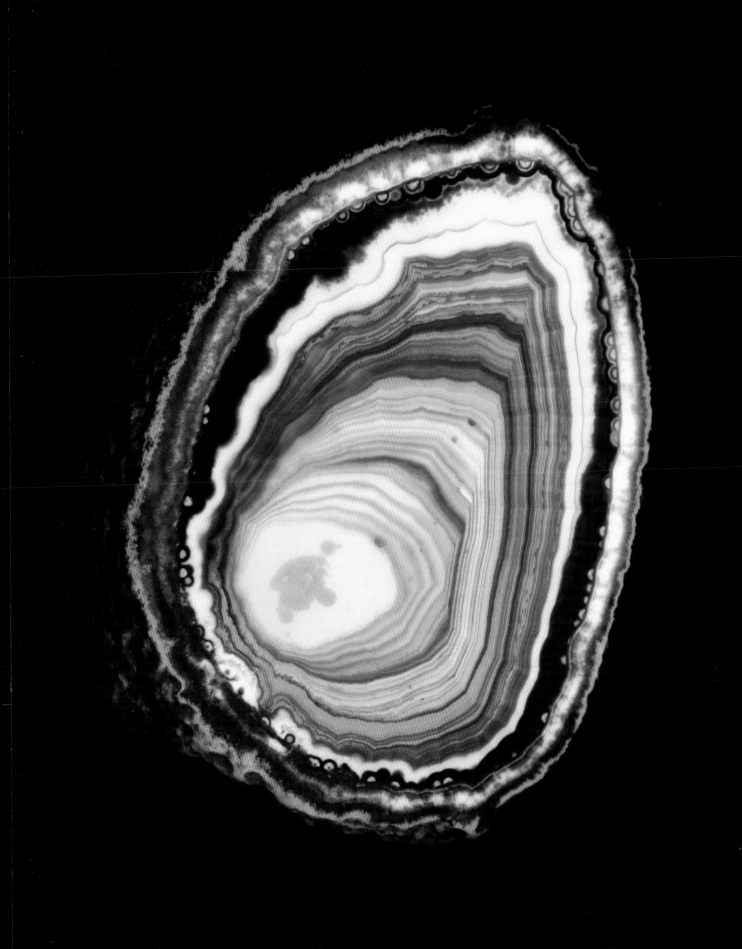

FIGURE 331

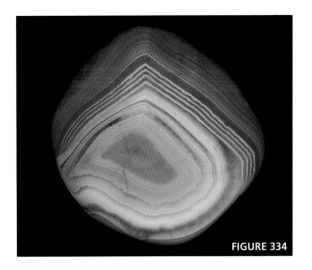

FIGURE 334

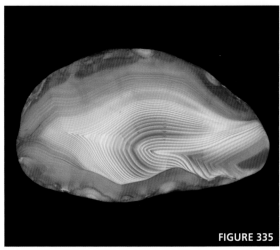

FIGURE 335

**FIGURE 334**
A thick, yellow band at the center of this agate is unique. Approx. 2.5" x 2.5" (6.4 cm x 6.4 cm)

**FIGURE 335**
A strange, greenish shell of chalcedony surrounds this agate. Approx. 3" x 1.5" (7.6 cm x 3.8 cm)

coloration is caused by tiny, dusty hematite growths "floating" in bluish gray chalcedony. Pink colors, though rare, are also a result of this sort of optical illusion, caused by tiny particles mixing with a colored band. In Figure 336, the pale pink coloration near the center of the banded pattern actually consists of tiny hematite particles in white chalcedony, and the same is true in Figure 337.

Greens can result of several possible causes. Many greens are caused by unoxidized iron inclusions. Though rare, such inclusions are the source of pale, translucent green banding, as in Figure 336. Lake Superior is also home to rarer causes for green coloration, such as in the stones pictured in Figures 331 and 338. While the origin of their shades of green is largely unknown, it is very likely that these colorations stem from inclusions of minerals like chlorite. Finally, occasionally there are agates found with strange opaque coloration. Like paint agates, these agates likely have a large amount of unweathered impurities, but what those impurities are isn't entirely known.

## COLLECTIBILITY

Rare colors in agates are all highly collectible simply because of their uncommon nature. But it is the truly rare colors that pique collectors' interests the most, such as the canary yellow agate in Figure 333 or the incredible orange, green and white banding of the agate in Figure 331. Specimens such as these, even when small or flawed, can be relatively valuable and remain one of the highlights of anyone's collection.

## NOTABLE VARIATIONS

Situated on the northern shore of Lake Superior is a set of unspoiled islands—the Wilson Islands—now protected by the Canadian government. On Wilson Island, a wild and pristine island nearly three miles offshore, small pebbles containing dark green and white banding can be found. These incredibly rare specimens were first described by A. E. Foote in 1873 and were named "zonochlorite." It was later noted by other researchers that zonochlorite did not seem to

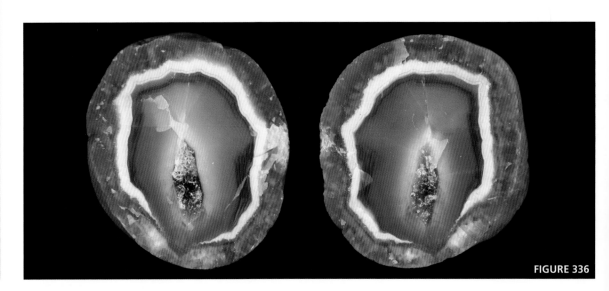

FIGURE 336

**FIGURE 336**
The two halves of this beautiful little agate were separated to reveal very strange colors for a Lake Superior agate. Approx. 1.5" x 1.5" each (3.8 cm x 3.8 cm)

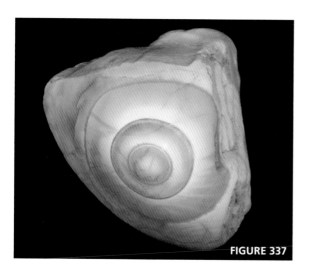

FIGURE 337

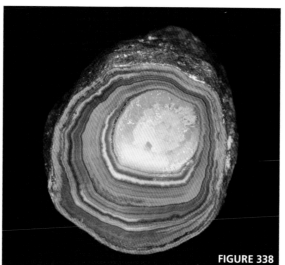

FIGURE 338

**FIGURE 337**
The pink coloration in this specimen is caused by tiny particles of hematite in white chalcedony. Approx. 2.5" x 3" (6.4 cm x 7.6 cm)

**FIGURE 338**
A small, but incredible, agate nodule freshly removed from its host rock. Approx. 1" x 1" (2.5 cm x 2.5 cm) Specimen courtesy of Christopher Cordes.

consist of a single mineral, but rather several minerals divided into bands. Though information on zonochlorite is very sparse, lab tests show that it is actually composed primarily of pumpellyite, a mineral from Lake Superior more commonly known as "greenstone," but that it also contains impurities of clinochlore, a variety of chlorite. In addition, zonochlorite's high hardness of about 6.5 on the Mohs hardness scale means that quartz is likely present as well.

The authors would like to point out the significant similarities between the specimen of zonochlorite in Figure 341 and the agates found near Grand Marais, Minnesota, that are shown in Figures 338 and especially 331. Though the zonochlorite lacks the orange iron–rich coloration, its banding is astonishingly agate-like. The authors possess several other specimens that corroborate this. Therefore, it is proposed that zonochlorite is actually a chemical replacement of agate, or an agate that has been significantly altered by other minerals entering its structure. In addition, the agates from Grand Marais, Minnesota, may also have been undergoing this process until they were collected from the rhyolite in which they formed. Though significant research would be necessary to prove this, the visual similarities are overwhelmingly in favor of this idea.

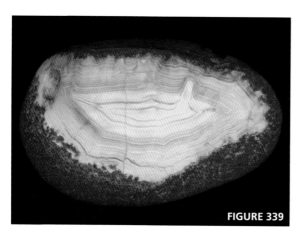

FIGURE 339

**FIGURE 339**
Opaque tan- or cream-colored agates like this are sometimes called "porcelain agates." Approx. 3.5" x 2.5" (8.9 cm x 6.4 cm)

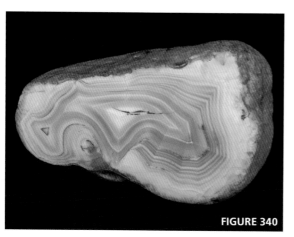

FIGURE 340

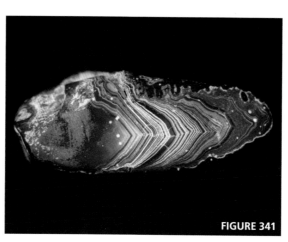

FIGURE 341

**FIGURE 340**
Strange, opaque gray banding surrounded by a pale orange chalcedony shell. Approx. 3" x 2" (7.6 cm x 5 cm)

**FIGURE 341**
A specimen of very rare zonochlorite from Wilson Island, Ontario. Approx. 1" x 0.5" (2.5 cm x 1.3 cm)

# Surface Colorations

*Yellow, red or white coatings are a common occurrence on the surface of glaciated agates*

**CHARACTERISTICS:** Very thin coatings of red hematite, yellow limonite, or white bleaching on the surface of an agate

**SYNONYMS:** None

**DISTRIBUTION:** Agates found in glacial till, particularly in east-central Minnesota and northern Wisconsin, most commonly exhibit various surface colorations

**RARITY:** Red and yellow surface colorations on agates are common, but white surface colorations are a bit more uncommon

......................................................................

## DESCRIPTION

When an agate forms, it derives its color from the impurities trapped within its twisted chalcedony fibers. But the color exhibited on an agate's surface may not be the same color found deeper in a specimen. After the glaciers tore them from their basalt matrix, many agates were subjected to mineral-bearing solutions, sunlight and harsh chemicals that changed their external coloration while leaving the colors of their internal banding intact.

Most collectors, no matter what their experience level, will have come across an agate that exhibits surface coloration. Particularly common on agates found in glacial till formations, surface colorations are exactly what they sound like—agate coloration that exists just on the outermost surfaces of an agate. There are three distinct types of coloration, including coatings of red hematite and yellow limonite, two iron-bearing minerals, and less commonly, white coloration that appears as if the agate's natural colors have been bleached from the bands. These coatings of red, yellow or white coloration are only "skin deep," and can easily be worn away, which is why this variety of agate coloration is not common on Lake Superior's shores.

Agates with surface coloration often contain areas where fresh chips, cracks, or breaks have revealed the chalcedony's true colors hidden below. In addition, even when very heavily coated with a surface-coloring mineral, most of the white chalcedony bands remain unaffected and retain their original color, as is well illustrated by the small agate in Figure 344. Whatever this agate's original colors may have been, they are completely hidden.

**FIGURE 342**
This beautiful adhesional banded agate exhibits a red hematite stain on its upper surfaces. This agate is actually gray in color, visible in the bottom right of the image where polishing has worn through the surface coloration. Approx. 2" x 3" (5 cm x 6.4 cm)

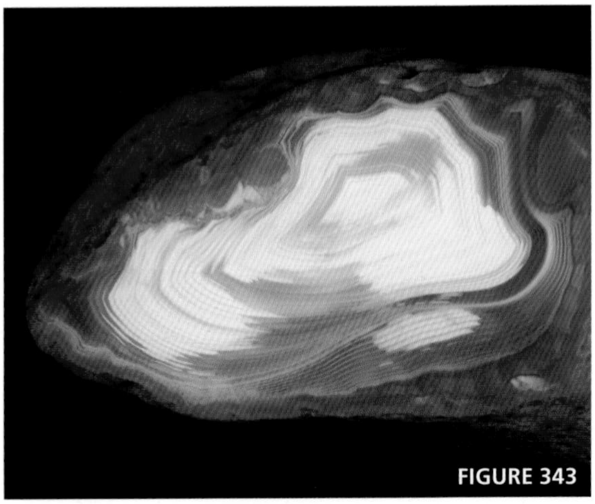

**FIGURE 343**
White bleaching has removed the color-causing impurities from the upper layers of this agate. 2x magnification

**FIGURE 344**
This agate is entirely stained with yellow limonite except for the white bands which contain fewer pores and therefore hold less color. Approx. 1.5" x 1" (3.8 cm x 2.5 cm)

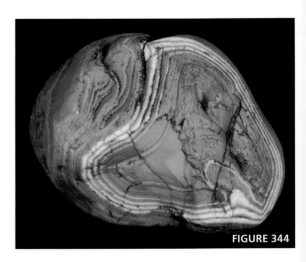

FIGURE 343

FIGURE 344

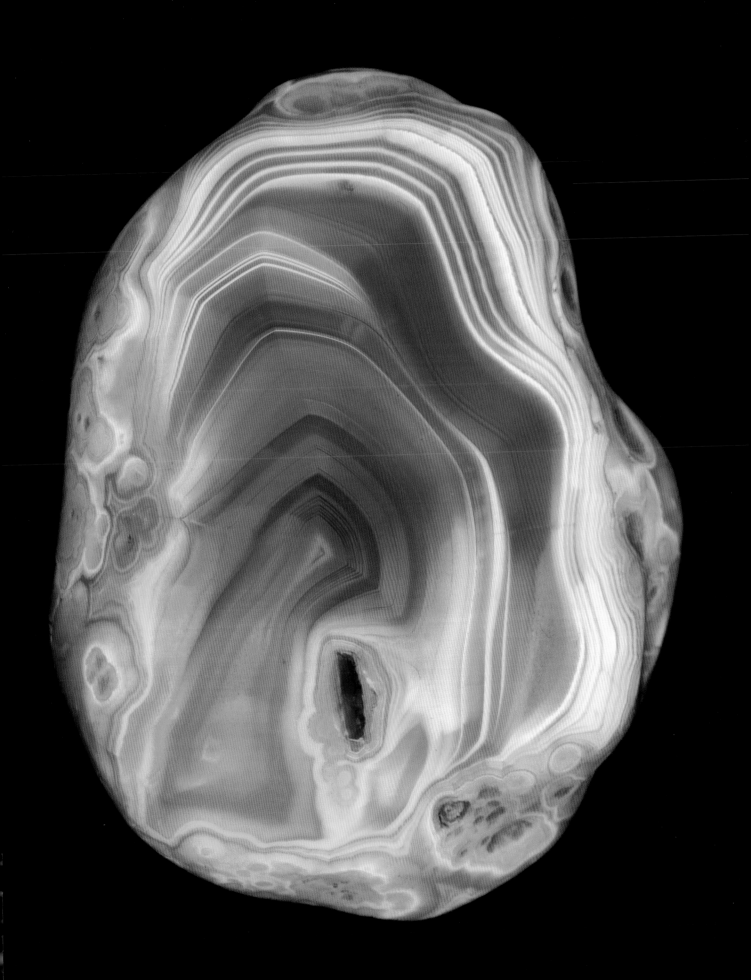

FIGURE 342

## FORMATION

We often see surface colorations directly on the interior bands of an agate, as in all of the figures shown in this section of the book. Because banding is not exposed until the agate is removed from the basalt and broken open by weathering, we know that surface colorations develop long after the agate is formed. But red and yellow iron-mineral coatings are much different than bleached, white surfaces, so they will be discussed separately.

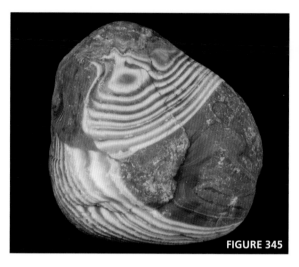

FIGURE 345

FIGURE 346

Since the glaciers dropped freshly exposed agates and other rocks into massive till deposits, agates likely gain their surface colorations from being buried in gravel, sand and clay. The Lake Superior area contains enormous amounts of red, iron-rich clay, especially within glacial till, so any agates buried in the till were in close contact with

an abundant source of iron for over 10,000 years since the retreat of the glaciers. As the clay eroded, its iron was carried with groundwater to the agates which may have soaked in this iron-rich water for very long periods of time. Because chalcedony is porous, the red hematite or yellow limonite (or both) were pulled into the agate, staining its surface. However, the white chalcedony bands retain their original color because white chalcedony is much more dense and contains fewer pores for impurities to collect in than do colored chalcedony bands.

In the case of the white surface coloration (called bleaching) a much different process occurred. Bleaching in agates has been thought to be a result of sunlight fading the colors on the surface of the agate, but this is highly unlikely. More realistically, bleaching is likely the result of the earth in which an agate is buried. The clays in

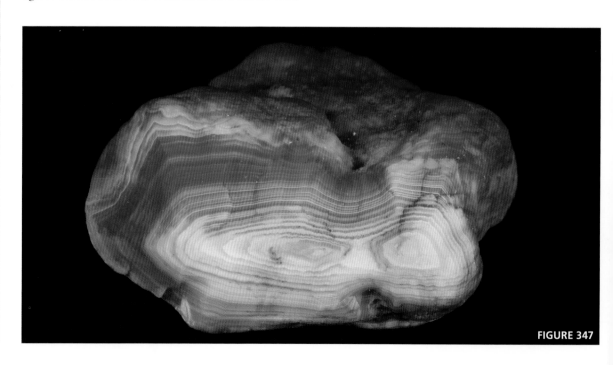

FIGURE 347

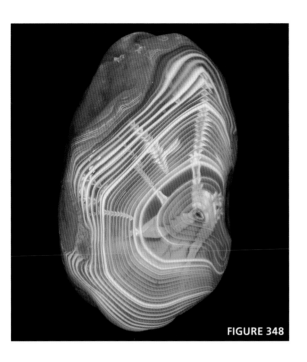

FIGURE 348

areas of glacial till generate very nutrient-rich soils that contain nitrogen and phosphorus, which are excellent for plant growth. However, the presence of plants means that decomposing plant matter creates acidic conditions, resulting in acidic water that may affect agates buried in the underlying till. These harsh acids may pull iron impurities from the outer layers of an agate, leaving only white chalcedony behind. This theory is supported by observations that show that bleaching is often observed affecting the cracks and fractures within an agate more than it affects flat, unbroken surfaces, suggesting that it was a liquid chemical, not the sun, that bleached these agates.

## COLLECTIBILITY

Typically, the only types of surface coloration popular with collectors are those that enhance an agate's otherwise drab or uninteresting coloration.

Red hematite is best known for this, and Figure 342 is a perfect example of how it can actually benefit an agate. Lake Superior agate collectors most often seek the brightest, most colorful agates with vibrantly contrasting banding, such as deep red bands alternating with white bands. But there are many more agates with dull, nearly colorless bands in shades of gray and white that lack any significant contrast. These kinds of agates frequently go ignored by collectors. But in the case of the agate in Figure 342, the surface of the gray bands was coated with hematite which seeped into the porous chalcedony, staining it red. Expert polishing has left much of the thin coating intact

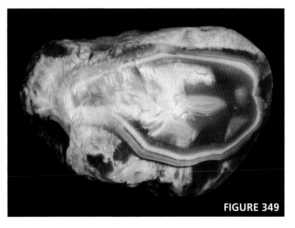

FIGURE 349

while letting some of the original gray chalcedony show through, giving an otherwise uninteresting agate contrast and making it more desirable. Similarly, the agate in Figure 347 would be more valuable if the red hematite coating had covered the entire face of the agate, rather than just half. But as it is, it is an interesting example of how drastically surface coloration can change the appearance of an agate.

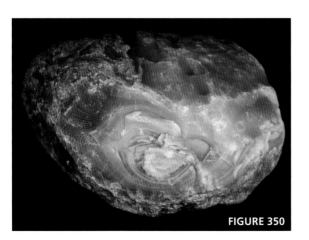

FIGURE 350

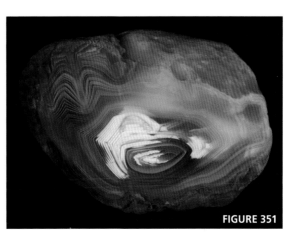

FIGURE 351

FIGURE 348
Before this agate was polished, its entire face was bleached white. After polishing, however, white bleaching only still exists in the deep cracks on its surface. Approx. 2.5" x 3" (6.4 cm x 7.6 cm)

FIGURE 349
Common bleaching in an agate, obscuring its pattern and original color. Approx. 2.5" x 1.5" (6.4 cm x 3.8 cm)

FIGURE 350
The highly weathered and cracked surface of this agate made it susceptible to bleaching. Approx. 3" x 2" (7.6 cm x 5 cm)

FIGURE 351
After polishing, bleaching only remains in the deepest cracks within the agate's face. Approx. 3" x 2" (7.6 cm x 5 cm)

# Weathering

*These agate varieties are the only ones defined by what happened after formation*

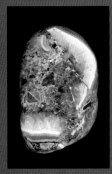

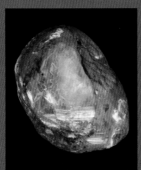

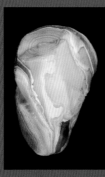

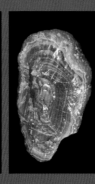

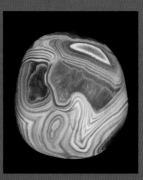

**BRECCIATED AGATE**

**FAULTED AGATE**

**PEELED AGATE**

**VENTIFACTS**

**WATER-WASHED AGATE**

Agates may be extremely hard, but they are very brittle, and after millions of years of being subjected to temperature changes, glacial ice, flowing water and other erosive forces, most Lake Superior agates have been chipped, fractured and worn down. Many times, the process of weathering will destroy an agate, but occasionally it can actually enhance its beauty or interest. When any of the previously described varieties of agates are weathered, they may develop certain superficial characteristics that collectors consider to be distinct varieties of agates.

## INTRODUCTION

At 1.1 billion years old, Lake Superior agates have seen immeasurable amounts of abuse from wind, water and, of course, the punishing weight of the glaciers that scoured the agate-forming rocks. Agates are older than most life on earth, and it truly is a wonder that so many Lake Superior agates still exist today. The fact that they have not been completely pulverized or worn to dust long ago is a testament to quartz and chalcedony's incredible resistance to weathering. But no Lake Superior agate was left unscathed, and every specimen, no matter how perfect a particular agate may seem, contains some kind of scar received over its arduous journey through time.

After formation, nearly every Lake Superior agate cracked due to weathering; these cracks resulted from a variety of causes: pressure within the vesicle, shifting rock, the freezing and thawing cycle, the crushing weight of glaciers, or a number of other weathering events. For collectors, finding agates without visible, distracting cracks is a top priority, as painfully obvious fractures like those in Figures 353 and 354 detract greatly from both a specimen's beauty and value. Some cracks in agate provided a large enough space for iron-bearing waters to easily enter and

stain the agate. This is clearly illustrated by the agate in Figure 352, which shows how the fracture acted as a conduit for the iron minerals to leach into the white chalcedony banding. A similar process occurred in the agate pictured in

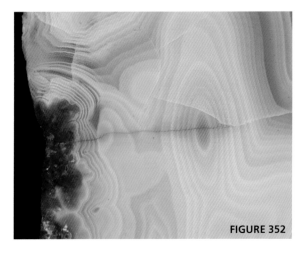
FIGURE 352

Figure 355, but much more severely. This agate is characteristic of the intense amount of weathering agates from northern Michigan endured. The elaborate network of fractures make this agate look as if ready to crumble, and if forced to undergo a few more years of freezing and thawing, it likely would have.

**FIGURE 352**
Cracks can become conduits for color-causing impurities.
3x magnification

**FIGURE 353**
The large, distracting cracks hurt the value of this agate from Michipicoten Island.
3x magnification

**FIGURE 354**
Dark stained fractures are common.
3x magnification

FIGURE 353

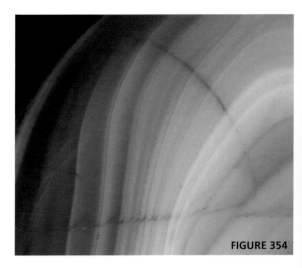
FIGURE 354

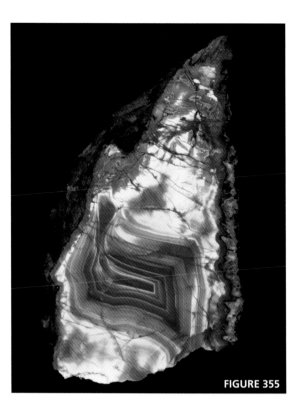

FIGURE 355

giving them a smooth texture. Similarly, ventifacts are agates that have been sculpted by windblown particles of sand. The extremely hard nature of chalcedony means that when abraded slowly over a long period of time, the agates were actually polished naturally.

Brecciated agates and faulted agates, both often referred to as "ruin agates," are examples of agates that were crushed and shattered after their forma-

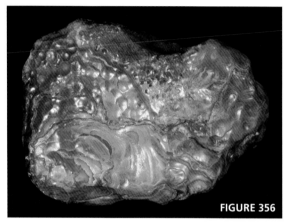

FIGURE 356

tion. However, additional silica "healed" these agates, essentially gluing them back together and creating some of the most interesting examples of the way weathering can affect agates. Finally, there are peeled agates, in which freeze and thaw cycles have caused their banding to separate and "peel" apart.

Weathering is inevitable for agates, but sometimes it can actually help display the natural beauty of an agate without the need for cutting and polishing. In this chapter, we will look in detail at the agates' appearances and features that result from these weathering events.

No matter how they were created, fractures are a certainty in nearly all Lake Superior agates, and specimens in which none are visible are highly praised. But not all weathering detracts from an agate's collectibility or value. In fact, wear and tear has actually increased the value of some agates.

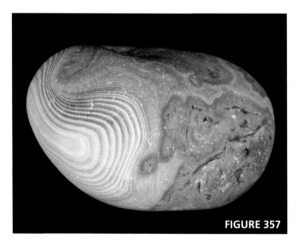

FIGURE 357

## PRIMARY VARIATIONS

In the Lake Superior area, there are five particularly collectible agate varieties that result from weathering. Water-washed agates are definitely the most desirable and have been completely rounded, exhibiting no sharp edges, jagged corners or deep pits. As their name suggests, they were worn smooth by fast-moving currents of water, which rolled them along other rocks and sand, slowly wearing away their high points and

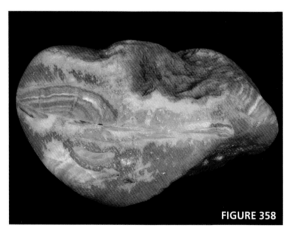

FIGURE 358

195

# *Brecciated* AGATE

*Agates that have been crushed or broken and later healed by silica are known as brecciated agates*

**CHARACTERISTICS:** Agates that have clearly been crushed and resolidified

**SYNONYMS:** Ruin agate, agate breccia, crushed agate, debris agate

**DISTRIBUTION:** Brecciated agates can be found anywhere in the usual range of Lake Superior agates, but particularly in areas that saw increased volcanic activity, such as Michigan's Keweenaw Peninsula and Minnesota's North Shore

**RARITY:** Very fine examples of brecciated agate are uncommon

## DESCRIPTION

In geology, the term breccia refers to rock formations that consist of broken, angular fragments that have been cemented together. Brecciated agates are no exception and are one of the most unique examples of weathering in agates. Some ill-fated agates, such as that in Figure 359, were partially crushed while still in the vesicle, cracking and shifting their banding and causing their macrocrystalline quartz to crumble. However, some other agates were even less lucky. The specimen in Figure 360 consists of banded segments of a gray agate suspended within a body of macrocrystalline quartz, and Figure 361 exhibits an agate that was pulverized and later encased in yellow chert. Clearly, all of these agates suffered violent fates, but their remnants survive to tell the tale.

## FORMATION

The integral moment in the formation of a brecciated agate is, of course, the event that crushed the agate. Most of the time, this was probably an earthquake, which would have been more common in volcanic areas after the basalt was formed. In the case of the agate in Figure 359, the agate was still in the vesicle at the time of being broken; this is clear because all of its fragments are more or less present. Silica solutions still remaining in the rock then filled in the cracks and spaces within the agate, crystallizing and cementing the fragments together to "heal" it and form a solid unit once more. The agates in Figures 360 and 361 were not in their vesicles, however, which allowed other forms of quartz, such as chert, to form in between the shards.

## COLLECTIBILITY

Oddly, these "ruined" agates are quite collectible, and aesthetic specimens can be valuable.

**FIGURE 359**
A spectacular example of a brecciated, or "ruined," agate. This specimen contains an outer shell of nearly intact banding, but its interior is crushed and contains banded fragments. Approx. 2" x 2.5" (5 cm x 6.4 cm)

**FIGURE 360**
A classic brecciated agate. Approx. 3.5" x 2" (8.9 cm x 5 cm)

**FIGURE 361**
Fragments of a red and white agate encased within chert. Because chert is generally derived from sediment, this specimen was possibly formed when the agate was broken within a body of water. Center fragment approx. 2" x 1.5" (5 cm x 3.8 cm)

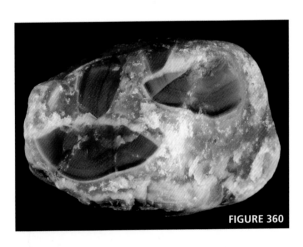

FIGURE 360

FIGURE 361

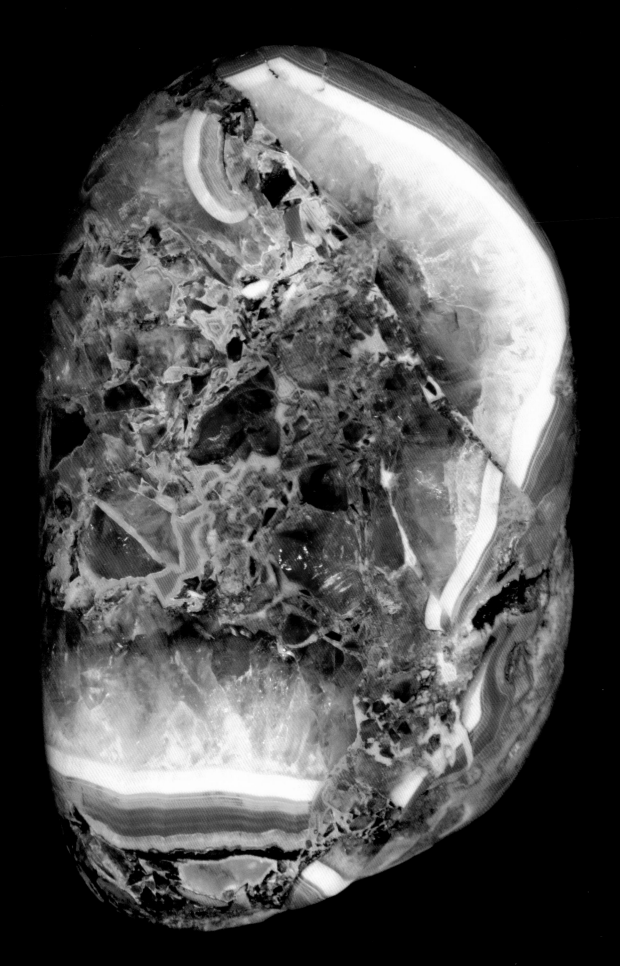

FIGURE 359

# *Faulted* AGATE

*Pressure and seismic activity have broken some agates, causing mismatched banding and cracks*

**CHARACTERISTICS:** Agates with banding that is interrupted, appearing as if the bands were broken and then healed back together, often mismatched in the process

**SYNONYMS:** Ruin agate

**DISTRIBUTION:** Faulted agates can be found anywhere in the usual range of Lake Superior agates, but especially in areas that saw increased volcanic and seismic activity, such as Minnesota's North Shore and Michigan's Keweenaw Peninsula

**RARITY:** Faulted agates are uncommon

## DESCRIPTION

Closely related to brecciated agates, faulted agates also contain evidence of the violent forces that sometimes acted upon agates. Unlike brecciated agates, however, faulted agates were not crushed or reduced to rubble; they were merely cracked. The result are agates with banded patterns that appear interrupted by a crack or fissure. The "scar" is often filled in with differently colored chalcedony or quartz, making it highly visible, as in Figures 363 and 364.

One of the most unique traits of faulted agates is known as shifted banding. Though not present in all faulted agates, many exhibit "mismatched" bands. These regions of a faulted agate appear to have been broken in two, then shifted slightly so that the banding is staggered and no longer matches up properly. This is exhibited well by the agate in Figure 362, in which the gravitational banding at the bottom of the agate was broken and the pieces shifted.

## FORMATION

Faulted agates formed in much the same way as brecciated agates—they were subjected to seismic activity. The intense periods of volcanic activity that created Lake Superior's basalt and initiated the formation of agates generated strong seismic events as well, which came in the form of earthquakes. These earthquakes, along with other events derived from volcanic activity, were believed to have shifted the rock, putting pressure on the vesicles and breaking the agates inside. Brecciated agates were unlucky; they were often completely crushed and fragmented into many pieces. Faulted agates, however, were broken, often badly, but their fragments remained in the

**FIGURE 362**
A stunning example of faulting in agates. Approx. 2" x 3" (5 cm x 7.6 cm)

**FIGURE 363**
A large, dark quartz-filled crack in a white agate. Approx. 3.5" x 3" (8.9 cm x 7.6 cm)

**FIGURE 364**
While containing little banding, these two intersecting cracks are composed of white chalcedony. Approx. 2.5" x 2.5" (6.4 cm x 6.4 cm)

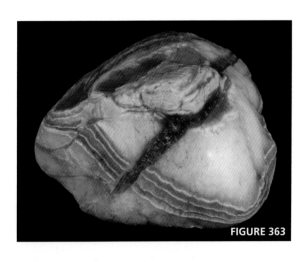

FIGURE 363

FIGURE 364

FIGURE 362

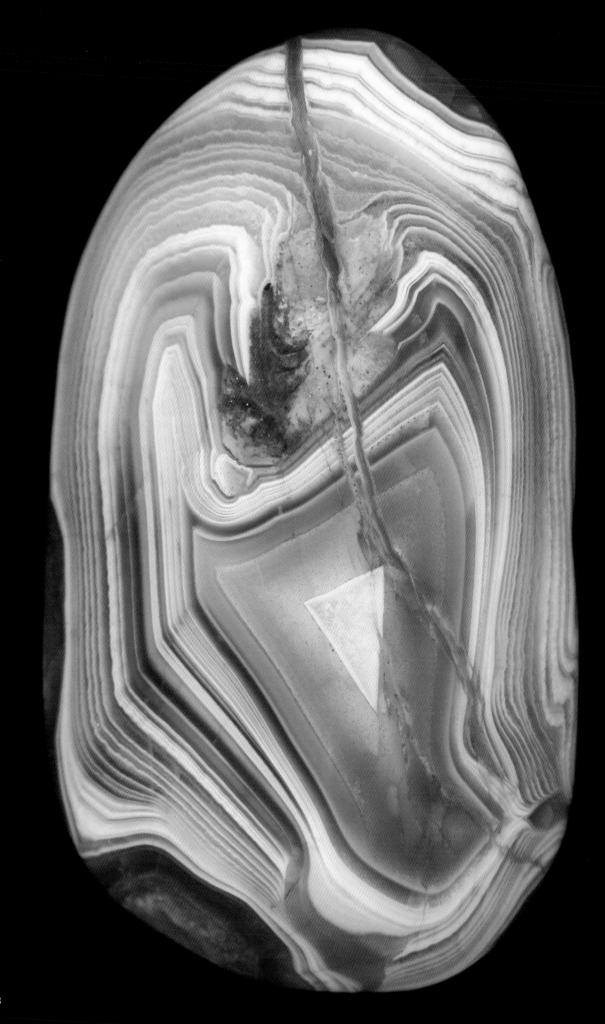

FIGURE 368

FIGURE 365

vesicle. After breaking, the loose pieces of agate that may have been present were sometimes able to move and shift, possibly because the vesicle was filled with water or other fluids.

Because these agates remained in their vesicles, silica solutions in the surrounding rock could still interact with them. The cracks and voids within the broken agate were then filled with additional silica which crystallized into chalcedony or granular quartz, effectively "healing" the agate back together. When this happened, any sections of the agate or fragments of banding that had

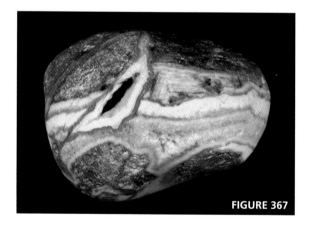

FIGURE 367

moved and shifted were frozen in place. Faulted agates therefore formed in a similar manner to brecciated agates—both were subjected to violent seismic activity—it was just a matter of degree.

Figure 362 shows that the process of an agate breaking and healing did not always begin after the agate had finished forming. Note how the gravitational bands are faulted, but the overlying macrocrystalline quartz is not. This agate had only formed a few of its parallel bands before it was broken, and the incoming silica filled around the shifted bands and crystallized to form quartz. It should also be noted that the traits exhibited by this agate are problematic for differentiation theorists. There is adhesional banding visible on the left side of the photo—if agate banding was

formed via a chemical reaction within a body of gel that caused it to organize itself into layers, then why were only a few solid bands present at the time of faulting? Walger's accumulation theory better explains this occurrence, as it assumes that each band was formed separately, with each new band fully hardening before the next begins to develop. Therefore, because only a few adhesional bands and gravitational bands are seen in this specimen, the agate must have been incomplete at the time it was faulted, and is therefore evidence against differentiation theory.

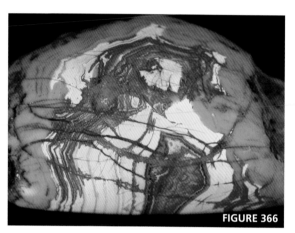

FIGURE 366

## COLLECTIBILITY

Given they are broken and "ruined," it may seem odd that faulted agates are collectible, but they actually can be quite sought after. Specimens with large, intrusive cracks and faults, such as in Figures 363 and 368, are less desirable because such large fissures considerably disrupt the banding patterns, but specimens with finer cracks that resulted in a shift in banding (such as in Figure 362) are not only enjoyed by collectors, but can actually be quite valuable. In addition, paint agates from the northernmost tip of Michigan's Keweenaw Peninsula (see Figure 366) contain a large amount of fractures and faults, resulting in a network of iron-stained cracks and mismatched banding. As highly weathered as these agates are, however, this is the characteristic appearance of Keweenaw agates. Therefore, while specimens with less damage are more desirable, such intense faulting is expected, and it doesn't necessarily negatively affect their value. In fact, some collectors looking to expand their collection and make it representative of agates from all around Lake Superior welcome the highly "ruined" appearance of Keweenaw agates, as it is one of their most recognizable attributes.

**FIGURE 365**
A close look at subtle faulting. 2x magnification

**FIGURE 366**
The characteristic shattered appearance of a Keweenaw agate. 2x magnification

**FIGURE 367**
This unique skip-an-atom agate was faulted and cracked, but the crack was only partially filled, leaving a geode. Approx. 3" x 2" (6.4 cm x 5 cm) Specimen courtesy of Terry and Bobbi House.

**FIGURE 368**
This large, disruptive crack extends throughout the face of this agate and onto its back side. Note the section of slightly mismatched banding near the center. Approx. 2" x 3.5" (5 cm x 8.9 cm)

# *Peeled* AGATE

*Millions of years of freezing and thawing have caused some agate bands to separate along their length*

**CHARACTERISTICS:** Agates with smooth chalcedony surfaces, appearing as if the layers have been peeled apart

**SYNONYMS:** Peeler

**DISTRIBUTION:** Peeled agates can be found anywhere in the usual range of Lake Superior agates, though particularly in northern Minnesota

**RARITY:** Peeled agates are fairly common

## DESCRIPTION

There are many ways an agate can weather and break down, all of which are fairly universal. Any agate-bearing location around the world can produce a faulted agate, for example. But one type of weathering in agates is fairly unique to the Lake Superior area; peeled agates are common around Lake Superior, but are found in few other places in the world. Indeed, if you want to add a "peeler" to your collection, you'll want to look to Lake Superior. Peeled agates are named for their characteristic appearance. Specimens exhibit smooth, rounded surfaces, as if the upper layers of an agate had been peeled off of the lower layers.

While they didn't peel in the sense that we would peel a fruit or vegetable, there certainly was a separation of an agate's layers, which revealed the distinctive smooth surfaces. But what you're really seeing when you observe a peeled agate is a three dimensional representation of the bands. Too often when we view the beautiful concentrically banded faces of agates, we forget that those bands are actually agate shells, one inside another, that extend throughout the entire stone. When those shells are separated and the agate peels, we are treated to a rare view inside the agate and to the sides of the shells that have never seen the light of day in one billion years of existence. For this reason, peels offer tremendous insight into the formation of agate bands. For example, the specimen in Figure 371 appears to have common, smooth concentric banding around its edges, but its center peeled to reveal the lumpy, rounded interior structure that we would normally never see.

Peels can theoretically occur in any type of banded agate, but they are generally only seen in adhesional banded agates and gravitationally banded agates, signifying that something about them may make them more prone to peeling. In addition, peels tend to reveal a white or colored chalcedony band.

**FIGURE 369**
The large peels seem to wrap around this agate, giving it a unique cylindrical shape. Approx. 2.5" x 4" (6.4 cm x 10.2 cm)

**FIGURE 370**
A common peeled agate. Approx. 2.5" x 2" (6.4 cm x 5 cm)

**FIGURE 371**
This polished agate has a peeled center. Approx. 4" x 3.5" (10.2 cm x 8.9 cm)

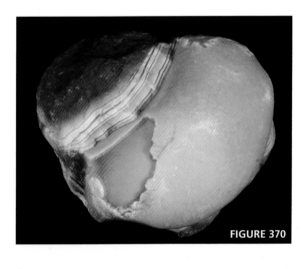

FIGURE 370

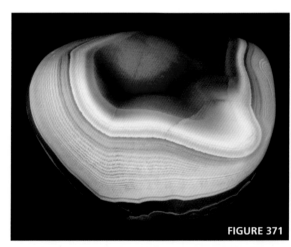

FIGURE 371

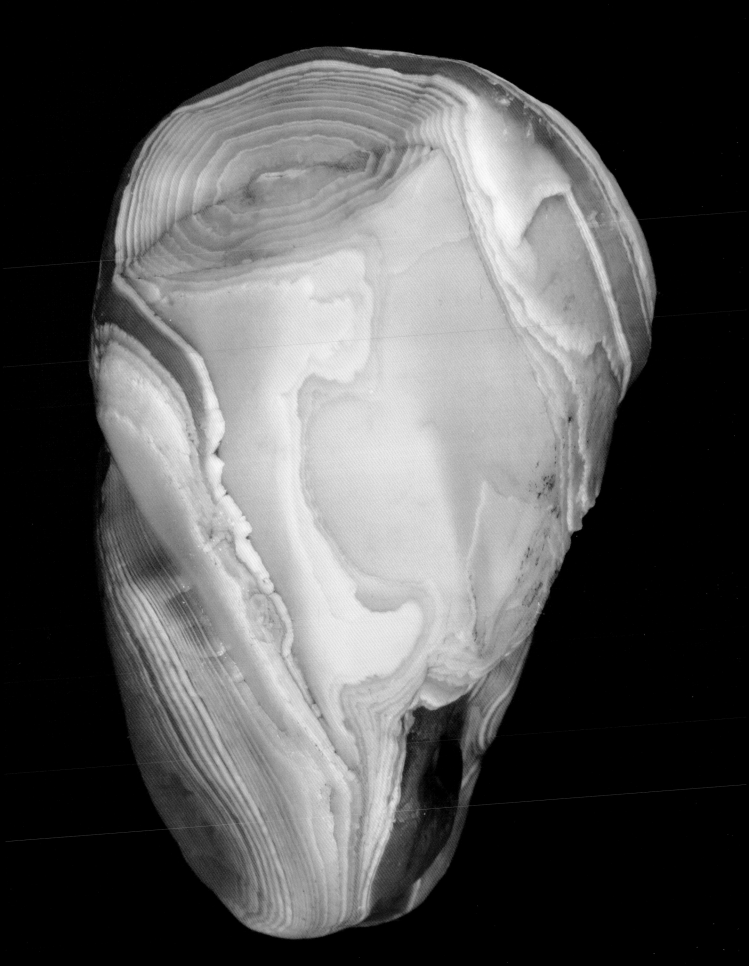

FIGURE 369

**FIGURE 372**
A large peel that didn't reveal much banded patterning. Approx. 3" x 3" (7.6 cm x 7.6 cm)

**FIGURE 373**
A small peeled paint agate still embedded in basalt. Agate approx. 1" x 1" (2.5 cm x 2.5 cm) Specimen courtesy of Jim Cordes.

## FORMATION

Agates are not quite as compact and solid as they seem. There are microscopic spaces between the chalcedony layers that are virtually invisible even

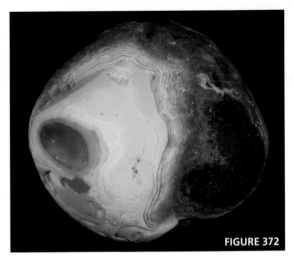

**FIGURE 372**

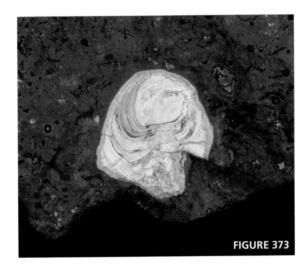

**FIGURE 373**

under very powerful microscopes. But such layers do exist, and the pervasive nature of water means that it can easily seep through the pores in chalcedony and collect in these miniscule spaces. When the temperature became cold enough for the water to freeze and expand, the tiny interlayer spaces widened slightly. These years of freezing and thawing, combined with other forms of weathering (such as being tumbled around in lakes or rivers) caused the spaces between the layers to widen enough that the upper layers of an agate were able to break off.

In some specimens, such as in Figures 372 and 373, this may have occurred in stages, resulting in a stepped series of peels, while in others, such as the agate in Figure 374, the peeling event was catastrophic and happened as one major separation.

Virtually every peeled agate shares one characteristic that's easy to observe: they never seem to peel in such a way that reveals a colorless microgranular quartz band. This suggests that the tiny spaces between chalcedony layers and microgranular layers are larger and allow for more water to infiltrate them, or that there is a weaker adhesion between chalcedony and granular layers. Similarly, peels can also occur between the horizontal layers of a gravitationally banded agate. Because the horizontal bands are comprised of tiny grains of

**FIGURE 374**
This wild, twisting peel reveals the true shape of the interior banding. Approx. 3.5" x 2.5" (8.9 cm x 6.4 cm)

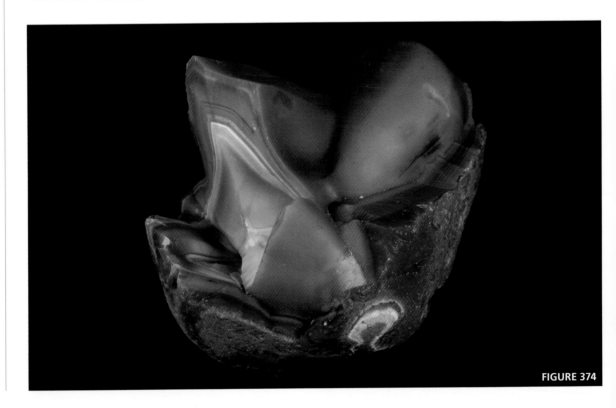

**FIGURE 374**

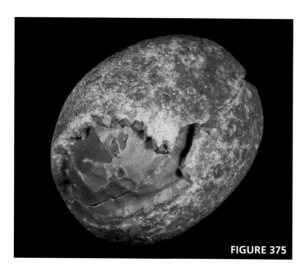

FIGURE 375

quartz rather than true chalcedony, Petránek suggested in 2004 that this causes a lack of coherence. The tiny, compacted grains do not remain as a whole band as easily as "woven" chalcedony fibers do. This is also the likely reason why microgranular bands separate from chalcedony bands in adhesional banded agates.

## COLLECTIBILITY

"Peelers," as they are known among Lake Superior agate collectors, are generally somewhat collectible, though this depends greatly on a particular collector's taste. Some love the smoothed, sweep-

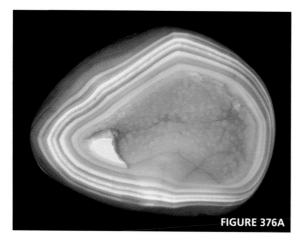

FIGURE 376A

ing curves of heavily peeled agates while others typically only enjoy peels when they add to the beauty or visual interest of a specimen. If an agate is heavily peeled, but still reveals little agate banding or pattern, such as the specimen in Figure 372, then it is generally regarded as less collectible. But if a specimen exhibits strange and striking peeled surfaces, like the wild appearance of the agate in Figure 374, then the specimen will catch more attention and likely appeal to a wider range of collectors. No matter what their appearance,

peeled agates are generally worth less than their unweathered counterparts.

## NOTABLE VARIATIONS

Occasionally, you will find a perfectly round cup-like shape in the surface of a peeled specimen (especially in heavily weathered agates). These strange holes are caused by entire agate eyes that

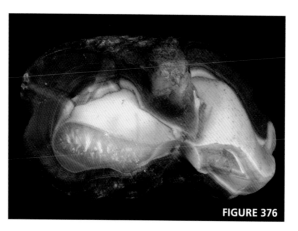

FIGURE 376

have peeled and separated from the agate. Collectors often say that these eyes have "popped out," which is actually an accurate description. These specimens are fantastic examples not only of the eccentricities of agate peeling, but also of the hemispherical nature of agate eyes.

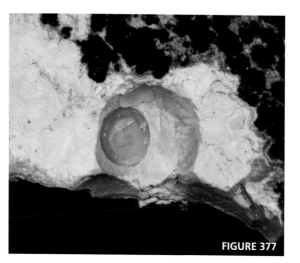

FIGURE 377

# Ventifacts

*Agates that have been naturally polished by windblown particles are known as ventifacts*

**CHARACTERISTICS:** Agates with an extremely high luster, as if polished, though often only on one side

**SYNONYMS:** Wind-polished agate

**DISTRIBUTION:** Ventifacts cannot be found in any particular area, though gravel pits in Minnesota may yield more specimens

**RARITY:** Naturally polished ventifacts are quite rare

## DESCRIPTION

There is no question that Lake Superior's agates have endured untold amounts of weathering and erosion, but few are naturally polished as a result. The authors' collection contains several agates that appear to be ventifacts. A ventifact is a stone that has been shaped and worn by windblown particles, such as sand. In this case, the result is agates that are very shiny and smooth, but typically only on one side, as is the case with the agate in Figure 378. Presumably the shiny side was exposed to the wind while the remaining portion of the agate remained protected, likely buried in glacial till. Because an agate ventifact

can be of any agate variety, the key identifying trait simply is the natural polish, which can sometimes be surprisingly brilliant and reflective.

## FORMATION

If a windblown stone is hard enough, such as an agate, the abrasive sand will slowly remove tiny amounts of material from its surface, effectively polishing it instead of simply wearing it away. This is commonly observed with hard, quartz-rich petrified wood from the southwest United States, which often exhibits the shiny surfaces and strangely eroded pits and holes characteristic of ventifacts. Lake Superior may seem an unlikely place for windblown sand and silt to abrade an agate long enough to polish it, but there is no reason why it could not have happened. In addition, we cannot know how long a particular agate has been exposed to the elements. Perhaps the glaciers dropped these agates directly onto the earth's surface rather than burying them in till.

## COLLECTIBILITY

Some collectors are skeptical that these agates have actually been polished by the wind, but the fact remains that they are Lake Superior agates that have been naturally polished, and that makes them highly collectible.

**FIGURE 378**
Even under highly controlled lighting, the natural polish of this agate ventifact shines brightly.
Approx. 2" x 3.5"
(5 cm x 8.9 cm)

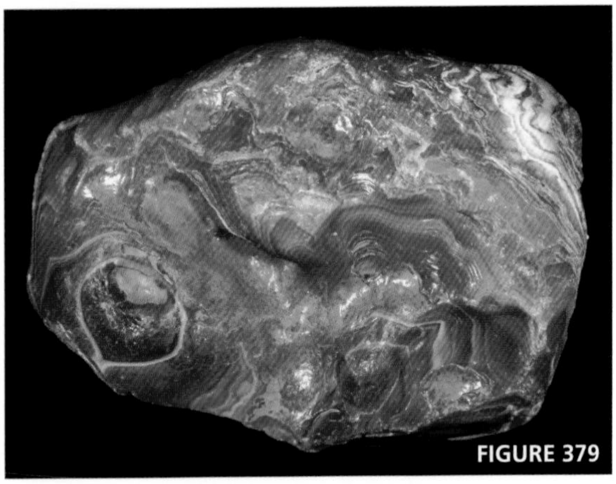

**FIGURE 379**
The surfaces of this red and yellow agate were sculpted by wind.
Approx. 3" x 2"
(7.6 cm x 5 cm)

**FIGURE 380**
Most of this agate is not wind-polished except for the odd, dark "bowl" near its center, which appears as if carved by wind.
Approx. 3" x 3"
(7.6 cm x 7.6 cm)

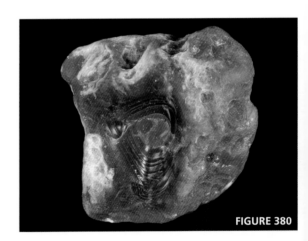

FIGURE 379

FIGURE 380

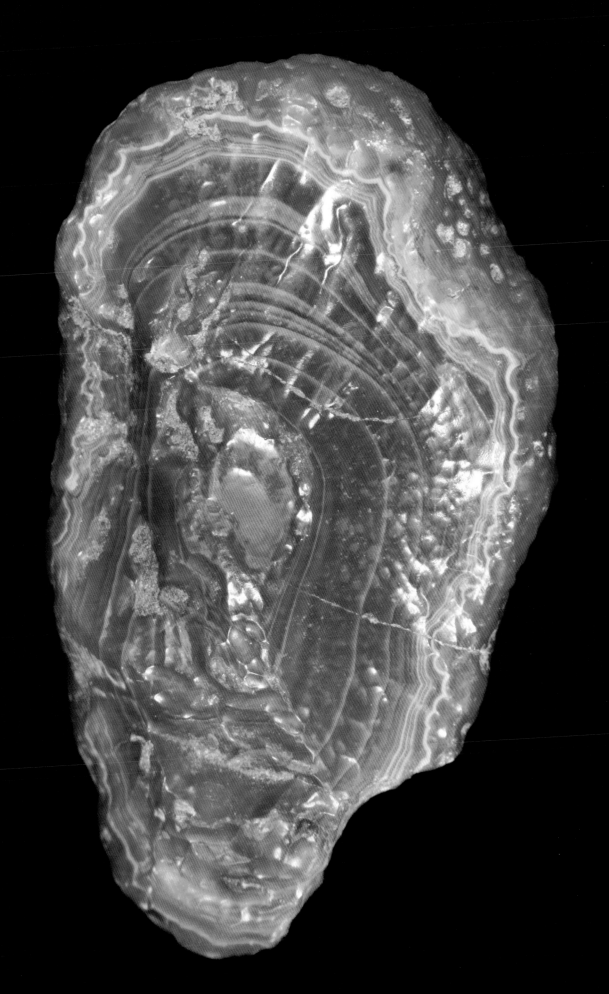

FIGURE 378

# *Water-washed* AGATE

*Smooth, rounded agates naturally shaped by water currents are said to have been "water-washed"*

**CHARACTERISTICS:** Very smooth, naturally rounded and worn surfaces exhibiting no "extra" bumps or pits

**SYNONYMS:** Water worn agate, river agate, rounded agate

**DISTRIBUTION:** While they can occasionally be found in gravel pits, rivers and lakeshore all around Lake Superior are obviously the best places to find water-washed agates

**RARITY:** While most Lake Superior agates will exhibit smooth edges, completely rounded water-washed agates are quite uncommon

## DESCRIPTION

Undoubtedly the most popular of all weathered agates are those that Lake Superior agate collectors call "water-washed." These stones, which can consist of any variety of agate, exhibit rounded surfaces with beautifully exposed banding. Of course, all glaciated Lake Superior agates are weathered in a similar manner, but water-washed agates are exceptionally smoothed and shaped. All high points, jagged edges and corners are worn away, and some water-washed agates are even approximately spherical or ovoid. But other than their round, sculpted shapes, the most striking feature of water-washed agates is their lack of the thick, reddish outer husk characteristic of Lake Superior agates. As a result, water-washed agates exhibit highly visible banding patterns around all sides of a specimen, which is exemplified by the agate in Figure 381. This is all due to the significant weathering these agates have endured at the bottoms of lakes and rivers. Not coincidentally, water-washed agates are typically found in riverbeds and on the shores of Lake Superior. Water-washed agates can also occasionally be found in gravel pits and other areas of glacial till.

Most water-washed agates are not very large, rarely measuring larger than an adult's fist. This is due to the fact that in order to become sufficiently smoothed and worn to be classified as a water-washed agate, a large amount of material had to have been removed from the stone, which resulted in a drastic decrease in size.

## FORMATION

As their name suggests, water-washed agates develop their smooth, rounded appearance after they are freed from their host rock and are natu-

**FIGURE 381**
This specimen is a remarkable example of a water-washed agate and exhibits all the qualities collectors love to see. Approx. 3" x 3" (7.6 cm x 7.6 cm)

**FIGURE 382**
A small water-washed agate. The odd red shapes surrounding the pattern are actually remnants of the agate's husk. Approx. 2" x 1.5" (5 cm x 3.8 cm)

**FIGURE 383**
A beautiful brown and white water-washed agate. Approx. 2.5" x 2" (6.4 cm x 5 cm) From the Jon Moin collection.

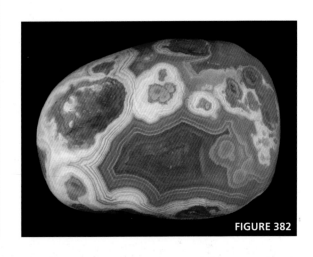

FIGURE 382

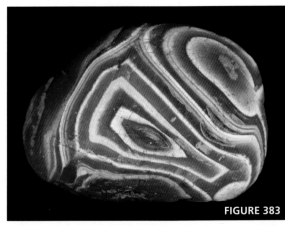

FIGURE 383

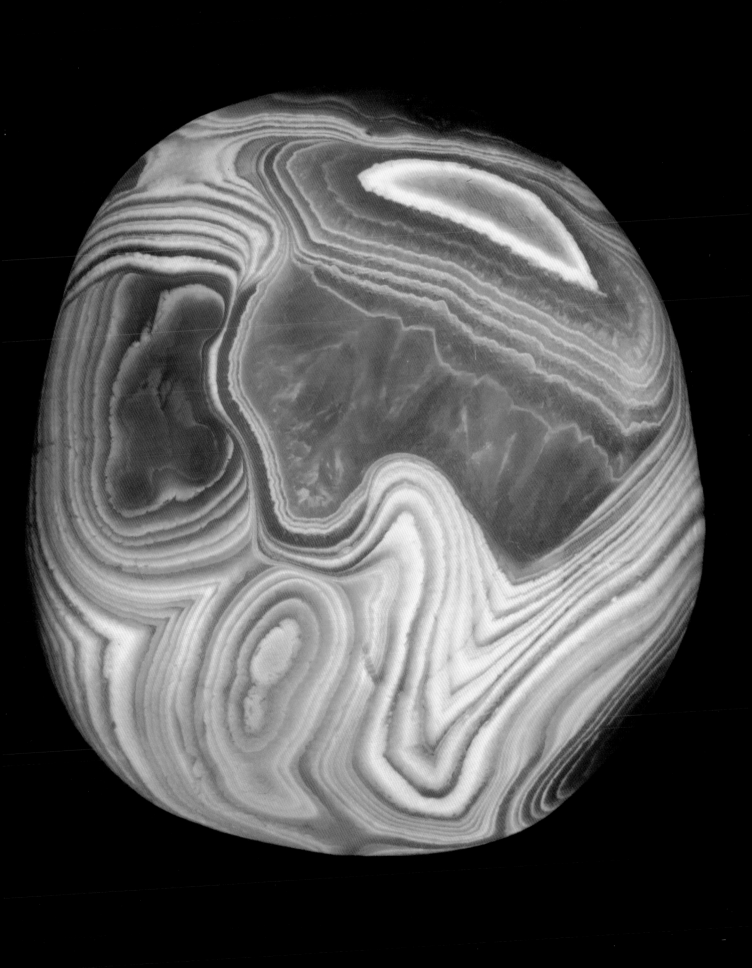

FIGURE 381

FIGURE 384
A red water-washed agate. Notice the small geode hole near the left side that hasn't yet worn away. Approx. 3" x 2" (7.6 cm x 5 cm)

FIGURE 385
This agate, found on Wilson Island, Ontario, has become so waterworn that it is nearly polished. Approx. 2" x 1.5" (5 cm x 3.8 cm) Specimen courtesy of David Gredzens.

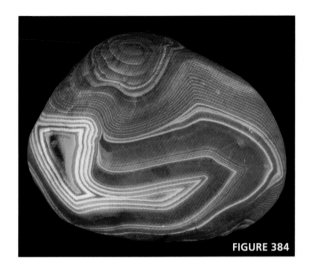

FIGURE 384

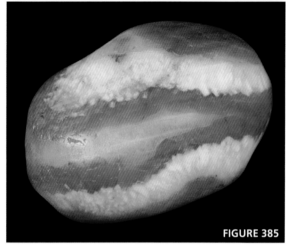

FIGURE 385

rally tumbled and rolled in rivers or lakes. Considering that the glaciers responsible for exposing the agates also melted to produce the billions of gallons of water that formed the thousands of lakes and rivers in the area (not to mention Lake Superior), it is easy to understand why some agates could have experienced such weathering. Fast-moving rivers or Lake Superior's strong currents have smoothed these agates for thousands of years, gradually bumping and wearing their high points and corners against rocks and sand, wearing them down until the entire agate is rounded.

Because they are so weathered, water-washed agates generally lack the outermost layers of chalcedony, including the thick husk, except within any deep pits or holes that remain in the agate. The loss of these layers reveals the banding hidden just below the surface. But unlike most

agate specimens, which are broken or cut perpendicularly to the bands so that a face exhibiting a concentric pattern is seen, water-washed agates are worn along their surfaces, nearly parallel to the banding. Therefore, instead of displaying only one face of agate banding, a well-worn water-washed agate will show banded patterns on all of its exterior surfaces, elegantly wrapping from one side of the specimen to the other, as in the case of the agate pictured in Figures 386 and 387.

Specimens that have been worn and weathered in rivers for an exceptionally long time, such as the agate in Figure 385, are smaller in size due to the extensive removal of material, but are incredibly smooth and can sometimes appear nearly polished. In water-washed specimens that are less eroded, small depressions and holes sometimes remain on the surface of an agate, such as the small geode

FIGURE 386
Because this agate was worn on its outer surfaces, wild, swirling patterns were revealed. Approx. 2" x 3" (5 cm x 7.6 cm)

FIGURE 387
The back side of the agate in Figure 386 is entirely different, showing red circular shapes that are actually part of the original husk. Approx. 2" x 3" (5 cm x 7.6 cm)

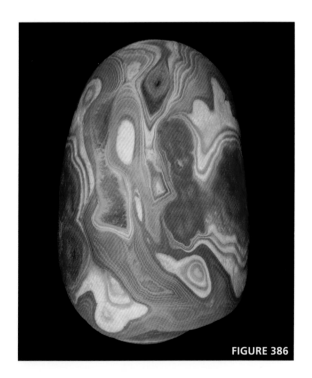

FIGURE 386

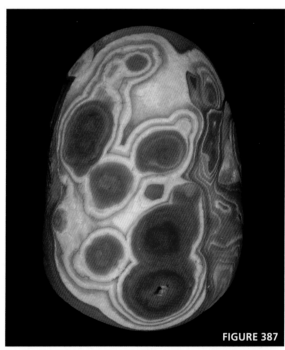

FIGURE 387

cavity in the agate pictured in Figure 384. These pits survive because not enough material has been removed yet from the agate. Given more time in Lake Superior or subjected to a strong river current, all cavities would eventually be worn away as the agate continued to decrease in size. However, as previously mentioned, water-washed agates can occasionally be found buried in glacial till. Though these specimens may be far from rapidly moving water sources today, water-washed agates found in gravel pits were likely shaped by the short-lived but fast-flowing rivers that developed at the front of a melting glacier.

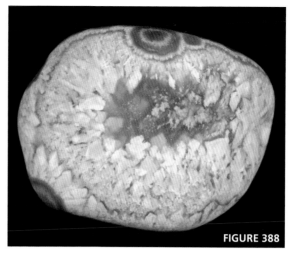

FIGURE 389

## COLLECTIBILITY

Water-washed agates are among the most collectible and desirable of all Lake Superior agates, and in fact some collectors build their collections primarily of water-washed agates alone. Their biggest draw is that they are all banding—there is no husk to obscure their patterns, no broken edges or gouges to distract from the beauty of a specimen, and they consist entirely of banding so a

specimen doesn't have just one single face, but instead can be viewed and displayed from dozens of different angles. And for collectors, the busier and more wild the patterns displayed by a water-washed agate, the better. The specimen in Figure 381, for example, was worn in such a way that the banding appears as overlapping swirls and twisting shapes that wrap around the stone and extend onto its back side, making it a highly desirable and valuable agate.

Due to the abundance of agates with common adhesional banding, most water-washed agates are of that variety. But different types of agates, such as sagenites or skip-an-atoms, can be found water-washed as well, and are equally as sought-after, especially when specimens exhibit bright colors and well-formed structures or patterns.

FIGURE 390

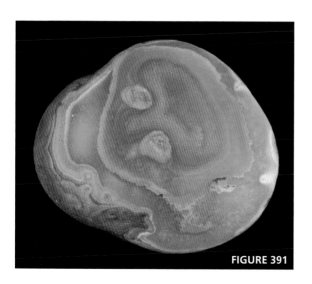

FIGURE 391

# Final Topics

*Closing comments on Lake Superior agate varieties and formation theories*

**THE IRIS EFFECT**

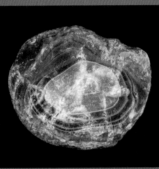

**BEFORE POLISHING**

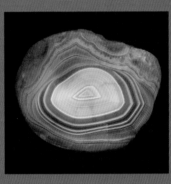

**AFTER POLISHING**

**SAGENITIC AGATE**

Lake Superior agates are like no other agates in the world. Given that there are so many defined agate varieties, it would stand to reason that every Lake Superior agate could be classified, but there are actually rarer varieties that are much more difficult to define and individual special cases that are altogether impossible to classify. But no matter what an agate's structure, banding pattern, colors, inclusions or weathered surfaces may be, collectors will still continue to find, polish and appreciate the Big Lake's ancient agates while researchers continue their 300-year-old quest to solve the agate enigma.

## ODD AGATES

Thousands of Lake Superior agates are found each year, and virtually every one of them falls under the label of one of the previously described varieties. But some of them do not. Some contain features so puzzling or unique that they are not easily classified. Unfortunately, collectors most often seek perfectly formed adhesional banded agates, allowing many "ugly" agates and their oddities to go unnoticed. But if you take the time to inspect and scrutinize every agate and all of its features, you will certainly find dozens of specimens that seem to defy description and will cause even lifelong collectors to scratch their heads.

## "CLAMSHELLS"

The authors have observed two Lake Superior agates with a very peculiar and very specific structure. Nicknamed "clamshell" agates because of their shape, these stones exhibit odd, rounded and deeply striated peaks or cones on either side of the agate, arranged symmetrically. According to Pabian and Zarins in their 1994 publication, formations such as these are formed of radially arranged feldspar crystals intergrown with quartz, and are most abundant on the surface of thunder eggs. But the presence of these feldspar forma-

tions in amygdaloidal agates is very strange, primarily because they somehow produced a protrusion from the surface of the agate rather than an impression into it. Figure 394 exhibits one of the cone-shaped features with deep striations as well as an extremely odd and well-formed circular "brim" at its base. This observation, combined with the fact that they grow in symmetrical pairs, suggests that these formations grow under very specific conditions, but we're not yet sure exactly what. It is likely that these are the freed agate cores of thunder eggs, but without more specimens we can't know for certain.

FIGURE 392

FIGURE 392
A large "clamshell" with two of the curious cone shapes on either side of a body of macrocrystalline quartz and red chalcedony. Approx. 3" x 2.5" (7.6 cm x 6.4 cm) Specimen courtesy of Wally Crabtree.

FIGURE 393
A small "clamshell" with dark-colored cones surrounding a vein of red chalcedony. Approx. 1.5" x 1" (3.8 cm x 2.5 cm)

FIGURE 394
An incredibly detailed cone formation from the top of the agate in Figure 392. Note the deep striations and strange "brim" around the cone's base. 2x magnification Specimen courtesy of Wally Crabtree.

FIGURE 393

FIGURE 394

## IRIS AGATE

Irises in agates are caused by translucent chalcedony bands that are so thin that light bounces between them in such a way that a rainbow-like spectrum of colors is produced. Iris agates are not an unknown phenomenon; in fact, they are well understood. Brazilian and Mexican agates, in particular, commonly produce the iris effect, but it is extremely rare in Lake Superior agates. The banding has to be infinitesimally fine—some Mexican iris agates have been found to contain over 10,000 bands per inch. However, the agate must be sliced very thin and held in front of a very bright light at specific angles for the iris effect to appear. Figure 396 shows one of the few Lake Superior iris agates in the authors' vast collection to date. Measuring only one millimeter thick, this agate slice only exhibits the iris in three different bands.

Irises in agates are interesting and beautiful, but it is likely that the iris effect is not actually as rare in Lake Superior agates as it seems. Few collectors slice their lakers because cutting a Lake Superior agate can drastically reduce its value; however, if careful sawing were done to more agates, it would undoubtedly result in more known Lake Superior iris agate specimens.

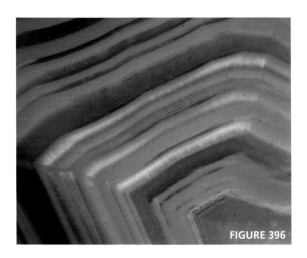

FIGURE 396

## "SCRAMBLED" CHALCEDONY

The authors have several agates that share another strange trait. The outermost layers of chalcedony appear "scrambled" or "mixed up," exhibiting swirls and smears of color rather than the translucent spherulitic band found in regular agates. Under a microscope, it is easy to find chalcedony fibers within the "scrambled" areas of agates, like the one pictured in Figure 395, but they are

disorganized and are arranged into small clumps or fan-shaped formations. Yet, in all of the authors' examples, the interior banding is more or less of the common adhesional type, signifying that whatever change occurred in the outer layers did not affect the interior of the agate. It is likely that this was a result of conditions in the surrounding rock at the time of formation, but how those conditions differed can be anyone's guess.

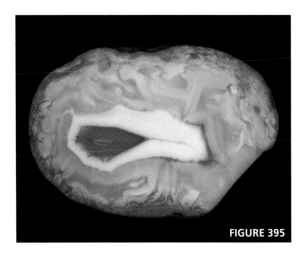

FIGURE 395

## LIESEGANG RINGS

While Liesegang's experiments with colloids led to a refuted theory of agate formation, it turns out that he may not have been completely wrong when he applied his mysterious rings to agates. Very rarely, agates from around the world, including Lake Superior's, contain what appear to be Liesegang rings as peculiar curved bands isolated in interior portions of an agate. These bands are not chalcedony, however, but are simply iron impurities that have curiously arranged themselves across many bands. Because these stripes of color are superimposed over the agate banding, they may well be Liesegang's inexplicable rings.

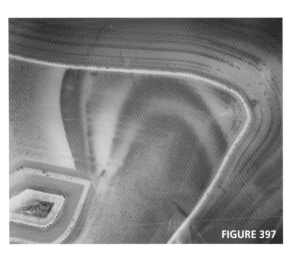

FIGURE 397

**FIGURE 395**
What caused the outer layers of chalcedony to "scramble" as they have here? Approx. 2.5" x 1.5" (6.4 cm x 3.8 cm)

**FIGURE 396**
Backlighting reveals the rainbow colors of this iris agate—a very rare find in Lake Superior agates. 8x magnification

**FIGURE 397**
Could these strange swirls of hematite that seem to cross perpendicularly across many bands actually be Liesegang rings? 3x magnification

# Before and After

## WORKING WITH AGATES

Readers will certainly have noticed that many of the specimens shown in this book are cut and polished, and they may want to know how to polish their own agates. It takes a great deal of expensive equipment and an even larger amount of experience to properly work with agates. Because agates consist of quartz and are therefore extremely hard, only diamonds are capable of cutting and giving agates the high shine collectors desire. Polishing with diamond removes a lot of material from an agate and the process is not reversible, so it takes an experienced eye to know when and where to polish a specimen.

There is a misconception among novice collectors that polishing agates is a foolproof way of increasing their value. This is most certainly not true with Lake Superior agates. In fact, many amateurs are shocked to discover that the large agate they found and polished was likely worth ten times more when rough. Serious collectors typically will always prefer an agate in its rough, natural state, and only polish a specimen if doing so will increase its beauty. For example, the specimen in Figure 398 is certainly interesting, but the white bleaching and many cracks are distracting. After polishing, shown in Figure 399, the agate is able to show off all it has to offer.

**FIGURE 398**
This dark gray and brown agate has white patches of bleaching and cracks that significantly distract from the pattern. Approx. 2.5" x 2" (6.4 cm x 5 cm)

**FIGURE 399**
After polishing, the cracks and white bleaching are removed, revealing the beautiful fortification pattern hidden within. Approx. 2.5" x 2" (6.4 cm x 5 cm)

**FIGURE 400**
This agate naturally shows a large quartz-rich face. Though this specimen would not necessarily need polishing, it isn't worth much in this state due to the scarcity of agate banding. Approx. 4" x 2" (10.2 cm x 5 cm)

**FIGURE 401**
Because it didn't have much to offer collectors in the first place, polishing improved this stone by cleaning up its face. Approx. 4" x 2" (10.2 cm x 5 cm)

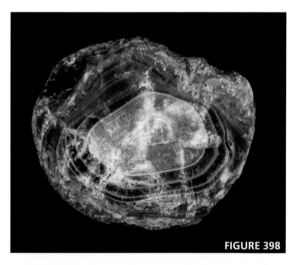

FIGURE 398

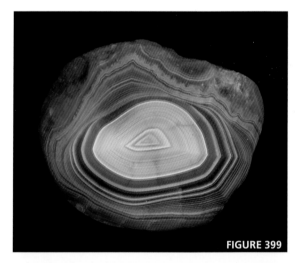

FIGURE 399

FIGURE 400

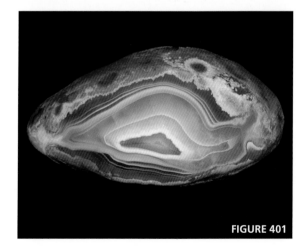

FIGURE 401

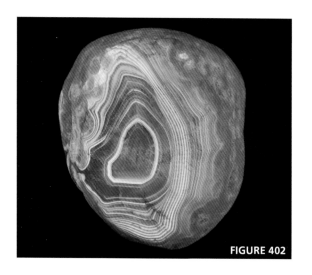

FIGURE 402

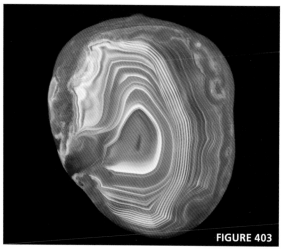

FIGURE 403

The authors are often asked by amateurs, "What is inside my agate? Will it have more banding if I cut it?" The answer is simple: If your rough specimen already shows banding, then it has already been broken open by weathering and you do not need to cut it. Cutting may reveal a different pattern that could be better than what is already showing, or it could be worse. This is always a gamble. Many collectors have turned very valuable agates into stones worth only pennies after needlessly cutting, or even breaking, an agate in half. When in doubt whether or not you should work an agate, ask yourself, "Does this agate show a beautiful pattern already?" If the answer is yes, then cutting it may only cut its value.

## CARVING AND SHAPING

Agates have been used decoratively for millennia in jewelry, carvings and even knife blades, but agate's high hardness and very brittle nature can make it extremely difficult to work with. As with polishing, efficiently working with agates requires diamond-bladed saws and drills which can be out of the price range of novices or casual collectors. In addition, the amount of skill required to expertly cut and polish agates, such as the cabochon in Figure 405, only comes with years of practice. But even decades of experience won't prevent a brittle, fractured agate from crumbling just as its polish is nearly finished.

The primary use of Lake Superior agates, other than simply keeping them as collectibles, is as decorative stones in jewelry. Figure 404 shows a piece of jewelry designed and fabricated by both of the authors while Figure 405 shows a cabochon ready to be put into a ring or pendant. Other hobbyists have the incredible patience to carve or shape agates, exemplified by the beautiful agate marble shown in Figure 406.

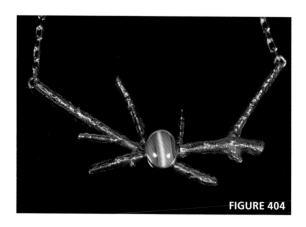

FIGURE 404

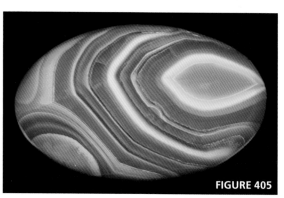

FIGURE 405

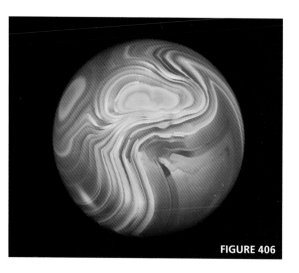

FIGURE 406

**FIGURE 402**
This beautiful red adhesional banded agate is fairly desirable, but the small size of the face and cloudy fractures near its center limit its collectibility.
Approx. 3.5" x 3" (8.9 cm x 7.6 cm)

**FIGURE 403**
Polishing may have removed some of the bright red surface coloration from the face, but the cracks are gone and the polished stone is nearly flawless.
Approx. 3.5" x 3" (8.9 cm x 7.6 cm)

**FIGURE 404**
A sterling silver pendant designed and fabricated by the authors.
Approx. 3" x 1.5" (7.6 cm x 3.8 cm)

**FIGURE 405**
The high contrast banding of this cabochon would make for a gorgeous piece of jewelry.
Approx. 1" x 0.5" (2.5 cm x 1.3 cm)

**FIGURE 406**
This beautiful agate marble was painstakingly made for the authors, from a paint agate, by John Harris.
Approx. 1" round (2.5 cm round)

# What is an Agate?

## CONCLUSION

If one thing is certain, it's that the study of agates can be a complicated and nearly impenetrable topic for newcomers to explore. The research isn't often compiled in one place and it isn't always easy to decipher, and old research must be dissected in order to distinguish the facts that are still relevant from those that are outdated. On top of that, too many theorists insist that their ideas are the answer to the question of agate formation. But there is no "correct" answer yet. Throughout the course of this book we have shown that the accumulation theory of agate formation may be better suited to explain many of the varieties of agates seen around Lake Superior, but there is no reason why differentiation and accumulation theories need to be in opposition to each other. Combining aspects of both theories seems to be our most viable option for decoding the agate enigma, but we should also consider that different varieties of agate likely formed as a result of different processes.

The application of Liesegang rings to the formation of agates was, at the time, a groundbreaking theory that initially seemed like the most viable idea available. But it wasn't until more than 100 years after Raphael Liesegang's discovery of the mysterious rings that a mathematic model was proposed that could sufficiently explain them. The formation of Liesegang rings is a chemical reaction between just two pure substances and is very easily reproduced, yet it still took more than a century to explain. Agates are decidedly more complex; they are a combination of silica, alkaline elements, iron mineral impurities and aluminum and formed in an environment with acidic conditions, low temperature, low pressure and possibly dozens of other variables. This formation process has never been replicated. So it's not surprising that a sufficient theory of agate formation doesn't exist, despite more than 300 years of scientific research. There are simply too many facets of agate development for it to be easily explained. Looking only at agates and their banding is to consider the product of an elaborate chain of events. Like skipping to the last chapter of a novel, it's easy to come up with ideas of agate formation, but without an understanding of all the prerequisite pieces of the puzzle, there can be no true comprehension of the whole. Today, we know that Liesegang rings are not the cause of agate banding as Liesegang thought they were, but that is only one possibility eliminated from a long list of potential causes of formation. If only agates were as simple a formation as Liesegang rings, we would probably have an explanation by now.

Many theorists have stated that we will never know how agates form until one can be grown in a laboratory setting where every step of its growth can be observed. This is indisputably true, but producing synthetic agates would be to deny that which makes agates unique. Any learned collector can instantly recognize a Lake Superior agate just by looking at the way the iron minerals stain its bands or how its exterior surfaces are weathered. The same is true for agates from anywhere in the world because every location produces agates that are distinct in appearance, giving them not only an easily determined source, but an identity. And while many visitors to the Lake Superior area search for agates for their beauty or perhaps because they heard that they can be valuable, few realize that what makes the Big Lake's agates so distinct is a growth process that took place an immeasurably long time ago, before any life existed on land, followed by more than a billion years of weathering.

So what is an agate? We don't have an answer for this persistent question yet, and this may be true for decades to come. For now, we must be content in referring to agates as the concentrically banded form of chalcedony, but what they really are is one of the most beautiful mysteries of the natural world.

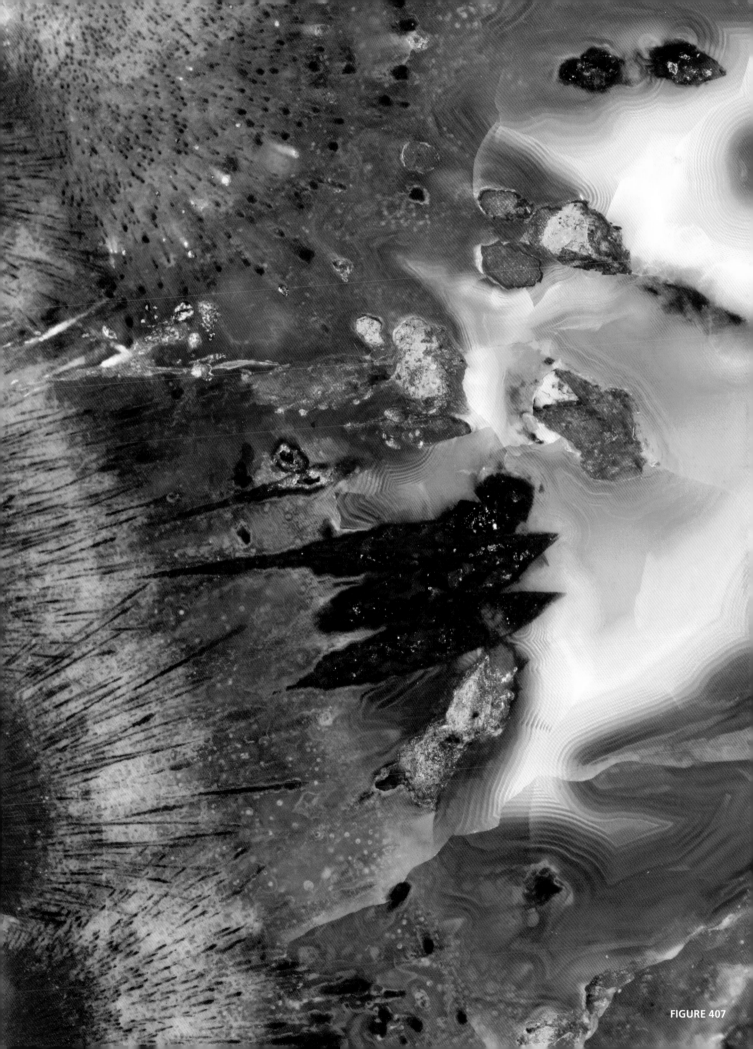

FIGURE 407

# GLOSSARY

Agate: The concentrically banded variety of chalcedony

Alkaline: Said of bases, or compounds containing alkali elements such as calcium, sodium and potassium; having the opposite properties of acids

Anhydrous: Without water

Band: A distinct layer within a mineral formation

Barite: A soft mineral consisting of barium, sulfur and oxygen that forms blade-like crystals

Basalt: A dark gray or black iron-rich rock formed by lava spilled onto the earth's surface

Bleaching: Color turning white due to exposure to chemicals or sunlight

Calcite: Calcium carbonate; a soft, calcium-rich mineral that forms six-sided prismatic crystals

Carnelian: Red or reddish orange chalcedony, with or without banding

Celadonite: A soft bluish green mineral that forms as a lining within vesicles

Chalcedony: The microcrystalline variety of quartz composed of microscopic plate-like crystals arranged into parallel stacks

Chert: A rock consisting primarily of tightly compacted microscopic quartz grains as well as clay

Chlorite: A soft, dark green to black mineral that forms as a lining within vesicles

Coagulate: Change to a solid; clump up

Colloid: A homogeneous substance containing large molecules of one substance suspended in another substance; a gel

Color center: A hole in the crystal lattice of quartz which can hold vibrating, color-causing atoms

Concentric: Said of circular shapes that share the same center

Conchoidal fracture: Cracks with a circular shape

Copper: Red-brown metal

Crystal: A solid body with a repeating atomic structure formed when an element or compound solidifies

Crystal lattice: The internal structure of a mineral composed of linked molecules

Crystallization: Forming a crystal; a mineral solution solidifying to form a distinctly structured unit

Crystallization front: The forward-moving edge of a crystallizing mineral mass

Deuterium: A rare isotope of hydrogen with twice the mass of normal hydrogen atoms

Druse: A mineral crust consisting of many small crystal points, particularly quartz

Element: A substance that cannot be broken down further; elements are the primary constituents of matter

Erosion: Wear away, due to weathering

Feldspar: An abundant group of minerals that is a primary component in most rocks

Fibrous quartz: Microcrystalline quartz with a fibrous structure

Flint: Black colored chert

Flocculate: To form small clumps or masses, often used to refer to a solution turning into a gel

Gel: A jellylike substance; see *colloid*

Geode: A hollow, rounded rock or mineral formation

Glacial lobe: A rounded protrusion of ice extending from the main body of a glacier

Glacial till: The rock, gravel and sand deposited by melting glaciers

Glaciated: Said of agates that have been worn and rounded by glacial activity

Glacier: A slow-moving mass of ice formed in cold climates by the compaction of snow

Goethite: A brownish yellow hydrous iron oxide

Granular quartz: A quartz formation consisting entirely of small, compacted quartz grains

Hematite: A common, red to black iron oxide

Host rock: see *matrix*

Husk: The thick, outermost chalcedony band of an agate that is composed of chalcedony spherulites

Hydrous: Containing water

Impurity: A foreign mineral within a host mineral that often changes the properties of the host, including color

Infiltration channel: A channel by which a jet of silica solution entered a vesicle

Iron: A common, hard, magnetic metal

Isotope: A particular form of an element

Jasper: The colored varieties of chert

Lapidary: The art of cutting and polishing stones; one who cuts or polishes stones

Laumontite: A common, soft zeolite mineral typically found in shades of orange, pink or gray

Limestone: A soft, sedimentary rock comprised primarily of calcite

Limonite: The name given to yellow-brown unidentified hydrous iron oxides

Macrocrystalline quartz: Quartz crystals large enough to see with the naked eye

Magnetite: A black, magnetic oxide of iron

Massive: Occurring in solid, compact concentrations

Matrix: The rock in which a mineral forms

Microcrystalline quartz: Quartz crystals too small to see with the naked eye

Microgranular quartz: Microscopic irregular quartz grains in a compact mass

Mineral: A naturally occurring chemical compound or native element that solidifies with a definite internal crystal structure

Molecule: A group of atoms bonded together

Native Element: An element found naturally uncombined with any other elements, e.g. copper

Nodule: A round, compact mineral formation

Oxidation: The act of an element or mineral combining with oxygen to produce another substance; also oxidize

Oxide: A combination of oxygen with another element, particularly a metal

Prism: A crystal with a length greater than its width

Pyrite: Iron sulfide; a common, brass-colored iron- and sulfur-bearing mineral the forms perfectly cubic crystals

Quartz: Hard, white mineral formed of silicon dioxide; the single most common mineral on earth

Rhombohedron: A geometric shape resembling a leaning or tilted cube

Rhyolite: A light-colored quartz-rich rock formed when lava spilled onto the earth's surface

Rock: A massive aggregate of many minerals

Rough: Used by collectors to denote natural, unpolished agates

Sard: Brown or yellow-brown chalcedony, typically without banding

Sardonyx: Sard with parallel layers

Siderite: An iron- and carbon-rich mineral closely related to calcite

Silica: Silicon dioxide molecules, often in the form of quartz or dissolved in a solution

Spherulite: A very small spherical formation

Stilbite: A common zeolite mineral that primarily grows in fan-shaped crystal groups

Stromatolite: Ancient bacteria colonies, often preserved in jasper and chert

Thomsonite: An uncommon zeolite that forms radial eye-like arrangements of needle-like crystals

Till: see *glacial till*

Vesicle: A cavity created in an igneous rock by a gas bubble trapped when the rock solidified

Vesicular: Said of a rock containing vesicles

Waxy: A mineral with the reflectivity of wax, such as a candle

Weathering: Being subjected to the forces of nature, including wind, water and ice

Zeolite: A large group of soft silica, aluminum, alkali and water-bearing minerals that form as a result of basalt weathering in the presence of alkaline groundwater

# REFERENCES AND RECOMMENDED READING

## Articles:

Abbott, W.J.L. (1887) The Formation of Agates. *Proceedings of the Geologists' Association.* **10**, 80–93.

Cohen, A.J. (1985) Amethyst color in quartz, the result of radiation protection involving iron. *American Mineralogist.* **70**, 1180–1185.

Götze, J., Tichomirowa, M., Fuchs, H., Pilot, J. and Sharp, Z.D. (2001) Geochemistry of agates: a trace element and stable isotope study. *Chemical Geology.* **175**, 523–541.

Götze, J., Plötze, M., Tichomirowa, M., Fuchs, H. and Pilot, J. (2001) Aluminum in quartz as an indicator of the temperature of formation of agate. *Mineralogical Magazine.* **65**, 407–413.

Heaney, P.J. and Post, J.E. (1992) The Widespread Distribution of a Novel Silica Polymorph in Microcrystalline Quartz Varieties. *Science.* **255**, 441–443.

Heaney, P.J. (1993) A proposed mechanism for the growth of chalcedony. *Contributions to Mineralogy and Petrology.* **115**, 66–74.

Keller, P.C., Bockoven, N.T. and McDowell, F.W. (1982) Tertiary volcanic history of the Sierra del Gallego area, Chihuahua, Mexico. *Geological Society of America Bulletin.* **93**, 303–314.

Lakshtanov, L.Z. and Stipp, S.L.S. (2010) Interaction between dissolved silica and calcium carbonate; 1, Spontaneous precipitation of calcium carbonate in the presence of dissolved silica. *Geochemica et Cosmochimica Acta.* **74**, 2655–2664.

Léger, J.M., Haines, J. and Chateau, C. (2001) The high-pressure behaviour of the "moganite" polymorph of $SiO_2$. *European Journal of Mineralogy.* **13**, 351–359.

Masuda, T., Morikawa, T., Nakayama, Y. and Suzuki, S. (1997) Grain-boundary migration of quartz during annealing experiments at high temperatures and pressures, with implications for metamorphic geology. *Journal of Metamorphic Geology.* **15**, 311–322.

Moxon, T. (2002) Agate: a study of ageing. *European Journal of Mineralogy.* **14**, 1109–1118.

Moxon, T. and Ríos, S. (2004) Moganite and water content as a function of age in agate: an XRD and thermogravimetric study. *Mineralogical Magazine.* **16**, 269–278.

Moxon, T., Nelson, D.R., and Zhang, M. (2006) Agate recrystallization: evidence from samples found in Archaean and Proterozoic host rocks, Western Australia. *Australian Journal of Earth Sciences.* **53**, 235–248.

Moxon, T. and Reed, S.J.B. (2006) Agate and chalcedony from igneous and sedimentary hosts aged from 13 to 3480 Ma: a cathodolumines-cence study. *Mineralogical Magazine.* **70**, 485–498.

Moxon, T. and Carpenter, M.A. (2009) Crystallite growth kinetics in nanocrystalline quartz (agate and chalcedony). *Mineralogical Magazine.* **73**, 551–568.

Moxon, T. (2010) Agates from Western Australia Found in a 3,480-Million-Year-Old Host Rock. *Rocks & Minerals.* **85**, 66–72.

Oehler, J.H. (1976) Hydrothermal crystallization of silica gel. *Geological Society of America Bulletin.* **87**, 1143–1152.

Petránek, J. (2004) Gravitationally banded ("Uruguay-type") agates in basaltic rocks— where and when? *Bulletin of Geosciences.* **79**, 195–204.

Pilipenko, P.P. (1934) Zur Frage der Achaten-genesis. *Byulleten' Moskovskogo Obshchestva Ispytateley Prirody, Otdel Geologicheskiy.* **42**, 279–299.

Reeves, T.K. and Carroll, Herbert B. (1999) *Geologic Analysis of Priority Basins for Exploration and Drilling.* U.S. Department of Energy. 29 pgs.

Shaub, B.M. (1955) Notes on the origin of some agates and their bearing on a stylolite seam in petrified wood. *American Journal of Science.* **253**, 117–120.

Walger, E. (2009) The formation of agate structures: models for silica transport, agate layer accretion, and for flow patterns and flow regimes in infiltration channels. *Neues Jahrbuch für Mineralogie—Abhandlungen.* **186**, 113–152.

Wang, Y. and Merino, E. (1990) Self-organiza-tional origin of agates: Banding, fiber twisting, composition, and dynamic crystallization model. *Geochemica et Cosmochimica Acta.* **54**, 1627–1638.

## Books:

Carlson, Michael R. *The Beauty of Banded Agates: An Exploration of Agates from Eight Major Worldwide Sites.* Edina: Fortification Press, 2002.

Clark, Roger. *South Dakota's Fairburn Agate.* Appleton: Silverwind Agates, 1998.

Cross, Brad L. and Zeitner, June Culp. *Geodes: Nature's Treasures.* Baldwin Park: Gem Guides Book Company, 2006.

Kunz, George Frederick. *Gems and Precious Stones of North America: A popular description of their occurrence, value, history, archaeology, and of the collections in which they exist, also a chapter on pearls and on remarkable foreign gems owned in the United States.* New York: Scientific Publishing Company, 1890.

Liesegang, R.E. *Die Achate.* Dresden and Leipzig: Theodor Steinkopff, 1915.

Marshall, John D. *The "Other" Lake Superior Agates.* Beaverton: Llao Rock Publications, 2003.

Moxon, T. *Agate: Microstructure and Possible Origin.* Auckley, South Yorkshire, England: Terra Publications, 1996.

Moxon, T. *Studies on Agate: Microscopy, Spectroscopy, Growth, High Temperature and Possible Origin.* Auckley, South Yorkshire, England: Terra Publications, 2009.

Ojakangas, Richard W. and Matsch, Charles L. *Minnesota's Geology.* Minneapolis: University of Minnesota Press, 1982.

Ojakangas, Richard W. *Roadside Geology of Minnesota.* Missoula: Mountain Press Publishing Company, 2009.

Pabian, Roger K. and Zarins, Andrejs. *Banded Agates: Origins and Inclusions.* Lincoln: University of Nebraska, 1994.

Pabian, Roger K., et al. *Agates: Treasures of the Earth.* Buffalo: Firefly Books, 2006.

Zenz, Johann. *Agates.* Haltern, Germany: Rainer Bode, 2005.

## Extended Reading:

Bates, Robert L., editor. *Dictionary of Geological Terms, 3rd Edition.* New York: Anchor Books, 1984.

Bonewitz, Ronald Luis. *Smithsonian Rock and Gem.* New York: DK Publishing, 2005

Chesteman, Charles W. *The Audubon Society Field Guide to North American Rocks and Minerals.* New York: Knopf, 1979.

Coenraads, Robert R. *Rocks & Fossils: A Visual Guide.* Buffalo: Firefly Books, 2005.

Johnsen, Ole. *Minerals of the World.* New Jersey: Princeton University Press, 2004.

Mottana, Annibale, et al. *Simon and Schuster's Guide to Rocks and Minerals.* New York: Simon and Schuster, 1978.

Pellant, Chris. *Rocks and Minerals.* New York: Dorling Kindersley Publishing, 2002.

Pough, Frederick H. *Rocks and Minerals.* Boston: Houghton Mifflin, 1988.

Robinson, Susan. *Is This an Agate?* Hancock: Book Concern Printers, 2001.

Schumann, Walter. *Gemstones of the World, 3rd Edition.* New York: Sterling Publishing Co., 2006.

Schumann, Walter. *Minerals of the World, 2nd Edition.* New York: Sterling Publishing Co., 2008.

Wolter, Scott F. *The Lake Superior Agate.* Eden Prairie: Outernet Publishing, 1986.

Wolter, Scott F. *Amazing Agates: Lake Superior's Banded Gemstone.* Duluth: Kollath-Stensaas Publishing, 2010.

Zeitner, June Culp. *Midwest Gem, Fossil and Mineral Trails of the Great Lakes States.* Baldwin Park: Gem Guides Book Company, 1999.

# INDEX

# About the Authors

**DAN R. LYNCH** has a degree in graphic design with emphasis on photography from the University of Minnesota Duluth. But before his love of the arts came a passion for rocks and minerals, especially agates, developed during his lifetime growing up in his parents' rock and mineral shop in Two Harbors, Minnesota. Combining the two aspects of his life seemed a natural choice and he enjoys researching, writing about, and photographing rocks and minerals. Working with his father, Bob Lynch, a respected veteran of Lake Superior's agate collecting community, Dan writes and produces their series of rock and mineral books and field guides. Dan's meticulous research allows him to create a relatable text that helps amateurs "decode" the complex and sometimes unapproachable sciences of geology and mineralogy. He also takes special care to ensure that his photographs compliment the text and always represent each specimen exactly as it appears in person. He currently works as a writer and mineral photographer in Bellingham, Washington, with his beautiful fiancée, Julie.

**BOB LYNCH** is a lapidary and jeweler living and working in Two Harbors, Minnesota. In 1973, he sought more variety in the gemstones used in his jewelry, so he began working with and polishing rocks and minerals. When he moved from Douglas, Arizona, to Two Harbors in 1982, his eyes were opened to the incredible beauty of Lake Superior's agates and he quickly became an avid collector. In 1992, Bob and his wife Nancy, whom he taught the art of jewelry making, acquired Agate City Rock Shop, a family business founded by Nancy's grandfather, Art Rafn, in 1962. Since the shop's revitalization, Bob has made a name for himself as a highly acclaimed agate polisher and as an expert resource for curious agate collectors seeking advice and specimen appraisal. Now, the two jewelers keep Agate City Rocks and Gifts open year-round and are the leading source for Lake Superior agates, with more on display and for sale than in any other shop in the country.

The "Minnesota Agate"